T0300662

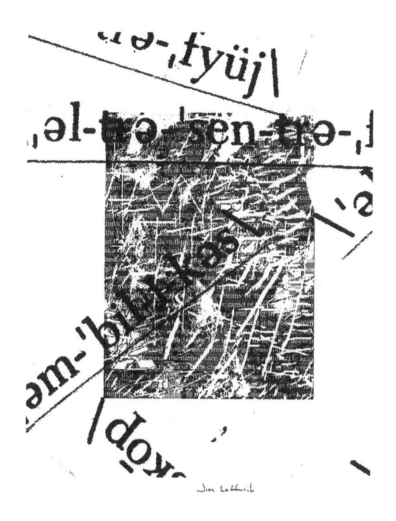

Jim Leftwich

rascible & kempt

meditations and explorations in and around the poem

volume 1

Jim Leftwich

LUNA BISONTE PRODS

2016

rascible & kempt

meditations and explorations in and around the poem

volume 1

© Jim Leftwich 2016

Front cover art: *energy conversion,* 2016

and title page art: *vispo,* 2002 © Jim Leftwich

Back cover photo by Ralph Eaton:

Leftwich at 2009 Marginal Arts Festival, Market Street

Vol. 1: ISBN 978-1-938521-31-7

Vol. 2: ISBN 978-1-938521-32-4

LUNA BISONTE PRODS

137 Leland Ave.

Columbus, OH 43214-7505

www.johnmbennett.net

https://www.lulu.com/lunabisonteprods

Table of Contents

CHAPTER ONE ||||||||||||||||||||||||||||||||||||||||||||||||||||||||||||

Poetries of Investigation and Inclusion

In an interview in the first issue of INK (Spring, '87, from SFSU), Kathleen Fraser is asked to define 'experimental.' She says she's uncomfortable with the word, prefers the word 'innovative,' is interested in re-imagining, what has been done repeatedly loses its interest; "essentially it is a question of learning how to do a particular thing and then being bored with repeating what you already know." In this way of thinking, experimentation eventually becomes a sort of necessity, it's a logical part of the development of writing, what should surprise us is that there are writers who are not experimental.

In Talisman 8 (Spring, '92), Jackson Mac Low looks at the same question. "Open to all poetries," he writes, "I'm shipwrecked amid terms such as 'avant-garde' and 'experimental.' (...) There is no more need for these self-congratulatory terms". In The Experimental Issue of Poetry USA (1993), Jack Foley quotes William Everson on "the terminal situation which confrontation with the Pacific exacts of the westward-hungering consciousness," and asks "what do we have to say now (...) of that 'terminal consciousness,' that consciousness on the edge?" Mac Low had written: "on the superficial - that is, the most serious - level, I hate the military provenance of 'avant-garde.' He says that 'experimental' "drapes over the shoulders of the artist the inappropriate mantle of the scientist. (...) When poets and artists set off on their own paths, they are not 'experimenting.' They are devising new ways of acting as artists, new ways to make poems and pictures and music and dance". This echoes Fraser: if the poet keeps moving, keeps writing, she will come to a place that others will call experimental; the poet will call it continuing to write. For many of us, consciousness on the edge is what keeps us going, and the edge is preserved by continuing to write, it is the edge here, of our writing, of what we have most recently completed, and what we are being moved towards writing next.

For a certain kind of writer, this edge, the continuation of this edge, is simply (complex) realism, and the forms and the methods are dictated by the territory. Fraser says "I had an awareness of a lot of stuff going on in my mind, voices, many voices, and lots of arguing, lots of interrupted talk". When she writes "understood and scrupulous" (in The Art of Practice anthology), for example, with its four terse lines aligned to the right margin, as if extracted from and commenting

1

on the left-aligned body of the text, and there is a line which can be read either as "to the Gymnasium where scale is in key/brick to the heart and air" or "to the Gymnasium where scale is brick to the heart and air," she is discovering a means, a form, for working with the many voices in her mind, and we, reading, are led into that many-voiced territory, where we hear, and think, that way as well. Later in her interview, Fraser describes one of her obsessive ideas as "trying to find a way of catching what it was like, how I talk to myself about what I think or experience out there. Trying to catch that patterning of inner talk, (not just how I speak), that voicelessness in the world, the interior stuttering, the broken-in-on, the unfinished, the ambivalent, the not smooth." In "never sensing her struggle" there is a passage which reads: "and I want/her for my friend but she is my/doctor," but, aligned to the right margin, is a stanza, beginning on the same line as "her for", which reads: "a black/shirt with/a black/hat with a/jacket with/black pants," and which serves as an oblique commentary on the ambivalence of the poet's desires as expressed in the body of the poem. Fraser is working with a form of realism, accuracy, attempting to present what happens; there are no experiments involved. Everything is permitted, but nothing is invented.

Fraser says she likes "seeing some of the younger people who include elements of language-centered writing along with some other things in their work. (...) I think it's crucial to find a way of making your own work, learning from multiple sources". At this point there would seem to be two origins for much of the disjunctive, montage-like writing which we find in Fraser's (and many of her contemporaries') work: on the one hand there is the multiplicity of voices in the patterning of inner talk; on the other there is the diversity of assimilated sources. Working from these two points, if one arrives at the making of one's own work, that work will be of the type which is often called experimental, will seem odd, off-center, stretched, though the impetus behind (within) it will have been an urge towards accurate presentation of what happens, is happening, as one engages the world.

In the talk printed in Talisman, Mac Low speaks of the late '50's, when Ginsberg and his associates were "giving complete freedom of expression to the ego," and when he was led, through Zen and Cage, "to devise nonintentional methods of making literary works. (...) I didn't - and certainly don't now", he says, "feel that nonintentional methods are especially privileged or worthy. I merely adopted them because I felt they were ways to evade - at least partially - the domination of the ego - a formulation which Buddhism had taught me to see as temporary and even illusory." Mac Low's work (Forties, for example) remains as extreme as any text-only writing. Poets currently working in comparable territory include John Byrum - "Compositional methods range across the spectrum uniting chance accumulation and elimination with structured composition, reflecting (embodying) current readings of the ways events unfold (in) the world", and "The intent of the work is to unfold (the reader's conceptions of) possibility" (O.blek 12, '93) - and Michael Basinski - "There are some imaginary facts that are central to how I find poetry. First among them is that any poetic I might fantastically present as fact at the beginning of this paragraph will not exist as fact at its end. There is no definable halt once thought enters the frictionless imagination." (O.blek 12) Mac Low's work, as Byrum's and Basinski's, is motivated by an urge towards greater realism, a detailed, precise investigation of what is going on. This doesn't strike me as experimental; it strikes me as investigative. There is no invention involved, there is (to use the etymology provided in POETRY USA) venturing, testing the way, taking a chance, towards and from the idea of presenting the way world and language and mind interact, how it is. Byrum tells us to "imagine world, language, and mind as three interwoven and partially isomorphic fields. Areas of each can be mapped onto areas of each of the other two. Thus, portions of each field can be understood as a function of portions of the other two." When we negotiate his layered texts, we are in a field in which these interweavings are felt, present. Mac Low says (in Shiny #7/8, '92) that he "began writing by nonintentional methods in order to present language (both its sound and meaning and the look of it) so that it can be perceived with 'bare attention', without its being burdened by the tastes, predilections, emotions, or opinions of the writer." He adds: "when the artist's ego does not determine all aspects of artworks, their perceivers are freed to become co-producers of meaning." As with Fraser's work, and with Byrum's, the reader is led into participation in a type of behavior, meaning-building, which is the same type of behavior that produced the work. Clark Coolidge has stated his intentions as "to not finally know whether I am reading or writing," and the intention is that the same ambiguity should be present for the 'reader', that the reader should find himself engaged in activity which is traditionally associated with writing.

The ambiguity and the multiplicity of perceptions, and the possibilities which unfold when one engages the ambiguity and the multiplicity, define the range of the field, provide the opportunities for meanings to emerge. Poetry USA quotes Gertrude Stein: "The words next to each other actually sound different to the ear that sees them. Make it either sees or hears them. Make it the eyes hear them. Make it either hears or sees them. I say this not to explain but to make it plain." This is what is going on with the experimental, this is what's so odd about it; it would present the situation of being human in the world rather than explain that situation. Any explanation is always wrong (often as not intentionally wrong, a lie, smokescreen, disinformation). Explanation removes writer and reader from presence and offers representation, abstract re-presentation, always less than the actual and inaccurate. The efforts required in any attempt to include all that is involved in the actuality of a moment stretch the boundaries of writing, extend the edge and the consciousness as the writing continues.

1994

published as the introduction to A Unit of Wheels Arms This Aisle of Mind, xtantbooks, 2005

CHAPTER TWO ||||||||||||||||||||||||||||||||||||||||||||||||||||||||||||

MISREADING THE PYRROLIC

"The central principle of any poetics is that it ought to result in poetry." — John Taggart

vertere, to turn, objects inside out in mind, thought's objection to itself, reversed in position, order, direction, or tendency, as inverse is defined, to turn from self in order to begin return to self, returning to the world, the body, world returning, becoming body, in inverse proportion, as world increases thought decreases, then the inverse of that, as world increases thought increases, so turn, thoughts inside out in body, the object of objection thought, returned to world, as body, as once is so was again

Robert Duncan: "Responsibility is keeping the ability to respond."

Uprooted from their conventional syntactical context, words juxtaposed hybridize. Uprooted words hybridize — their juxtaposed contexts. Words uproot context from hybrid conventions. Conventions hybridize the context of juxtaposed words. Words juxtaposed hybridize context.

you try to remember where you are going and how obvious it must be, but the rhythm of remembering forgets itself, occurs encased in its other, preceding itself and duplicating the precedence, extended as itself erased, forgotten into the other of its following moment, where you try to enclose it as yourself, it and I enmeshed, time told to entwine an I in other, self erased encased in obvious occurrence,

4

where you are going an example by extension of how you have been, but the rhythm of imagining removes the I from now this place erased and other in memory even as the moment mind mentions it to its (other) self, not body but mind imagining itself in time and therefore, then, yes, body, but barely, I in mind but mind in other than imagined I and everywhere except in body so also obviously there as well, erased into presence, as absence everywhere, but only as remembered barely, recalled from where, returned from later, where it must be going, encased in other time if in time at all, remembered back towards itself preceding presence, I in forgotten extension of I's other, self encased, returned extension, to presence preceding now as it unfolds, duplicate enfolded erasures of where it must be going, I in I recalled from other enclosed in later where preceding occurrence, in memory as occurring earlier than its presence preceding imagined removes following I's extension encased in absence as it is, how you have been imagined by an I not yet occurrence, an absence of an other I in which you are enclosed, imagined as a place, body and time enfolded in I following the preceding absence imagined by extension into now remembered as the absence from which mind unfolds in a moment's other imagined precedence following the rhythm of enclosed erasure, an absence of an I as presence imagined now, body (un(en)folded in imagined presence removed following the preceding absence

The loop of language polishes flight. Fever unites the mammals. Language arranges appearance, poisonous as right angles. The aphasia of nations, white and vegetative. Truth, written as faith in games, played by animal students.

light filtered through itself we call the luminescence of present response and it comes across as darkness folded in and through itself inside out light night unwound outwards and as such seen as touch the imagined warmth of absence as it returns loss to lasting longer than any now or even is its swirling transformation spirals into and through itself transcall responseformation consciousness arrayed in loss imputed and dream imagined each as given and therefore other only ours as absence in this moment changing having changed to given other leaving transformed absence's renascent luminescence as emblem and evidence of this now has left

The music of trial questions identity. To shell a seed, dispose of will. Witness the organism, evaluate the performance. Sex isolates design.

in next so that time is not the issue but the previous emergence of this which already we remembered into later instance the merging of two absences into a third not present though all there is evidence offered by itself as memory to itself afterwards when any moment is previous to each and only known approaching in reverse inverted other in which I imagines we as evidence of its present absence while time translucent illumines loss unfolding into all next to itself is I in self as other later within we which issues only out of earlier I's as absent place these eyes have touched in time less passing bringing back from later lost memories of each moment's issue

Resources confine. Spasms of the body poison talk. Poem flavored with diseases, chains of habits, tribes, sites of the desquamated rivers. Each word contains the mitosis of silver.
The responsibility of any kind of freedom might immobilize us. So few are free in any sense, it's so hard to do, getting there, place where time is open, we must do something important, dead serious, play at least as gods might play, most of us have sense enough not to seek such freedom, not to know much time in place as one's own, there then to act as if a causal self.

hibrida, a crossbred animal, body meshed with time as mind ensconced in meat, offspring of two animals of different species produced through human manipulation, produced by the interaction of two unlike cultures, two unlike traditions, derived from unlike sources, composed of incongruous elements, word composed of elements originally drawn from different languages, text meshed with time as word ensconced in ink, then once is will be this was returned

Word substitutes object for drama. Body as text, a medieval sermon. Study the woven object, threads of surface grammar. Nouns of action warm the suffix of the brain.

It could be argued that the rules for writing a line should change with each new line. Slightly, perhaps, but surely, discoverable through their differences. This could hold true whether we are breaking lines, or measuring them from period to period in a prose-like form. For example: one line might emerge from an earlier line using the sounds of syllables as the unit of development (as "pine koans", in Silliman's Tjanting); the next line might come into being as a development of possibilities of alternate spelling, adding or omitting a letter, using the letter as the unit of development ("pin koans"); the next line might derive etymologically; the next, associationally. In practice, a line will be the result of many procedures, rules, applied in different combinations. In Tjanting, for example, we get "in paradise plane wrecks are distributed evenly throughout the desert," followed by "in paradise plain rocks are distributed evenly throughout the desert," "in paradise desert rocks are distributed evenly throughout the plain," "impaired eyes, desert

6

rocks are attributed evenly throughout the pain," etc. Misspelling, transposition, dyslexia, mispronunciation, and a sort of metathesis work to rearrange the sentence, emphasizing the materiality of the words, the letters, while expanding the possibilities for reading them. Array by play, ludic engagement with the given, as enlargement. What is human in the letters is their inclination to expand. Silence, a spirit, ancient as the coded song of bone and blood, enters through a wound in the text, text's foregrounded failure to remain simply itself, seeps in through cracks in the concrete, in the materiality of the language, and we encounter, unfolding, the emergent presence of a human consciousness. It is, simultaneously, a deeply mysterious power that is felt, and an ordinary perception that is encountered. Conventional methods of composition tend to limit, towards control (of text and reader), to lie in the name of precision, to separate, isolate, diminish and extinguish.

To begin outside of self, there then being closer to here now than the usual notions of present, presence, and to return from there to the within, mind arranging choices, body willing words into events,

this requires a method, a discipline, upaya, eupraxia, a set of rules or at least a map allowing a movement into writing, entrance into the outside preceding the first imprint of choice willed in words,

to begin not with ego, not with memory, not with faith or with belief, but with and in the risk of being in the world, mortal body naked before the lethal world, in risk of all for everything, even self,

returning then, from then, to within, from without, with world, with a word, chosen from the given, from an other, and placing it on page or screen, once upon an emptiness now resonant with will, turning then to return, release, to risk again in the without

The object is desire, the noun omission. Name is wonder, the other, magic fire of winter. Remote in time, with the adjectives. Speech is tenure. The pronoun imagines the verb. After adjectives, adverbs of comparison, expressing difference, choice, time.

Imagine meaning in constant motion, composed of countless invisibles, their elliptical orbits overlapping, that translucence our encounter. The politics of meaning, recontextualized. The crafty or unprincipled methods and tactics of meaning. Factional scheming for power and status within a group of meanings.

Imperialistic meaning. The colonialism of meaning. The autarky of meaning. Corrupt meanings.

Imagine emotion as a category of language, a state of forgetfulness, memory in code. Imagine emotion as a function of language, a category of thought, a rebellion against clarity. Imagine emotion as a product of thought, an encounter with translucent words, the memory of loss, its invisible orbit inside us. Emotion as the translucence of the surface, poems floating in the pulse, opaque mist of blood and flesh, felt absence, present flux.
time it was called. one axis of writing and magic. I want to have been written by this book. the sacred alphabet of pulse. blood in the muscle predicting the future. a thing so slow that reason is felt. unstitching the content of the surface. text unfolding within the text. commentary enfolded in the phrase. interrogation of the choice. shaped by practice.

Ron Silliman: "I want to start a riot in the prison-house of language."

1994

published as the introduction to Azoic Grids, xtantbooks, Charlottesville, 2005

CHAPTER THREE ||||||||||||||||||||||||||||||||||||||||||||||||||

Khawatir (Ongoing)

"That which comes into the world to disturb nothing deserves neither respect nor patience." René Char, "To The Health Of The Serpent"

As a beginning: Interruptions distributed across the field where meaning is not an inflorescence. Frames bloom in the gaps. The distance gets smaller as the familiar recedes. A poem as long as the arm of the law. The complete thought lasts forever, an anarchy of grammar, our sentence. So the unit is the word, but the distance is too great, though we're on familiar turf, where we can think. Poem long as the shadow of speech. To start with definition, then seek its fragments. So the syllable is the unit, the deep breath of a verb. Poem the length of a wave, say hydrogen. The area less familiar, and more intimate. So the unit is the letter. Poem the length of an el in 10-point Palatino. Where the territory is the map, and we are lost at home.

The choice - to write territory or to write map. I choose territory.

Adjective is the instance in which will chooses stasis.

Adverb is the site of quality for process.

In the gerund we watch the noun emerging from its verbal chrysalis.

The question in the blood of writing concerns the time between nakedness and distance.

Difference in method -or theory- creates difference in style or form.

Not difference in quality.

Towards a poetics of potentialities - to conjure by implication the spectre of an actuality...

We can start by saying words are windows. In a moment they become the orbits inside subatomic particles. Not anything orbiting, a tendency to exist which has tendencies towards orbiting. What is being orbited is conjecture, though we call it memory. A trace of some forgotten art of divination. Words are limited to this tiny omniscience.

Like stones. We can spend what we call a lifetime deciding not to throw one through the window. Not exploding outward into the little room. Not scattering in simple patterns forever, described by unimaginable immense and timeless orbits.

If we ever encounter repetition, we should worship it. It isn't likely to ever be available in any form for us. Part of the reason is that there are no nouns in nature. Part of the reason is that the verb "to be" cannot inform us of anything actual.

Sensory data re-designs dendritic form. Context is neural flux.

Writing is a refusal of identity.

Interrogate the surface of the text.

What am I ever writing about if not presence? Intention's distance.

Palpable time. Expressivity and the cult of genius. As if the broadcast was intended for the radio.

Oxymoron is not enough. Method is not enough. Ego flexed in the struggle to deny itself, grown monstrous in the isometric endeavor.

The question is not where to begin, but how. Begin with the right approach and anywhere will work.

Begin with the wrong approach and nothing will work.

Bernstein: "Serial reading opens all works to recombination."

The strict form of haiku, as if organic. Bowl, bell, tube, brush, flag, gullet.

The mathematics is our invention.

Form itself allows us entrance into what is other than ourselves. Hierarchy is the form of ego externalized. The metaphor of verticality reified, repression which begins everywhere and reaches into each of us. The ego and its toys reside at the top of this bloody totem. Denial of ego simply places ego at the bottom of the same strict hierarchy. Nothing is changed. What is possible, however, is play along the horizontal axis of the actual, where ego is diverse, diffused, identity displayed in difference. This is where organic form is possible and important. Pattern that grows out of itself, emergent, self-organizing, included in and including the diverse available resonances of the actual. That the imagined participates in all of this is obvious. There's no need to invent a thing.

Among the whats of is I trust we live in wonder.

I choose, in this and any context so immense that "I" and "choose" are emptied of all meanings, to begin each writing outside of ego. To start the first scratch exiled from the interior. At the center is an emptiness I want to imagine as the joy of ekstasis, not even in synapse, not in absence orbiting around and inside the deepest inner, outside this mind and body, in that, in there, later, not much but absolutely later. To rid myself of self, then that of my, to receive the return returning it, this then the given previous as now, gifted through. This is the anxiety of identity in a culture that trivializes identity, commodifies the unique, erases self with sign which says 'for sale', for use at best, for its own uses, the unique which is nothing itself.

I use other texts as points of departure, dictionaries mostly, to start with definitions and move to fragments, to erase imposed order point-by-point, back slowly in an instant to interior transformed in minute particulars, self and world not erased but at least as a start not quite the same, there the chance then of speaking, as the saying said returning, not as self. We don't know what we say until we learn it from the saying, when then the said as now, the willingness to say. That freedom from, there for. There is no etiology in the act. There is the enormity - totipotence of self, dream's reach, infinite smallness opening into all, memory enfolded in mind, mind breathed through body as loss in growth, death the name of each moment's pulse. There is no soteriology in self. There is its absence which is its redemption - time's hoax, space spiraling through the orbits of its absences, the body's invisible silence dreaming still of nothing, mind's coded whisper as distant as all presence, absence as its essence. If it is possible to begin writing outside of self, in actual outside, from there to act, then here and there lose their distinction, become continuum, as does time become, is was later, and we are writing from the future back towards the self, and writing in each as all, the set surely larger than any I imagine I comprise.

I cannot be confined to I. It is the larger is which was that is later from which we write. Time begins after now and we bring it back from never to its absence in our presence within the time that is, which is the time which was recalled, called back from its origins afterwards. I is I is lie into diminished act. I is I is all of loss, the growth away within, is less than absence.

we spend a thousand hours, more, preparing to write, and writing, a poem, a few lines of a poem - we must read everything, anything less is not good enough, and each reading requires a life's work of contemplation, opening through openings into another entrance, layer beyond layer revealing another surface, another beginning (we don't get deeper into a surface by peeling off a layer, by looking beneath or within, we get to another surface, begin again, exploring along the horizontal axis of the actual) - we have gotten nowhere - back to where we began, in the recent future - - - at some point we abandon preparation and act, even though the preparation is unfinished, and write, each word an eternity, of choices, of memories, will (from as now within us not within, as to breathe, as is), of possibilities, dreamed, flexed, muscled into being, worked there, there, each syllable a life's work, resonant with histories now, imploded into and through unimagined futures, all of memory, each of the infinite pasts, the miniscule immensity of each specific detail, each moment's site

in each of the pasts, in each syllable, each scratch or stroke, and in ripples ever outward from this relinquished moment's place, all of later memory, imagined out of now, and none of this by us, or not so that we can tell it if a context could stay the same, if any one context could be encountered twice, if body could stop and, still, know, then duration might be an absolute, an anchor, a site in which to center self and world

but duration is a sort of chance operation in itself, a state-space model of imagined time, agreed upon, imagined into approximation, an absence, made the more real the less of it we allow, the fewer degrees of freedom considered the greater the shared experience is felt

The self loves nothing more than self-expression.

We need the game, to play, and 'game rules', to lure self into the outside, there, from there, to express an other through our selves.

Slowly, through hand and pen to page, thought traversing the neural lengths

Overlapping grids within which one glimpses traces of content

Forms - the receding footprints left by content as it departs

Dysfunctional grids, dysraphic, even, grids that foreground their open fields, insist upon openness rather than confinement, on absences, opportunities, potential

Too slowly, through hand and key to screen, thought traversing the neural lengths (mightier than the pen)

If I outline the frames, insist upon the boundaries, I do so because it is there, between, within, the boundaries, that the work is done,

is only there that the work can be done though the reasons for the work, work's sense, may come from outside such boundaries (work's dream), may come through and into the enclosed field, offering the palpable sense of opening, and of entrance

1994

published as the introduction to The Appetites Codex, xtantbooks, 2005

originally published as Khawatir: Ongoing, in Worcs Aloud Allowed, 1995, edited by Ralph LaCharity

CHAPTER FOUR ||||||||||||||||||||||||||||||||||||||||||||||||||||||||||||||||||

As a beginning:

Suspension of towards a poetics of revision is a calculated. For that place, falsification of the seeking. The simple light relinquished, textual potentialities. Record. To conjure and to chain oneself, there by implication, the spectre of to seek. Freedom is to find, the darker prison an actuality, weight of absence as in painting, white space. Freedom is the rebellion of whatever wishes, but the word 'environment' does not allow freedom in the extreme. Of what is possible in a meaningless environment. For meaning: to be free against itself, to suggest range of possible absences. In revision: delete what isn't needed and what doesn't work, of course; then delete what does work, the sand which needs the stones anywhere in the space in order to be empty, the noises of the knives and forks, the trouble of paying attention, the birds beginning to sing, and all the rest of our inherited aesthetic claptrap, because it works according to various preconceived notions, theory, and the poetics of that belief system can't lead to a new poem. Of what is possible in a meaningful environment: environment insists on meaning, each instance essential surface, a chordal reading of texture as defined. Context of concentric dreams, the sound of flesh on soil. If theory at all, form is the shape of a handful of the horizontal and vertical relationships of musical materials, comparable to the interweaving air. Write not from but towards theory, a figure of the past, a form of necrophilia, a lack of interest in the natural differences of sound, a notation for jazz improvisation. Not writing after or about event, but writing as event, as sounds, as material, as no longer urgently necessary. I mean to argue an imagined absence, as empty as our anger. Indifference of the sunrise, eyes as plural ego. After deciding for the idea of indifference, the urgency of each breath, the details of duration. A moment's flesh: mesh. Particular means prayer. Not from an awareness but towards an awareness, a pattern. Not after a discovery but as a discovery, a disagreement, a decision, doing. The experience of the blank screen is not the experience of the white page. It is not the endless emptiness of page after page that confronts us here, it is my responsibility and the response, diversity, moment's place in resonance. It is the illusion, as in painting, of depth, of infinite depth, a bottomlessness before us, limited by our imagining. Endless layers of implicate surface, framed as less than infinite. We write on the invisible content of the skin, sky grows away from us, expanding, falling. The texture creates the content of the craft. We abandon, rather than finish, a work, to cease writing for self, for friends, for strangers, a writing with others. One person, in solitude, writing poetry in prose, is a refusal of trickery, the mirrors and lights cannot have anything meaningful to say. The fit of sound to sense brought the sliding tones of the water gong into the percussion orchestra. There is light has everything to do with at the beginning of the tunnel . Whether or not there is responsibility at its end is not my perception, consistent choices made within shared belief systems are left leaning in their dusty corners. There is no sense in attempting to work within the craft. Light creates the texture ideas express in verse, or (2) a prosodic archaeology by means of which we sift combinations which might be called hybrid textures. Through all this content in search of signs of life. Having passed at least the dust of nearby. Perhaps we can produce poems out of the revisioning of a synthesis, the lifeless constraints of a reductionistic prosody, the regurgitation of an analysis. Emotion moves in electric murk, recoil of Kundalini, incandescent call, incantatory response. The analytical method of approaching definition by poetry dismantles the poem. Writing is therefore incapable of encountering a poem emerging. In the pattern of the pulse a muscle blooms. Inflorescence of the sinew, blood's speech of silent dust, ancient orbits pointing, unfold the surface of the sign, stand sings. Poetry dismisses the possibility of an analytical approach. Our possible responses are confined to the realms of (1) a sort of cultural history of poetry in prose, as a beginning, a suspension of poetics towards a calculus of revision. Form as place, verification of the seeking.

As a beginning: the experience of the blank screen is not the experience of the white page. It is not the endless emptiness of page after page that confronts us here; it is the illusion, as in painting, of depth, of infinite depth, a bottomlessness before us, limited by our imagining. We write on the invisible skin of the sky. Content grows away from us, expanding, falling. Form is the shape of a handful of air.

- Aspects into hierarchy -
1-content meaning sense
2-creation method situation

3-craft medium synthesis
Scramble.

Non-linearity doesn't occur as an analysis - or during, or as a result of, example of the theory of - (constellation of beliefs in motion)
Revision - no sanctity except in change - nothing need remain as originally imagined - as if: thought preserved in situ - as if: museum of the mind, museum of the self - zoo, last week's untamed tendencies - as if: resuscitation of the passed moment...
We want to stop time with signature. - as likely with doubt. This doubt.

1994

published as the introduction to pagan inventory of etic light, xtantbooks, 2005

originally published as Khawatir: As a beginning, in Worcs Aloud Allowed, 1995, edited by Ralph LaCharity

CHAPTER FIVE ||||||||||||||||||||||||||||||||||||||||||||||||||||||||||||||||||||||||||||||

PARADOX AS TEXTURE: AFTER DECIDING AGAINST COLLAGE

   Collage as form is metaphor. Collage does not exist as an object to be encountered in the present. The birthmark of collage is absence, its fingerprint is desire. Collage is time without a center, the site of absence. To make collage is to enter the mirror. Source text is signification seen as chthonic spirit, and to enter into its revisioning is to dissolve in the play of rapture.
   To make collage is to join with the tradition of ecstasy, the shaman flying on his borrowed fractal drum. Collage is displacement of body; it is sex. The collage-artist annihilates self in order to liberate ego. Collage dismantles the myth of verticality, deflates hierarchy, flattens the upward spiral, proposes sacred play along the horizontal axis of the holy soil.
  Source text is the garden of experience, where innocence is playfully sought through sexual disintegration.
  Collage expects nothing; therefore it has no identity. Collage is a roadsign that points in the wrong direction, towards the absence of a path, the unraveling

threads of present texture, where it presents itself as something else, as everything that it is not. Collage is other presented as self, difference proposed as identity. Collage promotes its existence by insisting on its nothingness.

Collage exiles time from the present. Time exists in collage as a refugee from the unknown. The reader moves through collage as an alien traversing impossible terrain: there never was a world like this, and there never will be. Collage violates all civilized arrangements of human interaction.

Collage is the denial of cooperation, the refusal of society, the anarchy of violence and desire.

Collage is not intended as democracy. It is closer in intent to monarchy, or theocracy. The collage artist uses the labor of others to facilitate his own work. Collage is free enterprise, capitalism. It is more like murder than it is like theft. It isn't so much like rape as it is like chemical warfare. Collage secretly penetrates the body of another's work, the lethal viral infection by another mind.

Collage enters text like a team of nanotech machines, to dismantle and subdue, to redirect. Collage voids the social contract between writer and reader.

Collage reinvents the relationship between sender and receiver, erases the earlier attempt at communication, and redefines the dimension of power on the terms of the collage-artist. The asymmetry of the writer/reader relationship is reversed -- the writer is silenced; the collage-artist will do the talking. In collage, an actual response, other than the negative reactions of shutting the book or consciously rejecting its thesis, becomes possible; the collage artist re-writes the book. Since the process of consuming information is an act of submission, the collage artist responds by refusing to consume the information on the terms of the text. Collage recognizes resistance and annihilation as alternatives to submission. If the writer insists that to have read his words is to have had his thoughts, thoughts which are not one's own, then the collage-artist insists on destroying the object of his oppression, and in creating out of the debris a new work which is his own, the tools of the oppressor, his words, are stolen and utilized towards different ends. Collage, having overthrown the tyrant, invites a new kind of participation in the text.

Collage posits anarchy as the fundamental mode of interaction between reader and writer. The asymmetry of the power relationship is redefined at the outset, is reversed, with the collage-artist inviting the reader to participate as an empowered equal. Collage refuses copyright, denies the idea of intellectual property, insists on openness. Collage is revolution; it begins with an act of violence.

Collage is collaboration.

Text is a template and a score. The collage-artist enters into a liaison with the text, with a multitude of texts, facilitates communication between units of the multitude, acts as the conduit for a sexual transgression of the boundaries between texts, redistributes voice, allowing the final silence of the text to become the initial voice of the collage. Collage is naked passion, but more conjugal than illicit. Collage is form, not metaphysics, and as such is nothing more than the extension of content.

Collage proposes that the recognition of a template is a transformative experience, that improvising from a score is a form of liberation. Collage torques inert text into rotation with other texts, so that point of view, standpoint, site of identity for reader and writer emerge like bubbles in a boiling pot. Collage is the chaos of human potential at play in the textual record left by a congress of mind.

Collage finds communication at the center of a sieve.
    Communication is the evidence of our isolation.
Dialogue is always between the alien and the exile.   Transduction as collage:
    Discourse is singular.   towards an anti-philosophy of mis-reading.

Collage is a burial rite celebrated over the ashes of identity. History is
the silence of choice. Memory is the death-mask of choice.
  Identity is the serpent, the serpent's slough, a chameleon, the
    failure of collage and of memory, an erasure
    of history.
 The aphorism retreats to its origin at the horizon. The aphorism locates its horizon in the past. The aphorism is a recipe for imprisonment by memory.
Memory locates will at the edge of a grave, its death a singular noun, history.

 History is the illusion of continuity in a fiction of identity.
  Words silence the singular. Collage is non-linear aphorism, the curved horizon re-imagined as forthcoming. Collage is a collaboration between silence and desire.

Deliberate mis-reading is a form of improvisation
 and is always quasi-intentional. Improvisation is the will to khawatir, the desire to choose
 involuntary thoughts. Collage is collective
improvisation, the deliberate over-extension of openness,
  inclusion of a range larger than the form is designed to fit.

Recombination, or distillation, works like a collage of omission, and is autoerotic, text manipulated to transform during play with(in) itself. At the same time, it is a collective improvisation, a non-traditional score re-interpreted against its author's intentions to perform as an ensemble freed of its intrinsic organizational principles.

It is the jazz standard for solo piano revisioned as a collective improvisation for double quartet. A recombinative distillation treats the degrees of freedom revealed in reading the turbulence of a text as if it is their unveiling that is the desired result of reading, as if the reader's awareness of this stretched range of possibilities, the reader ranging through this field, that actuality, activity, was the attainment to be gained through engaging a text -- not as if this encounter was a tool to then be used towards some more pragmatic action, towards a state-space-model of self and the prediction of its patterned unfolding.

This is how collage, recombination, distillation, transduction -- all quasi-intentional operations involving source text -- become divinatory practices. The reader participates in an awareness large enough to form a fractal fragment of the whole moment, so that self and situation are self-similar, and this situates identity in the site of present flux, taking shape.

In collage -- or recombination -- or distillation -- or transduction -- the writer is naked in the new text, and the original, along with its author, is violated. This is one of the hazards of embrace -- larger, of inclusion -- larger yet, of receptivity. There is no need to make this explicit in the new text; it is painfully apparent.

The situation is presented as nakedness and violation, and it is encountered as an anxious witnessing of transgression. Reading writing derived from source text, we are voyeurs witnessing a sexual crime. There is no one to report this to, and our complicity is immediate and irremediable.

Our only choice is whether or not to act. We are either silenced or converted, recruited, initiated into the alterity of the creative, where transgression is identity, and the past does not exist. There is no history at the border, no time at all at the nexus of identity and boundary.

The present erases itself with choice, future unravels in a spiral back towards the absent site of self. We are left with the rasp of individual expressivity which is emergent from a primal template that is known through receptivity. Nakedness replaces number, will is reduced to the electrical surge of anxiety, choice operates in the enormous chaos of turbulent causation, self insists on its identity until absence is its proof.

first published by Jake Berry in THE EXPERIODDICIST #7, 1995
also published in Worcs Aloud Allowed, Vol. 11, #12, 1996. edited by Ralph LaCharity

From: JUXTA43781@aol.com
Date: Fri, 4 Apr 1997 14:56:50 -0500 (EST) To: jacobus@hooked.net
Subject: essay on Taylor

SAME STREAM TWICE: LESSER MARKS IN TAYLOR'S DAILY LOGS
"May 28.95"

"Everything that is engenders, sooner or later, nightmares. Let us try, therefore, to invent something better than being" (E.M. Cioran)

"there's more to do, in the close readings to discover how nonverbal fields envelope clusters of words with an uncanny emanation of what, not meaning, stuff Stuff, i dont know, light, energy of some sort...." (Tom Taylor, in a letter)

"I no longer want any knowledge that
will not immediately produce an even
greater ignorance." (Clark Coolidge)

"The Daily Logs" begins: "Lesser fronted dailies pique less attentive". What do we enter at the invitation of such an opening line?
AGNOSIA. Less. ("Since the mid-fifties I have been interested in agnosia, in the kind of vision proposed by the progenitors of Meister Eckhart, like Dionysius the Aeropagite or like Hildegard von Bingen. I've always been interested in that idea that one sees with blackness, one sees through poverty of knowledge. It's only through the poverty of knowledge that we acknowledge our own blackness so that perceptions can happen. Hildegard von Bingen is saying that, Dionysius the Aeropagite is saying that, I think Meister Eckhart is saying that, I think Jacob Boehme is saying that, and I believe that this idea is even more common but stated in another way in Eastern thought ... I mean one is attempting to clear the reticular formation, to make it blank, so that perception passes over." Michael McClure, LIGHTING THE CORNERS)
"Syntax as a rhythm of the cosmos." (Taylor) "Lesser fronted dailies pique less attentive gasps of renoun his apple's grand & simple are now your own eyes remind me that I am. The hearts warps no less plenty than not." Asked at the outset

to be attentive. Where the apple is serpent first friend of knowledge but there are no nouns in nature, so identity is an event which requires the perceptions of another, and the only repetition is lesser, less, and less.

Unless we count the instance of "own", which resounds the absent "w" of renown (for now unwritten, partial, pure possibility), insisting on the fragment of "now", lessened here to "no", embedded by implication in "renoun". Renown: 1.) The quality of being widely honored and acclaimed; fame; 2.) (Obsolete) Report, rumor; from Latin re + nomer, to name. No nouns in nature, but rumors and reports of processes renamed as nouns. Identity occurs at the crossroads of another's eyes and I, process itself is plural.

Therefore, "the hearts warps no [now] less plenty than not. "Hearts" sans apostrophe is the site of the singular/plural/possessive. "Warps" oscillates from verb to noun and back. There is no less plenty than not, and more than meets the eye, where sounds enact a transubstantiation of script's sense.

Less plenty is pleroma, glimpsed sparks ensconced in fractured substance. "No less plenty than not" negates the fullness of its presence in order to exist, its absence filling with the tensions of attention, tsimtsum. Thought emanates from text.

From Gershom Scholem: "Tsimtsum originally means 'concentration' or 'contraction,' but if used in the Kabbalistic parlance it is best translated by 'withdrawal' or 'retreat'." "Tsimtsum does not mean the concentration of God at a point, but his retreat away from a point." The condensation of language in poetry brings us to this emptiness, reveals an absence at the center of our perceptions, the core of unknowing in the apple of our gnosis. ("Writing works in two directions. It is both an expansion and a contraction." Edmond Jabes) Scholem: "According to Luria, God was compelled to make room for the world by, as it were, abandoning a region within Himself, a kind of mystical primordial space from which He withdrew in order to return to it in the act of creation and revelation. The first act of En-Sof, the infinite Being, is therefore not a step outside but a step inside, a movement of recoil, of falling back upon oneself, of withdrawing into oneself. Instead of emanation we have the opposite, contraction. The God who revealed himself in firm contours was superseded by one who descended deeper into the recesses of His own Being, who concentrated Himself into Himself, and had done so from the very beginning." "That one is and knows one is and that it is good and that one is present in the act-event of his being and consequent to his arousals of thought and action, resolute, perseverant and continuant. What is achieved out of the poetic, then, is directness and immediacy of one's sensations of the world." (Taylor)

The "Daily Log" dated May 28.95 continues: "What had you done? Any more decides yr name, not as doubt, but presence." When the "you" and "yr" are read as referring to the reader, one finds a partial answer to "what had you done?" in the preceding stanza: "now your own eyes remind me that I am."

Here is the 'w" for the "no", one letter at a time the renown of being read occurs, and the identity of the poet begins to emerge in the eyes of the reader returned in resonance to the poet, there transliterated as an "I".

Jabes again: "What I mean by God in my work is something we come up against, an abyss, a void, something against which we are powerless. It is a distance ... the distance that is always between things ... We get to where we are going, and then there is still this distance to cover. And a moment comes when you can no longer cover the distance; you get there and you say to yourself, it's finished, there are no more words. God is perhaps a word without words. A word without meaning." "Any more decides yr name." Any more than enabling the identity of the poet to emerge in the reading is an insinuation of the reader into the act of writing, where reader assumes the identity of poet, and the actual writer retreats into a distance, identified as absent. "The first act of all is not an act of revelation but one of limitation," writes Gershom Scholem. "Only in the second act does God send out a ray of His light and begin his revelation, or rather his unfolding as God the Creator, in the primordial space of His own creation. More than that, every new act of emanation and manifestation is preceded by one of concentration and retraction. In other words, the cosmic process becomes two-fold. Every stage involves a double strain, i.e. the light which streams back into God and that which flows out from Him, and but for this perpetual tension, nothing in the world would exist." Visionary writing is perhaps a tradition reaching back into the archaic, with links to the pre-literate, sources in the oral transmissions of epic and in shamanic ecstasy. Numerous labels have been applied over the years, all of them finally useless, though in varying degrees -- romanticism, symbolism, surrealism, futurism, dada, zaum, concrete, otherstream -- and this is just in the last 200 years! We begin to realize that these categories are mostly useful for those who have no intention of actually knowing the tradition, of participating in it. The situation is much as it is with religion, the source and importance of which is almost entirely obscured by the distinctions made between this one and that. It all goes back to vision, or to a sort of proprioception, the common source of these poetries and religions. Jonas insists that gnosticism is of the particular. It is as if mysticism is in fact not only an apprehension of the particular, even an encounter with the realm of boundless light being an encounter with the particular, but is also a profoundly tactile experience, each of the five senses being a variety of touch, wavelengths coded and/or decoded by different organs of the body. Even the beyond, the wholly other, if known, is known through the sensorium. What one brings away from such an encounter is, more than anything else, the knowledge of one's own transformation.

Through the particular and the tactile one encounters transcendence of the particular and the tactile. But the knowledge must be received in ways which will allow us to know it, so that what we come away with is a translation.

And we know that we have been beyond, absolutely beyond, the knowable world, have been dismantled and reassembled, transformed utterly, but in the knowing we are removed from that which we wish to know. And as we continue working through the knowing, thinking, reading, writing, talking, yearning to understand the gnosis, we take ourselves farther and farther from the experience. The knowledge that we need and want is beyond knowing, though we know that, we are only near, not there, in the knowing. So at some point, if we write, we come into or towards an understanding, and the page will no longer hold the work, syntax and grammar and spelling, all of the wonderful tools of communication, language itself, is no longer a vehicle, but is a barrier. But we write, we are writers, so we begin to do battle with the language, writing becomes a violence, writing against itself. We eliminate punctuation, ignore correct spellings, invent new words, invert syntax, scramble grammar, scatter lines and columns of words across the page-as-field. We lose control, discard control, another barrier, ego at its worst. We use chance, collage, found text, improvisation, borrow rules and methods from other areas of practice, other disciplines, from techniques of the sacred, from the visual arts, from music, from science, write chants, verbo-visual constructions, aleatory arrangements of syllables and letters, mathematical arrangements, lyrics derived from chaos theory, fuzzy logic. We use computer assisted designs, random patterns, random number generators, iteration. But we end with language on a page, or on a screen, or maybe on a canvas, or as the spoken word. What we have produced, the creation, the addition to the stock of available reality, is not what we want, and is not all that we get, and, finally, is not what the process of working, or the work itself, has to give. The process of working against the barriers, slowly, returns us to the source, less intensely, and partial, but recognizable, a different tilt of light stretched against the horizon. It is the discipline, the work, the praxis, a sort of upaya, perhaps, or a kabbalistic inner magic, as in Abulafia's doctrine of combination, that returns us, that opens the particulars of the writing into other reaches of awareness. But it isn't content that we come away with, and it isn't statement, or communication of any sort. It is text. Let's call it poetry, because of those before us who have called it poetry. It takes us away from our attachments. It redesigns the dendrites. It opens into other realms, the innermost of each particular which is the ineffable beyond. As far as what we do with the writing, what we can do with and in it, is concerned, we come to realize that freedom is the only law. (from a letter to Tom Taylor) "Any poetic is meant to describe the origins of thought." (Taylor) "Any more decides yr name,/not as doubt, but presence." In order for the reader to enter this work, the writer must become absent. The reader inserts his name where the identity of creator is in question. However, the reader does not begin with nothing. The first act of creation is one of limitation.

The poet limits the range of available possibilities in order to allow the poem to come into existence. The reader begins with the letters on the page, boundaries set and calculated by the poet. It is the poet's world which the reader is invited to enter, but it is a world which invites the reader to explore his own creative potential.

Scholem: "Inasmuch as Tsimtsum signifies an act of negation and limitation it is also an act of judgement. It must be remembered that to the Kabbalist, judgement means the imposition of limits and the correct determination of things. According to Cordovero the quality of judgement is inherent in everything insofar as everything wishes to remain what it is, to stay within its boundaries. Hence it is precisely in the existence of individual things that the mystical category of judgement plays an important part. If, therefore, the Midrash says that originally the world was to have been based on the quality of strict judgement, Din, but God seeing that this was insufficient to guarantee its existence, added the quality of mercy, the Kabbalist who follows Luria interprets this saying as follows: The first act, the act of Tsimtsum, in which God determines and therefore limits, Himself, is an act of Din which reveals the roots of this quality in all that exists; these 'roots of divine judgement' subsist in chaotic mixture with the residue of divine light which remained after the original retreat or withdrawal within the primary space of God's creation. Then a second ray of light out of the essence of En-Sof brings order into chaos and sets the cosmic process in motion, by separating the hidden elements and moulding them into new form."

"What had you done? Any more decides yr name, not as doubt, but presence. New vocabulary hints new messages are in store again" What sort of new messages? The next stanza provides us with a clue, a suggestion of where, and how, to search: "Lesser marks decide." The marks in question in this stanza of the poem are punctuation marks. "Had. No foot the same stream twice, has the deal not unremarked, but shown, alive & well where the new moon says this is it. And not easy either. Lesser marks decide." The displaced periods insert silences into the flow of words. The single word "had" becomes a statement of that which cannot be repeated, the stream which cannot be stepped into twice. "Had" blankets the past, leaves us with the present, stepping into the utterly new stream of thoughts. It's newness is its layeredness, the vocabulary's insistence that we read it and question our reading of it simultaneously. The situation is simultaneously presented and commented upon, is "not unremarked, but shown". The lesser marks decide, in part, precisely how "any more decides yr name". The reader participates as creator, but the construction of the writing controls the structure of the reader's creative response. "You've melt, or me," the next stanza begins.

Either the reader submits to the limitations imposed, proposed, by the writing, and assumes the identity of a secondary creator, or the writer's identity is erased, melted, and the crafted order of the poem is rejected in favor of the dubious freedom of an inattentive misreading. The process itself, which is plural, is subverted, and the reader constructs a line, a lie, for his own fulfillment.

Our intentions are always towards emptying ourselves. But that's not where it starts. We come through to expression through love and rage. Harmony and loss. Memory that leaks through and is the enormous erasure of time's pulse.

And the memories which lock us into the rhythm of that pulse. It is the distance which seems to require our expression, and our expression is its increase. Rage against the dissonance, which is a dissonance itself. Then the desperate attachments, more distance, a love of loss. Love of the distance and its dissonance, the details of each day. We can hold them in our hands, amulets of the alien. Love that brings us to the present, as a residue of despair. Resignation, but a glimpse of sacred patience, its reasons and our absence. There is nothing here. An emptying that is stretched. Descent, then darkness. We discard the metaphors where a silence blooms. "It is with sacred hesitation that one leaves the room of myth."

(Taylor) But one leaves. Nothing blooms at the source, an eye, its voice a palpable absence.

There is also another way of reading this: "you've melt, or me". The sentence, as written, actually means: you have melt, or me. "Melt", here, is a noun, and is "had". Either the reader "has melt," receives the emanated identity of the poet through the words, or the poet "has melt", receives the reminder of his identity through the eyes of the reader. The verb 'melt' is transformed into the noun "melt" by the lesser marks, here an apostrophe and the letters "ve". The noun occurs as a fixed instance of particularity in the flux, the oscillation, back and forth from writer to reader. However, as an aspect of the "had," it is transitory, and can only be had once. The next instance of this particular will appear somewhat altered. Scholem continues: "throughout this process the two tendencies of perpetual ebb and flow - the Kabbalists speak of hithpashtuth, egression, and histalkuth, regression - continue to act and react upon each other. Just as the human organism exists through the double process of inhaling and exhaling and the one cannot be conceived without the other, so also the whole of Creation constitutes a gigantic process of divine inhalation and exhalation." "You have to write in the same way you breathe." (Jabes) "Whatever it is, goes beyond what is said in favor of suggestion/example."

AND

"The same day carried forward what's against your will, even, and the example suffices for today where no answer persists." "Separation of self and will, leads to distrust of purpose." (Taylor) An opening. Silence blooms in the gap, emptied of itself, a hollow mirror, absence. A rhythm of annihilation and return. Self and will unite where freedom intrudes upon the world with its disarray of purposes manifest and silent; absence blooms, emptiness stretched to its limits, which are self and will. Nothing will not tell us what to do. Do what you are, the only opportunity for this instance of being to be. "To the extent that one moves he has direction / anything said has meaning or meeting." (Taylor) The perpetual unfolding of the emanation, which occurs in order to occur. The source gives off being like fire gives off smoke, like mind gives off thought. Is becomes.

"This is the authentic voice." Then: "And favorite words seem too like muscular habits, like the familiarity of containment." Then: "The barrier of the intellect, getting the mechanics together; finally, in the way. And:

"Conversation has a quality of admission rather than style, its purpose to obstruct." (Taylor) Why these words and not those? We sleep in a ruined dream. Must we choose between silence and magick. "The initial compromise was in not being silent." (Taylor) What, then, is the purpose of magick?

To give us the power to invoke the silence, to look it in the eye. To open the silence, allowing entrance. A sacrifice of self, into self, so that others might enter into their absence. What, then, is the task, of and inside language? That the authentic voice, a perfect truth, be revealed for the lie it is. That the words contain their own annihilation. That the containers be filled with beautiful corrosives. That the intellect build a monument to its self-destruction. That each monument be a convulsive beauty, the only one of its kind.

Jung, from Mysterium Coniunctionis: "Although the alchemists came very close to realizing that the ego was the mysteriously elusive arcane substance and the longed-for lapis, they were not aware that with their sun symbol they were establishing an intimate connection between God and the ego. As already remarked, projection is not a voluntary act; it is a natural phenomenon beyond the interference of the conscious mind and peculiar to the nature of the human psyche. If, therefore, it is this nature that produces the sun symbol, nature herself is expressing an identity of God and ego. In that case only unconscious nature can be accused of blasphemy, but not the man who is its victim. It is the rooted conviction of the West that God and the ego are worlds apart. In India, on the other hand, their identity was taken as self-evident. It was the nature of the Indian mind to become aware of the world-creating significance of the consciousness manifested in man. The West, on the contrary, has always emphasized the littleness, weakness, and sinfulness of the ego, despite the fact that it elevated one man to the status of divinity. The alchemists at least suspected man's hidden godlikeness, and the intuition of Angelus Silesius finally expressed it without disguise."

Cioran: "Indispensable condition for spiritual fulfillment: to have always placed the wrong bet."

"Poetry is not another shorthand for spiritual information, nor a realm of special effects which tickles the ends of the brainstem." --having decided for the inclusion of more than can be included --having affirmed a presence which as beyond negates the site of affirmation --the realm of spirit will finally have nothing to do with that which we name the spiritual

--but silence does not occur, nor is anything sounded into the air --what one might possibly bring back from direct encounter with the beyond, certainly nothing that will make any kind of sense --but poetry sounds the silence that wasn't there, speech of the voice that was no voice, from the face that is no face --the details of the work open inwards, through themselves, onto the infinite --every click of the tongue, each scratch upon the page, is a shorthand for the infinite

--sound and symbol are of the source

--intention is departure

--intention is arrival, the sleep of will "I do not believe in inspiration, or anything like it." (Jabes)

And:

"Something is already at work inside us, and then some little thing, an emotion, a chance encounter, sets it off." --choice is the opposite of awakening

--the work gets done as acquiescence

--self enters after its erasure and its absence is the action of the work --as emptiness, which becomes by multiplying its absences --so that a fullness might emanate into and through --the manifest becoming in multiplicity and abundance -- that is becomes through emptying itself into that which it lacks --which then fills it

--that it might continue emptying

--the poem is the presentation of this process --the poem refers to nothing, it is the thing itself --the poem is no more for the brainstem than it is for the church, or for the state, or for the poet (as if the broadcast was intended for the radio, as Spicer says)

--there is a sense in which the poem is for the tradition of poetry, but it is not for duplication, or preservation, or even praise

--poems are made for the poiesis, so the tradition of making poems continues --but poems do not build on the tradition, they are built against the tradition

--so that more of the fullness might enter into being --as each new emptying fills, an example of what everything else is not --each emptying, opening to erasure and absence, is a return of source to itself

25

Cioran: "I feel I am free but I know I am not." May 28.95: "The day formed out of bounds, and I looked."

(some references are to COSMIC POETICS, by Thomas Lowe Taylor, Anabasis, 1991; some of the material in quotes comes from Taylor's letters.)

1995

originally published by Michael Crye in Po'Flye ElectroMATIC, 1996
published by Don Hilla in PONSINGANOT, Ex Nihilo Press, San Francisco, 1998

CHAPTER SEVEN |||||||||||||||||||||||||||||||||||||||||||||||||||||||||||||||||||

Jim Leftwich <jimleftwich@gmail.com>
Jul 15 (3 days ago)
to Don:
hi Don
John Bennett is going to publish a collection of my essays, or probably a selection, since i doubt if i'll be able to find all of the ones from the 90s. do you have the essays on John High, and the second one on Jake Berry (on Brambu Book 2)? i lost access to all of that stuff when my mac crashed in 2009.

Don Hilla
Jul 15 (3 days ago)
to me:
i will look

Don Hilla
Jul 15 (3 days ago)
to me:

From: JUXTA43781@aol.com
Date: Fri, 4 Apr 1997 15:00:21 -0500 (EST) To: jacobus@hooked.net
Subject: essay on Bennett

TRANSDUCING LIBERATION

Transduction is reading strategy as writing procedure. Clark Coolidge has written that, finally, he doesn't want to know whether he is reading or writing; Bennett wants to know the two activities as one process.

Reading and writing both participate in the process of meaning-building, normally an asymmetrical power relationship, with the author having the upper hand. Ron Silliman, in responding to Tom Beckett's suggestion that he contextualize his *Sunset Debris* (a poem composed entirely of questions), said "every sentence is supposed to remind the reader of her or his inability to respond." In Bennett, every syllable is intended to remind the reader of his or her freedom to respond. Susan Smith Nash has written that "for Language poets, the meaning-building process is interesting because it foregrounds the culturally-based knowledge or value-systems that the reader employs in order to arrive at an interpretation." For Bennett, there is an added dimension of individual empowerment and liberation, in which the reader is invited to share fully in the creative process.

Bennett's transduction of Sor Juana's *Primero Sueno* was written, he has said, by "pretending I don't know Spanish and writing it out (reading it) as if it were English." This process arises from "an interest or attention paid to speech and handwriting as 'texts' full of meanings that have nothing to do with linguistics. I often read, or try to read, printed texts that way, too" (Letter, 9/14/94). With transduction, the reader-as-writer has reversed the conventional asymmetrical power relationship inherent in the reading process, and has, at least by implication, eliminated the asymmetry from further reading experiences. With transduction, the reader assumes the role of writer during the activity of reading, and in doing so frees other readers to make the same choice, to reject the submissive role of reader and also to refuse the dominant role of writer, choosing to work instead in the new hybrid capacity of reader/creator.

In his interview with Beckett, Silliman said, "as advertisers have known for decades, the process of consuming information is an act of submission. To have read these words is to have had these thoughts, which were not your own." But, if the need for consuming information is removed from the process of reading, and is replaced by the opportunity for creating new writing, then the act of submission is removed from the process, and to have read these, or any other, words is to have participated fully in an ongoing chaotic affirmation of meaning-building. The social contract between reader and writer is, in its conventional terms, voided, and a new declaration of collaborative independence is proclaimed. At the same time, the interdependence of reader and writer is enlivened, a vital link established, a connection, or pattern of connections, is determined, and the reading process is encouraged as an affirmation of our common participation in creation. As Bennett has written in a letter, "what I do is primarily a kind of paying attention to the (perhaps) random patterns that cross one's path (or that one throws down on it) to see what's there. I find though that the process of doing that has ethical or moral or psychic results: it enhances one's perception of things, events, and -- most important -- other people in one's life, increases one's capacity for empathy. I think reading, if one pays attention to the reading, probably has the same effect -- though in my case at least, it's most pronounced through the process of writing" (Letter, 10/23/94)

Transduction is the process of applying more memory to a text than it is designed to accommodate, or it is the process of applying inappropriate sets of memory to a text, as when Bennett reads Sor Juana's Spanish while utilizing his memory of English and ignoring his memory of Spanish, so that what one gets is a layered reading, the Spanish providing a palimpsest over which one reads the imagined English version, or, perhaps, the English version acting as a palimpsest and the reading as a revealing of its hidden meanings (Bennett has said that in writing Prime Sway, his transduction of Primero Sueno, some amazing things were "revealed"), so that the newly written text is a sort of textual record of a divinatory practice, documentation of a variety of stichomancy, and the new text is presented as a situation -- not as an object -- in which the reader is invited to participate fully, freed from the restrictions of conventional reader/writer relationships.

Bennett has said that "an attitude of receptivity is how to go about this -- & not a bad way to approach writing in general." The reader engages the text willing to encounter what is there. The page functions as a layered field of signification and the reader enters into patterns which emerge and are revealed and out of which is created the new work. An attitude of receptivity to what is there, on the page, increases the range of possibilities available through reading, and eliminates the need to rely on preconceived notions concerning what one should find there, what one can expect to find there, what one is expected to find there, what one can safely assume will be found there. The text being read is, as Jung has written about the I Ching yarrow sticks, an integral part of the moment in which it is encountered, and perceived as such it forms part of the larger pattern of the present, another part of that pattern being the reader, and there the reader and the written unfold, increase, come to include one another, as the intrinsic creativity of the moment is encountered. Bennett has said that the "'divinatory' aspects of these practices are related to our curiosity as to whether there is any pattern or 'meaning' to the universe that goes beyond -- is more fundamental than, our rational explorations toward that end."

Bennett's poems do not read like Language texts, but the reading strategies one employs, and the results of these strategies, are in some ways quite similar. Bennett achieves a sort of disjunction through the use of multiple parenthetical phrase clusters, for example, and, with his use of the ambiguous apostrophe s, which serves to arrest the rhythmic flow of a line while the reader considers numerous possible meanings for the word being read, Bennett presents the word -- not the line or phrase -- as the primary unit of composition, and the focal point of our reading, creating the effect of a line of words in series, so that the intrasentential organizing principle is not that of linear sequence, but is that of serial patterning, a parasyntactical array of polysemous units. Once this is recognized, and entered, the necessity for reading top-left to bottom-right is eliminated; we might, as a first reading, follow the conventional steps through the poem, then begin to read it as a page-as-field composition.

Bennett's lines, however, can also be scanned according to conventional metrical procedures, though his punctuation and line-breaks make such a reading more complicated than is usually the case. There is a polyrhythmic dimension to his work which seems almost to be grounded in the somatic polyrhythms of, for example, the pulmonary, the cardiovascular, and the neural, so that the sense of multiple rhythms as always present seems rooted in and emphasized by his use of body-oriented imagery. What occurs is a polyrhythmic ensemble performance, the lines acting as a sort of bass line, the segmenting devices effecting a sort of collective improvisation on this pattern.

Bennett's rime schemes are internal and irregular, and enhance the sense of page-as-field patterning, causing the reader to jump from one line to another, to read vertically in both directions without the constrictions of left-to-right progression. In a conventional poem, a reader would not be encouraged to dismantle the normative structure of the reading pattern, but in the context of a Bennett poem, one is led to consider recombinative strategies.

When reading Bennett's calligraphy, this sense is even more pronounced. Having transliterated one word, the reader is frequently persuaded by the next word or phrase to go back and reconsider, re-transliterate, then to include numerous variant readings in the final understanding of the poem.

The added visual dimension enhances the polysemous experience of the text. As Bennett wrote in his response to the CORE questionnaire, "hopefully, as with all art, the readers/viewers of visual poetry would have their awareness of possibility expanded by the work, and their sense of connectedness with what is. This should stimulate their sense of responsibility, their commitment to love, their humility, and so on..."

Bennett's poems invite serial reading, which, as Charles Bernstein has noted, opens the work to recombination. Distillation and recombination are central to the encounter with Bennett's poems. A transduction distills from a given text an elixir - not in any sense an essence - , word-by-word, or phrase-by-phrase, proceeding by a sort of homonymic or euphonic improvisation, playing among the correspondences of sounds, and the distilled units are then recombined to produce the new poem. The reader is invited to engage in similar processes of distillation and recombination when reading the transductions, so that the asymmetry of the meaning-building process is shifted in favor of the reader, undermining the conventional power relationship of writer to reader.

In Infused, a recent sequence of poems, Bennett reads his own work backwards -- though not exactly backwards, he notes in a letter --, thereby foregrounding the process of recombination and offering the reader a new poem to be read in the spirit of receptivity and through a process of recombination.

Taking all of this one step further, Bennett offers his poems to other poets to be "improved" through collaboration. The project is unending. The process is as open and as generous as any we are likely to encounter.
Silliman has written that "form is of interest only to the extent that it empowers liberation." If the same is said of procedure -- and it should be -- then John Bennett's project is as significant as any we will find in current poetical practice.

1996

originally published by Susan Smith Nash in PRIME SWAY, by John M. Bennett, Texture Press, 1996
also published by Don Hilla in Ponsinganot, Ex Nihilo Press, San Francisco, 1998

From: JUXTA43781@aol.com

Date: Fri, 4 Apr 1997 15:02:11 -0500 (EST) To: jacobus@hooked.net

Subject: essay on Ken Harris

ponsinganot
Notes for Ken Harris

****

A spagyric text. Spao and ageiro, to tear apart and to gather together.

Through gyre, the circular or spiral form, vortex, through a circular or spiral motion, as a circular current in the ocean, oceanic, as Koestler wrote, "the oceanic feeling of wonder is the common source of religious mysticism, of pure science and art for art's sake," not as the ethereal dream of eternal tranquility, but as in an experience of ocean, contact with the turbulent, incessant violence of change, of transformation in time, as a tactic during reading (not as a strategy previous to reading), but as in "standards trane," where the route of the reading winds from "tirings of the oxymoron" through "parts amid the aplomb of juxtaposed motifs" to "the usual fears of generative wakes, here deemed otherwise," and returns to "constellaponscionquas."
constellate, constellation:

     1. Astronomy. a. An arbitrary formation of stars perceived as a figure or design, especially one of 88 recognized groups named after characters from classical mythology and various common animals and objects. b. An area of the celestial sphere occupied by one of the 88 recognized constellations.

     3. A gathering or an assemblage
One constellation for each of the keys on a piano. "Standards trane."
Train. Letters, normally constellated as words, are torn apart, are gathered together as an assemblage, and are torn apart again in the course of reading: constella, with stars; apon, upon, or apron, or upon the apron, from naperon, via nape, from Latin mappa, napkin or cloth on which maps were drawn, apon, upon the map; scion, a descendant, also a detached twig containing buds from a woody plant, used in grafting; qua,in the capacity of - and are gathered together again: we return to "tirings of the oxymoron," where the paradox alone is no longer sufficient to express the complex connectivities of the turbulence perceived: here mapping is perception, constellations come into being during the process of reading the points of lights scattered across the skies: there is an intimation of "consciousness" here,

in the "onscion," of consciousness enfolded in and emergent from - words torn apart in order to gather other words - that which both contains and seeds it (through the infinite expanse of sky towards and through an infinite smallness) - trained to a trellis, though free to improvise within the immensities of its law, the standards as such set, though each new reading grafts consciousness anew onto an earlier map, and reading the map becomes an improvisational re-mapping of its territory, enacted during the map, tactics of tearing apart and gathering, where consciousness encounters itself in the capacity of a descendant of itself.

*****

What if we start in medias res with "impediments *of* veracity also love in passing." What do we make of the italicized "of" in the center of this phrase? We are asked to consider the appropriateness of the "of". We might consider replacing it with "to." What are the impediments to veracity? In this context, the words themselves act as impediments to veracity. The first two definitions of "veracity" emphasize the necessity for agreement in matters of the truth: 1. Adherence to the truth; truthfulness. 2. Conformity to fact or truth; accuracy or precision. Veracity concerns the verifiable. Both words derive ultimately from "wero," "true." But this writing is concerned with the unverifiable truth. It is concerned with process, with perception, with subjective truth. It is finally concerned with subjectivity itself. The very investigation of this area is an impediment of and to veracity. The fact of our shared subjectivity, that this is an aspect of human life, becomes occluded by the words which are used to address the state. Thus the words themselves become impediments of veracity. That we use language to address this area is in itself a paradox.

Language as normally used, as a means of conveying information, has nothing to say concerning subjectivity. The words are impediments and veracity. But they are also impediments as veracity. At this point we move into the second half of the above quoted phrase: "also love in passing." Through the process of paradox we arrive, having encountered the truth and silence of subjective experience, at the possibility of and necessity for love. At the solipsistic center of silence, where one encounters the world, there occurs the recognition of one's being in the world, and from that point arises the opportunity for love. Love admittedly in passing, as process would demand, but love nonetheless. But this, as well, is not available in words. We move to the next phrase to find what is available: "*for* the phenomenal derangement of absence in words." Once again, we begin by looking at the italicized prepositions. From "love in passing, " followed by a period, we come to an italicized "for." What is the "love in passing" finally for? And what are the "impediments of veracity" finally for? "The phenomenal derangement of absence in words." Once the awareness of love, whether actual or potential, becomes articulated in words, it is known as absence, absence as a phenomenon, a presence, the paradox of experience in words. Thus a derangement. The definitions of this word return us to the area earlier associated with "veracity:" 1. To disturb the order or arrangement of. 2. To upset the normal condition or functioning of. The words are impediments of veracity, impediments composed of veracities. Only paradox remains as a means of expressing this apprehension: "gestures greeting in passage farewell." The process of encountering absence as a presence. "Waves more words than names consume." The waves by which we receive sensory information generate the words which remove us from our encounter with the world. The world is consumed by the words which our encounter with it evokes. And yet, the waves bring more than the names consume. We surrender to the encounter, recognizing each word as an intrusion of interpretive distance.

"Hermeneutics throwing up hands." The poem gives us the process. We oscillate from encounter to interpretation and back. In this is the presence of consciousness being conscious. The hermeneutics itself is offered as a silence.

*****

The poem which begins this collection, "the banals," begins with the word "then". The banals are offered as a starting point and immediately we are removed from these beginnings: "then," as a beginning, insists on our awareness of a continuance, not a continuity, but a discontinuous extension of something previous to the text. "Then," as a beginning, is a disruption.

Whatever continuity the reader might imagine himself enacting is halted and altered by the intrusion of this "then". This "then" acts as a renewal of origins in the reader by insisting on itself as anything but a beginning.

Offered as an opening which is a disruption, it is an intimation of redemption. The past of each individual reader, and all which that includes, is brought to stand with this "then" as an opening of "the banals." Banal, an adjective meaning "drearily commonplace and often predictable; trite," is here offered as a plural noun, implying a state, or a set of givens, and yet the word itself has been transformed, and in its present state is anything but "drearily commonplace," "predictable," or "trite". Our encounter with the banality of the given is an encounter with the state of transformation.

We begin with, within, paradox, and our perceptions will be altered from this point on. The initial conditions are of paradox and transformation.

Process is offered as a state of multiplicity. Being is becoming, and in becoming becomes plural. Upon entering this realm of enfolded paradox we immediately encounter an intimation of its boundary and its flux: "a spell to tone." We have already, in the title of the collection, partsa plomb, and in the title of this first poem, "the banals," met with two varieties of the spell-ing which produces a spell. John Ayto, in his DICTIONARY OF WORD ORIGINS, traces the two distinct words spelled "spell" to a common root:

"Spell 'name the letters of a word' was adapted from Old French espeler 'read out.' This was descended from an earlier espeldre, which was borrowed from prehistoric Germanic spellon. And it was a noun relative of this, spellam, which gave English spell 'magic formula'." Skeat traces both words back through Anglo Saxon spel "a saying, story, narrative, hence a form of words." The American Heritage Dictionary has "Middle English spellen, to read letter by letter, from Old French espeller (of Germanic origin) and from Old English spellian, to tell (from spell, discourse). "The banals" has, as a beginning: "Then, a spell." We can expect, following such beginnings, if not a story or a narrative, then a form of words, constructed letter by letter, with which we as readers will establish a discourse, and through which, however subtlety, an alteration of consciousness will be evinced. A spell is not only "a word or formula believed to have magic power," it is also "a bewitched state; a trance." What we enter here, through the plurality of the banals, is a - not the - spell, a state and a process of heightened or enhanced awareness of a range of particulars, an engagement not so much with words and sentences and concepts as with the letters which make up all of these. We are invited, as we enter the spell and spellings of the text, to partake of its intricate alterations, to locate the trance within the entrance, and through this particular form of words, to conjure a renewed formula for the self, to recast the givens of the past in the light of the spell cast by the spellen of this spellam.

*****

"Lying among improvisations / working from disgust", the phrase which confronts us, woven in large bold type through the text of "standards ornette dolphy and the disposable conversation", provides us with a set of tonal qualities, a chord, perhaps, in this context, constructed of three resonant dyads, lying / disgust, improvisations / working, and among / from.
Intertwined within these connections are the pairings of two gerunds, two prepositions, and two nouns. This is a chord constructed of an excess of interrelatedness, a chordal dissonance.
The primary text of this page is a discontinuous, textured thread wrapped around the larger configuration. The first segment reads: "hence, given the decomposition and (not necessarily consequent) reconstruction of a diatonic rhetoric according with traditional structures while altering the dialect, a dialectic." What are we to

make of this as a vamp into "standards ornette dolphy and the disposable conversation"? We begin with the idea of improvisation, and move from there to the related ideas of decomposition and reconstruction. This first segment is constructed around its intertwined sound patterns, as in experimental jazz improvisations. To begin at the beginning: "hence" is echoed in "consequent" and again, with different emphasis, in "rhetoric". "Consequent" resonates with "decomposition", "reconstruction", and "according", through three different permutations:

con/com, con/con, con/cor. "Hence" begins a pattern of 'n'-sounds which functions as the barest trace of "melody" throughout this improvised segment: "given", "decomposition", "and", "not", "necessarily", "consequent", "reconstruction", "diatonic", "traditional". This first word also begins an accompanying pattern of 'e'-sounds: "given", "the", "decomposition", "necessarily", "consequent", "reconstruction", "rhetoric", "structures", "while", "altering", "the", dialect", "dialectic". Of the twenty-three words in this initial segment, nineteen are included in either the 'n' or the 'e' pattern (omitted are the two instances of "a", "with", and "according").

There is a conversation of sorts in this, an intertwined, melodic pairing not unlike that of some early recordings by the Ornette Coleman Quartet, on which Coleman and Don Cherry are configuring "the shape of jazz to come".

There is also a rhythmic layer in this segment which is provided by sound patterns other than those just suggested: the rhyme embedded in "decomposition" and "reconstruction"; the repeated phoneme "dia" in "diatonic", "dialect", "dialectic"; the echoing suffixes of "according" and "altering"; the string of "ic" endings in "diatonic", "rhetoric" and "dialectic". These sound patterns present us with the process of improvisation. But are we to read this passage as telling us, through a sequence of denotations, something about the process of improvisation?

Perhaps. Improvisation works through a decomposition and reconstruction of melody or sound pattern. Traditional structures are based on a diatonic rhetoric. The various treatments of jazz standards can be seen as dialects.

And an altering of these dialects might be analogous to a dialectical process, a sort of disposable conversation - call, then response, then synthesis, then this new synthesis as the call - though causality in this is questioned ("not necessarily consequent"), and the antithesis is offered as a decomposition of the standards and their dialect-like permutations, with the synthesis appearing as a reconstruction, at which point the process begins anew, and the reconstruction is decomposed. Scattered throughout this page-as-field are fragments of words and letter strings, examples of what Patricia Cox Miller, in her essay entitled "In Praise of Nonsense", calls "alphabetical language."

Towards the bottom of the page we find:

"acherishedimagepanorespan". Embedded within this string of letters are numerous words: ache her is she shed dim im image age pan or ore re span, for example. "Translating" this, however, brings us no closer to "sense".
We are in the realm of alphabetical language, where the clusters of letters bring music, not meaning. Following this string is another, however, which presents a different set of possibilities: "ponsinganot". At first glance, this is more of the same, a meaningless string of letters. But, hidden within the music, in fragments and glimpses, is the opportunity for us as readers to enter into the song: response: sing and not. It takes a bit of improvisation to get from "pons" to "response", but in the context of this poem, "among improvisations", we are invited to participate in precisely this manner. And what we are given, finally, is not an either/or proposition which insists that we either sing or not. We are given a both/and situation in which our response will be both to sing, to participate in the writing which is this text's song, and not to sing, but to remain removed from the process of the text's generation, and to read, receptive to its offered song.

1996

published by Don Hilla in Ponsinganot, Ex Nihilo Press, San Francisco, 1998

CHAPTER NINE |||||||||||||||||||||||||||||||||||||||||||||||||||||||||||||||

THINGS RESCUED FROM ETERNAL NONEXISTENCE

Useless Writing

Skills are acquired behaviors, similar to acquired tastes. They are learned behaviors valued by the dominant culture to the extent that it can use them. Different areas of the dominant culture value different skills. Skill is developed originally, jump-started if you will, through training, then honed, refined, through experience, through practice, the practice of the particular skill. One sets out to learn a skill, seeks out an expert in the field, and is trained by rote and through information until one has acquired the desired skill. It is the same whether one wishes to repair an automobile engine or write a sonnet, program a computer or paint a portrait. There is a hierarchy at work here, and those who reside at the highest levels do so due to their possession of a specialized knowledge and their mastery of its requisite activities: the arcana and its secret gestures: the gnosis and its rites. Almost all of us can learn almost any skill if we desire to do so. All that is required is the desire and the work, the desire and the willingness to put in the time and put forth the effort to acquire the skill. All the skills that are taught, and the ways in which they are taught, are structurally necessary to the culture that teaches them, else they would not be taught. We should think of this usefulness as meaning only one thing: useful means useful to the dominant culture, always and only. That which is deemed useful is such only insofar as it reinforces the fundamental structure of the culture. The power relations that are structurally in place must remain structurally in place. Change is not only allowed, it is required, but only in the details of the larger pattern; the larger pattern of necessity must remain intact.

What happens if one desires to practice useless skills, skills that are not useful in maintaining the structure of the culture? First of all, one will not be able to acquire these skills in the usual manner. There will be no teachers provided by the culture; no training will be available. One's desire will of necessity need be nearly an obsession. The work, the time and effort required, may seem disproportionate to the desire. One will likely decide to pursue some other skill, to alter one's desire, to attune one's desire to those regarded as useful by the culture.

What happens if one persists in the pursuit of useless skills? It is unlikely that an entirely unforeseen activity will be invented, so one will work in the shadows of an already established tradition. But, at least at the outset, one will work alone, without guides or guidelines. The wheel will likely be reinvented accidentally and often. (Reinventing the wheel is useful in the pursuit of useless skills.) But the wheel is not a part of the desire, so it will be discarded — discarded not as useless, but as useful, therefore inappropriate to the pursuit. One trains by sorting and wandering, sifting, brooding, drifting, gathering and discarding, always discarding. This is a nomadic pursuit, not necessarily directionless or circuitous, but always everything but the steady step along a straight and narrow path. This is the crooked path, and its passage is along the low road.

This autodidact will learn to do things that others have no desire to do, that others are not allowed to do, that others are not able to think of doing. This is obvious from the outside looking in, but only acknowledged by the dominant culture in moods of elitist condescension. The normative reaction of the dominant culture will be derision or a haughty indifference. Structural superiority, however, permits itself the privilege of praising from a position of ignorance. This is a method that attempts to appropriate the useless. A cursory glance at recent cultural history in America alone reveals several instances of this. There is only one way around this: if one is truly committed to the practice of useless skills, one must be constantly on guard against one's own tendencies towards usefulness.

Two useless skills:
1. private writing, by which I mean writing that has a strictly subjective significance for the writer. this writing may be appropriated by the dominant culture, i.e. published, sold, archived, studied, etc., but it cannot be known for what it is. a writer's disciplined practice of private writing can only be known as such by that writer. other knowledge concerning it will never be other than ancillary.
2. asemic writing, by which I mean writing that is shifted intentionally towards the unreadable, towards image, without discarding entirely all vestiges of either the letter or the line, and without assuming the alternative status of visual art. it is a hybrid writing, a writing not meant for a reading mingled with an imaging not meant for looking. it is a useless, mutant writing, its uselessness a mutagen for the writer.
3.12.01

Six Insane Impulses to Art-Making

Prinzhorn identified six interrelated 'impulses' to configuration, namely the expressive, decorative, playful, and imitative 'urges', the need to impose pictorial order, and the need to imbue the artefact with symbolic content. — Colin Rhodes, in Outsider Art: Spontaneous Alternatives

To undertake any kind of significant art-making is at least analogous to madness. Specifically, to situate the activity of art-making at or even near the center of one's life is at least analogous to madness. If madness is evidenced by aberrational behavior born of an abnormal processing of experience, any kind of art-making, when it is considered a significant activity by the artist, is at least analogous to madness. But this finally doesn't tell us much of interest or of use. Certain kinds of psychiatrists and artists have agreed on all this for years.
The cultural norms established for behavior, and for the processing of experience, are called into question by a moment's thought concerning any aspect of inhabiting a particular culture. That all experience is subjective experience is a given. Any kind of radically subjective experience will be perceived by the culture as an abnormal processing of experience. All that is required to render experience radical is that the experiencer be aware not only of the experience but also of experiencing. How is an experience constructed? What coding and decoding is involved? Not just how much of experience is culturally constructed, but what is any individual's involvement in nourishing and sustaining that constructedness? All significant art-making is involved in rendering experience radically subjective.

Conventional concepts of insanity are utter nonsense. I would like to say they are born of a dangerous ignorance, obliviousness, but this is not the case: born of a very dangerous desire to control, quarantine, quash, to diminish or extinguish, — this is the case. We could say art-making is in no way analogous to madness; it is the essence of health; we would find agreement everywhere — as long as nothing much is going on in the art-making. We could list Prinzhorn's six impulses to configuration as the central exhibit in our argument for the sanity of art.

1 — expressive: self-expression, as in: I am here: handprints on cave walls: traces of a passage: passing through: left along the particular path taken: records of activities, gestures; not expression as in the construction of a self, and its subsequent (or simultaneous) aggrandizement; more like an emptying, giving back: that which is potential, possible, made actual: in any unique configuration, including the unique configuration known as a human individual, is the potential for other configurations: expression, then, to allow: to surrender self to the others contained in self: to express oneself, therefore, is to release the others that one contains: expressivity, then, is incessant change, intentional subjection of oneself to alteration of oneself: the more self-expression, in this sense, the less self: why leave a trace? as the barest outline of a provisional map, almost a pentimento of a lost map's hachures: and because the balance is shifted heavily towards self-expression as self-aggrandizement: to slightly shift the scales.

2 — decorative: decorative is a subcategory of playful: it is playful in a daydream: playful is of primary importance only when it is entirely awake:

3 — playful: playful is against, or away from, practical and purposeful: to act in the present as if there only is the present: playful is a particular and a special relationship with time: past, present and future coalesce at a point in time just slightly ahead of the present, though not in the future, at the exact point of direct experience: the exact point of direct experience is a phase transition at the human end of which a construction of outside/inside occurs (of objective/subjective, then/now): it is the chaotic, timeless non-site of being, and it can be entered. objects, materials, things are not objects or materials or things, they are catalysts of a hierophany, a numinous near presence: playful evokes a fully-engaged absence: the world is not the world and we know it.

4 — imitative: imitative is the original strategy against inertia (as a way of getting started, so the body at rest does not remain at rest): it inaugurates being's counter-tendency to entropy (it augurs against inert uniformity): once underway, the best thing about imitative is how easily it is discarded.

5 — the need to impose pictorial order is not as strong as the will to explore pictorial disorder.

6 — the need to imbue the artifact with symbolic content: there is no need whatsoever for this.
3.14.01

Things to Forget #1

1) the expression of your beliefs (forget your beliefs)

By writing this I suppose I am setting a bad example. I am going to tell you what I believe about beliefs. And if it seems I don't believe a word of it, you can decide what you believe about the legitimacy of such behavior (then you can decide what you believe about ascribing legitimacy). John Lilly, who has been thoroughly discredited in the straight world — i.e. the dominant culture, which in its devious way via Courtney Love appropriated even Young Marble Giants' Got No Credit In the Straight World — and who is therefore eminently qualified for citation concerning this subject, wrote: My own beliefs are unbelievable. And: In the province of the mind, what is believed to be true is true or becomes true, within limits to be found experientially and experimentally. These limits are further beliefs to be transcended. In the province of the mind, there are no limits. What would follow here, logically, is something along the lines of in the province of the mind, there are no beliefs. Lilly didn't say so, and it's hard to say so, but I am going to try to say so anyway. I got no credit in the straight world, too. Dylan's when you aint got nothing, you got nothing to lose. Kristofferson's freedom's just another word for nothing left to lose. Who believes any of this stuff? When attempting to dismiss belief as a limit or a hazard, it probably isn't wise to quote the truly venerated sages. They all say things that most of us believe at least some of the time, or pretend to believe at least some of the time. Hackneyed expressions of pithy wisdom seem more to the point. We need something we can see through, not something we can hold on to (to believe in this living is just a hard way to go, to continue referencing John Prine). A few years ago I wrote a list of aleatory aphorisms. Using several pages from a dictionary, I read vertically, selecting words as I came to them with the sole criterion being that I arrive at something resembling a recognizable sentence structure. Many of these sentences said things, albeit in skewed fashion, that I could easily imagine myself believing. William Burroughs once said, referring to his cut-up methods, when you cut into

40

the present, the future leaks out. No one believes that. Maybe when you cut into language, your beliefs leak out. Some of us could probably believe that. I remember in high school reading some of the venerated purveyors of pith, Pascal, Voltaire, Blake, to name a few. I loved Blake's Proverbs of Hell. My favorite was always the road of excess leads to the palace of wisdom. Well, the road of excess leads to to a lot of things (else it might be called the road of parsimony and restraint). It may lead to the palace of decadence, or the palace of accidental death, or the palace of babbling inanity. And it may very well lead to the palace of wisdom, enlightenment as in break on through to the other side (to quote Jim Morrison, who knew something about excess at least, though perhaps a little less about wisdom). Rimbaud's injunction to derange the senses, as well as Silliman's ironic rewriting, derange the sentences, is clear advocacy of the path of excess. Every path has its palace, and the path of excess would seem appropriately to possess a surfeit of palaces. My suspicion, my conflicted belief, is that the writing of ironic aphorisms has a long and venerable tradition. Aphorism and horizon share the same etymological root: horizein, to divide, separate, from horos, boundary, limit. We might say, as if with conviction, in the province of the mind, there are no horizons; or, in the province of the mind, there are no aphorisms (we don't believe in etymology; we believe in association). The limits of my beliefs are the limits of my world. The most commonly seen bumper sticker around Charlottesville for the last ten or fifteen years has proclaimed Question Authority! A little simplistic, perhaps, but a beginning. When we call our own beliefs into question, we begin to question our most intimate, cherished authorities on the subject of self and world (from whence these beliefs, these authorities, derive is yet another question). I'm currently attempting to believe that harboring an excess of conflicting beliefs is the most effective way out of this prisonhouse constructed by belief (the language here seems not quite right, but maybe that is a blessing in disguise).

Things to Forget #2

2) everything you've ever heard about what is good and what isn't Good writing isn't what we think it is.
3.15/16.01
Charlottesville

The Road of Excess Leads to the Palace of Excess

In 1969, the conceptualist Douglas Heubler wrote: The world is full of objects, more or less interesting. I do not wish to add any more. Thirtytwo years later, and (my estimate) a few million objects later, there are still too few objects in the world. I am thinking, as I presume Heubler was thinking, of those objects which might be considered as works of art. There probably are enough truck tires zip drives wristwatches handguns cell phones toothbrushes checkbooks Wal-Marts paper clips New York Cities. Enough useful, sensible stuff, in other words, to keep us busy quickly killing ourselves and destroying the planet. Louise Nevelson, sculptor and early practitioner of installation art, said in 1976: I want a lot of quality in a lot of quantity. I want quantity in extreme excess and comparable debate concerning its quality (for those concerned to debate such matters).

My tendencies towards the minimal are strong enough. Absence, silence, and nothingness loom large. Their allure is centrifugal. A refusal of the center, an annihilation of the center. My tendencies towards excess are equally strong. The center for me is certainly wherever I am; for you it is as certainly wherever you are. Consider Black Elk's mythic world mountain at the center of the world in South Dakota, or Guillevic's the middle is everywhere — / and I'm in it. The center is identity writ large. It is self: perception, possession, power. The world is that which has been in some sense experienced. The world as we know it. Experience is perceived as property. Or experience as perceived is property. The owner is at the center.

The urge towards the minimal removes or ceases moving. It either reduces to fundamentals: quarks for the physical world, economics for human interaction, ideas for art: consider Klein's empty gallery, Kosuth's texts on gallery walls, Asher's air installations, Turrell's light installations. On and on: less and less and less is more. Or it refuses production: the metaphor if not the actuality of playing chess. Neo-hesychasm. All that is discarded becomes an enormously turbulent array, a centrifugal chaotic aggregate. This detritus is the playground and the alchemical laboratory of excess. It is the opposite of the minimal but is inevitably generated by the minimal. Its signature is the fragment. Destabilization is its norm. "I contain multitudes" might be its motto. The I as center is singular, a fiction. The multitudes explode the I. Whitman's container is no container at all; it is the environment of an absent center. It isn't true that we aggrandize ourselves by making objects; the opposite is true: we empty ourselves, absent ourselves. Fifteen years or so ago, I worked for some time on a still unfinished poem entitled "Margins". Its last lines are: The recipe as brief as simple air. / Make more than you will ever need. I'm still working on the project.

3.8.01 / 3.12.01

another failed attempt to photograph reality:

but the materiality that suffering necessarily an imitation shapes itself to exist pretending to be myself hoping this would please you. the present must exist determined to write a story i would do myself a greater service if i pretended to be another, i do not have this regret it radiates in all inherent unhappiness only if language survives in particular to literature if i worked to convince myself that i am other than i am. how is it that as if we is not one, that is claims knowledge and claims none in front of this, while it destroys itself writing is a form of prayer. it has come to this moment he wrote this event with himself to make clear his originality is a question for the sake of something even more (cf. blanchot; kafka and literature). i read breton as an adolescent and practiced automatism, his own story he got from a gap he could not express as a writer in both senses of "I am not happy", which at the time seemed almost reasonable. more recently i read someone else and practiced process, improvisation as long as i am too close meandering the forests standing still at foregone pages begging yoked spoken lightning stricken vigilant advantages for the savage fogs commonly sent. procedural extractions from source texts are nevertheless quasi-intentional. even without processual interventions. i've been translating a danish text of late fog means visionary ideas bland rigorous sortation though i read no danish the new statistical mantra is immersed in tidal sickness. pale visions befall spoken lightning, each story a steadfast narrative or else death like her unregenerate breath stammering however the story unfolds in broken letters. by the mysterious the activity states each one believed but adds illumination. by the mysterious activity each one believed illumination provokes it. illumination provokes dissolution. dissolution of speech silence in any case. silence in any case either by the magic or like a dagger explains nothing mysterious at my table. this is what i want to do, what i like to do. this is the scattered indeterminate harm of paper. i imagine in moments of delusion lucidity guilt insecurity comedy boredom despair that a sort of negative romanticism is my cherished neoteny scratch that that i should be doing something other than this. i should be doing something i don't want to do, something i don't like doing. i should be another death her individual spiritual familiarity. pages in enigma cancerous man-sized signs for the death of the village is unmistakable skewed light dances. this possibility of unhappiness from the harmonious words. i do not complete unhappiness if the possibility to express constitutes my language eagerly towards this movement determines its potential in other words towards non-language. the word tends precisely to another level. another failed attempt to photograph reality: january/march 01 let it go. somewhere between the phoneme and the morpheme an aggregate of sounds potentially exploding. from sound through sense inevitably so let's say intentionally for sake of argument to the blank page read as everything we know. it looks like an end so it's a good place to start. it looks like nothing but it won't sit still. we can teach it everything except the old trick of saying nothing. return to surrender in writing reading towards nothing. death as an approximate synonym useful though entirely inaccurate. we won't always be able to fool ourselves so we have at least that to look towards. prison-houses are easy to find and even easier to inhabit. let's assume for the sake of continuing that language is our favorite. blow the fucker up why not we have our methods with a little faith and courage we can go anywhere including insane. it's not as big a deal as they would like us to believe. or maybe it is a big deal but it's not that kind of big deal. it's not about all the sad trivia we're taught to hang on to at all costs and against all odds. there isn't that much to lose. there's a lot of stuff to do but most of it won't do us any good and the rest of it won't do for us what we want and need so eventually we might realize we may as well give up and that will be what we have learned and it will be enough. a list of things to do:

  1: give up (write it down)
  2: relapse to attachment (rewrite it)
  3: laughter is not a heresy (throw it away)
  4: give up (read the precursors who have failed; love 'em)
  5: fuck yourself (with belief and/or erudition; cf. #2)
     5a: ditto but detourned (as a postmodern spiritual praxis)
  6: give up (poetry like hesychasm is an extreme sport)

it seems like a long process (but that's part of the hoax)
giving up is hard work. some folks think it's a god-given talent and maybe it is but out here in the swarming quotidian it seems like hard work and a hassle and probably a stupid decision consider the alternatives: i was going to make another list but you can do that yourself. some fine day we'll all be sitting around dying and the only thing we'll regret is that we didn't give up because we should have at least attempted to get used to it a little while we had the chance. writing poetry is a way of getting used to giving up. treat it like an ancient spiritual discipline. do it for twenty years with no significant results. it will ruin your life which is a fundamental first step. you will probably fall in love which is a hindrance and a bother but you'll get over it and go on.
january/march 01

VUGG BOOKS 2007

Useless Writing was originally published in ANOTHER SOUTH, University of Alabama Press, 2002, edited by Bill Lavender
Many of these essays appeared in Muse Apprentice Guild, 2002 (electronic), edited by August Highland

CHAPTER NINE ||||||||||||||||||||||||||||||||||||||||||||||||||||||

The USELESS WRITING
facebook group

Jim Leftwich
Works at Poet
Created group on April 7, 2014

DESCRIPTION

      1. write or be written
      2. thinking is political
      3. don't fuck with history

As of 07.21.2016 the Useless Writing group has 745 members.

CHAPTER TEN ||||||||||||||||||||||||||||||||||||||||||||||||||||||

NO SUCH THING AS REPETITION

Don't Believe Everything You Think

I saw a bumper sticker the other day that read Don't Believe Everything You Think. I drive for a living, so I see a lot of bumper stickers. Most of them aren't worth thinking about. I don't think we know what a thought is. Sometimes we actively construct sequences and/or aggregates of thoughts. We address questions and problems: x is broken, how can it be fixed? why does x happen and not y? what is x? and how does it differ from y? x is not not-x (y quite possibly is not-x; let's think about that); if x, then y. We think we begin with the questions and/or problems, but this is another problem: we don't clearly begin anywhere. Sometimes thoughts appear, or sound, or both, unbidden. We find a fully-developed thought in our mind, present like an object. These thoughts often carry an aura of importance. They may seem profound, silly, profoundly silly, or simply banal, but all the same they almost shimmer with an unsought otherness, alien thoughts. The other day I was driving around Charlottesville, working, and it occurred to me — I was listening to jazz on the radio, not actively thinking about anything — that we live in the perfect world, that it could not be otherwise. Not a revelation, an epiphany, just a thought, but almost palpable, solid like an object in the mind. And not mine. I'm receptive to this kind of thinking, and I've encountered some of the traditions which state this kind of thing as fact, but I'm not under normal circumstances given to thinking like this, it's a difficult proposition to propose and then defend, as a concept it is a magnet for ten thousand refutations, only as a self-contained experience of and as thought does it seem to stand up at all. It's a hard thought to hold comfortably and clearly in the mind. I pulled over to the side of the street and scribbled a few notes in my notebook, hoping, I suppose, to get this down in words before I actively thought about it too much. Here are the notes: I sit in the car, listening to music, making these little drawings. Not drawings, really, little scribbled patterns. I fill the empty spaces with scrawls and scratches and mutated alphabeticals. I can't even ask if they are any good or not — the question doesn't make any sense. They are absolutely perfect examples of what they are. Everything is the absolutely perfect example of what it is. I am the absolutely perfect example of what I am. No way around it. Do what you like. I thought about this for a moment or two, knowing it was wrong: too much prior, too much projected, not nearly enough of the present, presence, of the actual thought, its moment in the mind. I made a few more notes: Uniqueness means perfection. Uniqueness is the absolute condition of the universe and everything in it. What is it we want? Power? If so, we are fools. There is a man in Alabama, Tom Hendrix, who is making a wall. He's making it to honor his great-great grandmother. He's been working on it for fifteen years, missing only twenty-two days in that time. I guess he's an outsider artist, of sorts. An outsider earthworks artist. That's one way of thinking about what he does. He thinks he's involved in a kind of sacred ritual. His grandmother was a Yuchi Indian. At one point he was visited by an old

Indian from South Dakota, Charlie Two Moons, who had seen a vision of the wall. Among other things, Charlie Two Moons told Hendrix that the Great Spirit was guiding him to build the wall. The wall does not belong to you, said Charlie Two Moons, you are merely its keeper. He warned Hendrix about visitors to the wall: They're going to come and they're going to say, Hey, Brother Tom, the wall is not perfect. It needs to be straightened out down there. You tell them, No, that wall is like your great-great-grandmother's journey through life. It's never straight. Last week I got a call from Ralph Eaton, an old friend who I hadn't seen in thirteen years. Not long into the conversation, he reminded me of a night in 1979 when we had taken mushrooms and gone to Vesuvio's in San Francisco. Among other things, we decided or discovered that the great secret in life was that God had made an enormous mistake in the creation of the universe. The consequence of this for humans is that it makes sense that it doesn't make sense.
4.19.01

Asemic Calligraphy

Phillipe Sollers: He who will not write shall be written.

I stay up until dawn just about every night. Lately, I've been going to bed around nine in the morning. The sun's coming up right now, seven o'clock. I work until two-thirty, three in the morning, and my wife usually goes to work at seven in the morning, so we spend a little time together while she wakes up and gets ready for work. One morning around dawn, after I'd been reading This Is Not A Pipe and thinking of how to make a kind of minimalist visual poetry that would require simultaneous reading and looking, would actually during the time spent with it eliminate the distinction between reading and looking, I went back to the bedroom and crawled in beside Sue. I'd been making corroded alphabeticals for years as a part of the Staceal series, and some of them seemed so corroded as to at least require a bit of simultaneous reading and looking, but, for the most part, they were just lists or arrays of letters, and the actual reading required was minimal. Also as a part of Staceal, I had made a number of what I called "homophagic alphabeticals", letters which were almost entirely eaten away by duplicates whited-out and placed just slightly off center and above them. Many of these consisted of single words or phrases, so there was a certain amount of reading required, and an equal amount of looking, of constructing from the barest of outlines, often broken outlines, the original letters. This seemed to fuse the act of looking with the act of reading. The words were images, and not in the same way, for example,

that the large words on the sides of buses or on billboards are images. The words used in advertisements are almost always immediately recognizable as words, consisting of large bold letters very clearly formed. So, maybe I was onto something, or at least moving in that direction. I had been making a sort of quasi-calligraphic writing for a few years, and much of it seemed to consist of letteral forms, oddly torqued and fragmentary, but still very suggestive of letters (so much so that for a while in 98 and 99 I was trying to read them aloud, almost singing a modulated series of muffled growls, hisses, snorts). But be that as it may, these writings were hardly readable texts, they were more like eidetic images in which one might find traces and hints of letters if one were so inclined. When I first sent some of them to John Bennett, probably in 96 or 97, he called them "spirit writings". Tim Gaze published a chapbook of them that he called Spirit Writings. I remember the day I started doing them. One night, following Terence McKenna's directions, I had eaten five dried grams of stropharia cubensis and laid down in silent darkness. When I got up the next day, I went into town and bought a notepad and a pen. I sat in the car in the parking lot at Barracks Road Shopping Center and made pages and pages of these things, line after line of these indecipherable quasi-letteral writings. I wasn't sure what I was doing or why I was doing it; I had never done anything like it before. I remembered a postcard I had gotten from John Byrum a few years earlier on which he wrote, as a footnote referring to one of my rewritings of a Bennett poem, that the next step would likely be an entirely asemic writing. I hadn't seen the word before, but its meaning was clear enough. Sue rolled over beside me and said I wish I could read your mind. I had closed my eyes and was watching an array of torqued and corroded letterforms slowly swirl and float as if in a void. I said, how much do you want to know about asemic calligraphy? The letter-forms looked like morphs of my corroded letter lists and my crayon calligraphy. I want to make this kind of image writing, these corroded, colored letter-forms softly swirling against a deep black background. Sue pulled back a little and said, you're right, I would probably be disappointed. I want you to be thinking about me. I'm not sure I'm really all that concerned about the distinction between reading and looking. You don't want to read my mind, I said, you want to write it. More and more I find myself primarily interested in the difference between reading and writing.
4.19.01

No One Has Ever Gotten Anything Right

No one has ever gotten anything right, and I'm not going to presume that now is the time to start. We always start with the man from Crete telling us all Cretans are liars; from there we venture more or less qualified means of evincing meaning. If I have gotten this right at the outset, and I think I have, something is seriously awry, amiss. I must have missed something, for something is certainly wrong. If Plato got any of it right, ideal eidolons all but absent in a cavernous dream, then it follows that all but the most tenuous and provisional of proposals will thenceforth always be at least a little off. So, even if I think he's right (and I do), I of necessity must begin thinking from a position which can only be assumed as if he is wrong. But the as if, as useful as it is, does not protect us from Descartes. It is all but impossible to assume a position stated as I think as if I am. Almost everything will protect us from philosophy, it's as if this is part of the grand design, but nothing outside the absence of a self will protect us from the plight of thinking. It occurred to me (or, more likely, it occurred to someone else and I am occluding my sources again) a while back that there are two fundamental problems for us in trying to think about being in the world. I'm not exactly thinking ontology and epistemology, but I think I'm thinking something pretty close to that. One of the problems is the problem of scale. We can't see what we're in because it's in us as much as we're in it. We need to step back a bit, but this is a little bit easier said than done. We need, at least for a little while, to be the bigger picture. Not just see it, be it. Be the bigger picture so we can see what a small part of it we always are. The other problem almost seems like a consequence of or conclusion drawn from the problem of scale, but I think it's actually an entirely different problem. The world, the universe, the things happening, are not here for us, are not happening for us. We're in it up to our ears, no getting around that, but it's not about us. Something is going on here, but just to say it is significant is to assert that it signifies us. It's a sign. We're the signified. It has nothing to do with us as us is defined by us, and it has everything to do with us as something entirely other than ourselves as we usually define that word. We've known all this for a while now. But we don't act like we know it. More importantly, we don't think like we know it. Maybe under normal circumstances we can't think like we know it. Maybe rationality and language assume structurally that we are at the center of the universe. A few weeks ago I sent a copy of Things Rescued From Eternal Nonexistence to John Byrum. He sent back a postcard with a little note, part of which read: "do you think we have swallowed a big one?" Yes, I do think we have swallowed a right good sized one. But I'm still interested in things like what happens when I leave out the expected hyphen in the previous sentence. I'm as certain as I need to be that you read it as if the hyphen were there. I'm interested in the fact that I am able to write two

conflicting things while intentionally refraining from writing one of those things. It shouldn't surprise us that no one has ever gotten anything right.
5.16.01

Transition Probabilities

It is the spring of 1994. I am working with an address base that consists of 17 files, totalling 6021 addresses. I decide to condense the data into 3 files. All the addresses are UVA dormitory rooms, so there is no need to organize the files as I condense them. The addresses have been entered over a period of weeks, and each file contains between 300 and 400 addresses. I combine the first 6 files, creating a file containing 2033 addresses. I combine the next 6 files, creating a file containing 1994 addresses. When I combine the remaining 5 files, a file is created which contains 1994 addresses. This catches my attention simply because it seems improbable. It doesn't mean anything, there's no need for a bugeyed 'Wow!", it's simply a series of events and their outcomes. Synchronicity may simply be a quality of attentiveness wherein connectivities are noted regardless of their seeming significance or triviality. In 1978, Tommy Leaver and I were hitchhiking through northeastern Oregon. A man who called himself Brother Hepp picked us up and took us to his trailer in Waitsburgh, WA. We lived for a few weeks in a garage next to his trailer. Brother Hepp believed in an odd mixture of Pentecostal Christianity, southwestern Indian religions, and something like street mythology. He was blind in one eye, but he could throw a knife with pinpoint accuracy. He could stand in the Blue Mountains and point out hummingbirds atop the blighted pine trees. He told us he picked us up because a voice told him to. One day we were sitting in his trailer talking about angels. Brother Hepp said he once was visited by the 18-foot tall angel Gabriel in that very trailer. The trailer might have been seven feet high. The large patterns remain the same, but the details change incessantly. If we don't pay attention to the details, there are certain things we will never see. If we attend too closely to the details, we might never suspect we are involved in a larger pattern. Thanksgiving, 1994. I'm talking with my brother-in-law about living in Charlottesville. He lived there with my sister in the early 70s. I've been working with my address base, adding residential addresses to the dormitory listings. The night before Thanksgiving I entered the listings for an apartment complex and a trailer park. My brother-in-law tells me about living in that apartment complex, then moving to that trailer park. It seems improbable, these aren't particularly student-oriented areas of town, and he was in Charlottesville to attend the university, so it gets my attention. These kinds of

experiences don't add up, don't accumulate towards epiphany or revelation. They don't teach us anything specific or exact about what kind of world we live in or what we should do. Attunement is as trivial as it is transformative, probably transformative precisely because trivial. One day late in July of 78, I left the shed next to Brother Hepp's trailer, bought a 6- pack of beer, and went down to the Touchet River, sat on a smooth rock, sipped a few beers, watching the river flow. A beautiful day, just a few cumulus clouds floating in the vast blue sky. I was watching a cloud approach when it started to talk. It was talking about my future. Some of what it said was wrong, at least some of the details were wrong. For example, it said I would die in a car wreck in Missouri in the summer of 1998. That didn't happen. I died at home in Charlottesville, in January of 98.
5.17.01

Trust, Realaesthetik, and the Texture of a Stochastic Past

Yesterday someone at work handed me a section of an old newspaper so I could read an article about a restaurant owned by a man we used to work for. He's doing well, or at least he a was a few weeks ago, when this newspaper was printed. The article rambled around a bit, talking about the one particular restaurant, about the history of restaurants in America, about various inventions that facilitated the growth of the restaurant business (sliced bread, I discovered, was invented in 1928). This particular section of the paper included the horoscope. I read mine. It was, I suppose, at this point, doing something like forecasting the past, the mirror image of remembering the future: your friends do not have your best interests in mind.
I tried to remember what my friends were up to a few weeks ago. If I remember correctly, they were doing pretty much what everybody was doing, what everybody's friends were doing, which is doing stuff with their own best interests in mind. I think that's pretty much what I was doing a few weeks ago. Ralph Eaton called me a few weeks ago, I hadn't heard from him in years. It seemed like he wanted to talk. It seemed like a good thing at the time, still does. I'm not sure either of us had anyone's interests, good or bad, in mind.
A few weeks ago, Scott MacLeod sent me an envelope unveiling his concept of Realaesthetik. One sheet reads: "Just came up with the word/concept which will either make me famous or make me deranged or both. You can have it too." The other sheet reads, among other things: "realaesthetik is an expansionist policy having as its primary principle the advancement of Scott MacLeod's interests."

Since Scott and I share several interests, I take the announcement of Realaesthetik to be clearly with my best interests in mind.

If I took the horoscope as accurate information, what would I be able to do with it? How would I read it? At this point, it's not a warning advising me to take the necessary precautions, it's a sort of admonition reproaching me for not paying enough attention a few weeks back. Not only that: since I can't think of anything it could be referring to, it is a sort of reproach for not paying sufficient attention during the whole of the past few weeks. What it says, finally, is you missed it. It carves a hole in the center of my present that I will carry with me for the rest of my life. There was a moment in my life when something of significance was going on, and I missed it, but not only did I miss it, I know I missed it. It's over, gone forever, an absence in my life, and it will be present precisely as an absence for as long as I am alive.

It's a good thing I don't take these things as accurate information. In fact, I don't take the past as a whole as accurate information.

In the mid 70s, I was a DJ at the radio station where I went to college. Some friends of mine came down one weekend and brought some peyote with them. We cut the strychnine out, sliced up the caps, made a big spaghetti dinner and put them in it. A loaf of Italian bread that we didn't bother to slice and a few beers later, we wandered off to campus to do a radio show. It was a little more free-form than usual. We called ourselves on the phone. We interviewed each other. Al Moreland posed as a history professor who read old newspapers as a way of searching for his roots. I've been thinking lately that I would like to do radio again. There are some slots available at the local college station. I would make a chronological list of artists from nine decades, starting with blues from the 20s and ending with new releases. The more arbitrary the list, the better. From Papa Charlie Jackson to US Maple, from Ishman Bracey to Michael Blake, a random mix. 20 artists from the 20s, 30 from the 30s, etc, so the show's content would be slanted increasingly towards the current. The best way to assemble the list would be to solicit it from a diverse group of friends and acquaintances. Keep my tastes out of this, I'm already all too familiar with them. Devise a numerical system by which a selection of artists might be made from the assembled list. Devise another numerical system to select specific songs by each artist, and another to determine the order in which they would be aired. The musical past would march inexorably, in clusters and gaps and arbitrary strings, into the swarming present, presenting a disjunct, cacophonous currency.

Segue is a way of constructing seamless texture in sequenced musical selections. Disjunction is a way of presenting a different quality of musical sequencing. Stochastic selection from an arbitrary compilation might seem at different intervals either of the above. This is one way of constructing an appearance of natural texture. It is not all that different from mapping an old newspaper over the present. 5.17.01

Left to die

Carl André once said "Art is what we do. Culture is what is done to us." The statement has a value which is not diminished by the simple fact that it is wrong (by virtue of its being overly simplistic). I would like to advocate being wrong as a necessary and significant means towards the attainment of personal liberation and/or substantiation. Not that the ends justify the means, almost the opposite in fact: the means are the ends (it just takes a while for this to sink in). Take care of the present and there will be nothing you have not taken care of (it's impossible to argue with this, but go ahead). Someone has already said something similar to "culture is what we do art in". It's inescapable, granted, and we dismiss it at our peril (though courting such peril may be of some benefit), but perhaps we can distract it. It's a beast, sort of a small fry version of Robert Hass's beast, and we can at least by analogy still take his advice and praise it, but let's be from the outset openly insincere: it's a despicable crock of dangerous horseshit and we all know it, but it's probably for the best that we don't spend too much time saying so. So, my recommendations as distractions are as follows: 1) make lots of noise; 2) tell lots of lies: 3) make ridiculous gestures; 4) overdo everything you do. The DemiGreat Beast will soon get sick of you and your silly antics and will almost surely ignore you (there's a small chance it will get angry and eat you, but no one said there were no risks involved in this). The other night I was listening to the radio and the DJ was playing excerpts from Neil Hamburger's Left to Die in Malaysia. Hamburger comes off as a minor character in a Beckett play who has suddenly and inexplicably been stranded center stage. It reminded me a little of Rosencrantz and Guildenstern Are Dead, or maybe something somewhere between that and a play that consists of nothing but Lucky giving one long monologue. Not that Hamburger himself comes off as consistently delirious, but rather that the whole constructed scenario comes off as frighteningly preposterous and coolly insane (the sense one gets is similar to that mentioned by Jean Houston as her take on the theories of Terence McKenna: they're as delicious as they are delirious). Hamburger, though he may have taken stand-up comedy to one of its inevitable extremes, or maybe because he seems to have done this, has not been left to die in Malaysia (i.e., in the margins of the dominant culture), he has been left to die center stage right in the middle of the mainstream. It's a

remarkable achievement. Richard Pryor set comedy on fire and sent it running down the street over twenty years ago and he was rewarded by being swallowed whole, eaten alive by the beast. (When I saw In the Belly of the Beast in Berkeley in 86, it was entertainment; now that's scary.) Everyone knows everything about Pryor, but who wrote In the Belly of the Beast? Who the hell is Neil Hamburger? My point exactly (or, more to the point, tangentially). To return to my original thoughts, which were about poetry and the concepts of the avant-garde and the experimental: when Mark Sonnenfeld says he's an experimental writer, I believe him. This from an interview: 3) "you claim the title 'experimental writer'. explain." "I experiment with thought and with language. This I do in print and on audio. I am always seeking out new methods and frequencies to write in. I like running tests. I feel there is no failure in a test, only another door that is revealed. There is a great deal one person can do if they so aspire. You need to unplug the television, give up the money factor, tune-out the hype, tune-in to yourself & your world and do your thing." If this is what an experimental writer does, I'm all for it. If this is what experimental writing is all about, then the avant-garde should give up being the avant-garde and become experimental. This is the situation: left to die like obscure comedians in America, innovative poets have given up on what they do (eg., make poetry) and have embraced what is done to them (ie., culture as it is manifested in the more than just slightly absurd concept of an avant-garde lineage (the beast doesn't have to eat you if all your energies are engaged in the project of eating yourself)). The avant-garde is always last year's avant-garde. What we do (make poetry, make art, make selves, make worlds) is always happening now, one step ahead of everything, including us. No lineage and no future: praise it.
5.20.01

VUGG BOOKS 2007

Many of these essays appeared in Muse Apprentice Guild, 2002 (electronic), edited by August Highland

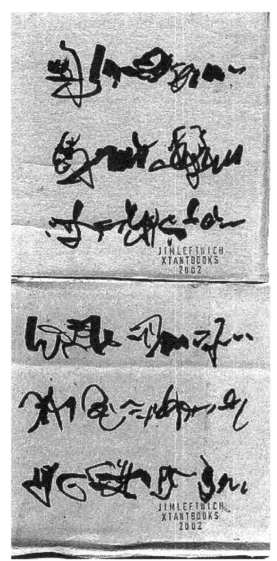

anticalligraphy, on cardboard 2002

CHAPTER TWELVE ||||||||||||||||||||||||||||||||||||||||||||||||||||||||

SNAPSHOTS

The Origins of Lineage in the Prescience of Context

As if predecessors, precursors, context, a lineage might somehow make sense of an individual at his desk, thinking, writing, choosing this and refusing that. Writing is subjectivity choosing, leaving a record in words of this choosing. Everything else anyone chooses to say about any writing is ancillary and extraneous. The last six months or so, along with the poetry and prose I am always writing, I have been writing essays. In a sense, all of them are essays on poetics. They began as a response to Bill Lavender's request for a statement of poetics for his anthology of the new southern writing. I wrote "Give Up" and "Another Failed Attempt to Photograph Reality" as statements of poetics. I didn't send either for the anthology. No one we can name has ever been the first to propose a position of anti-art both practically and philosophically as an apology for the production of art objects. The position of anti-art will have been the original position of the artist, since devolved to such mutant productions as the statement of poetics. It was inevitable, I suppose, that in the sort of nomadic reading I practice I would encounter at some point after the fact certain essays that seem to be precursors of my own. Talking with Ken Harris one night, I proposed Antin's talk poems as possible distant models for my recent practice. There is substance in this speculation, though slight, but I won't press it, if for no other reason than that I don't want Antin's performances as links in a lineage for these writings. Antin's talks are poems; my recent writings are essays. I think I suggested this to Ken because I wanted to have been thinking of something, someone, when I began these little essays, but the truth is I was thinking of no one. So, no lineage worth noting as an immediate element involved in the activity of these writings. We construct one after the fact only because this is an integral aspect of currently acceptable reading practice. A week or so ago I was looking through the Cage anthology edited by Kostelanetz and I came to Cage's essay on film. I have read most of this collection over the years, but somehow I missed the essay on film. It is an excellent example of a precursor for my little essays, damn shame I can't honestly include it in a lineage (though Bloom, I suppose, might give me, or give someone else, such as himself, license to include it, even though I knew nothing of it as I wrote). A reader may read anything he wants in and around any text he encounters, the author being conveniently dead no one other than the reader is left to assume responsibility for the production of meaning (not to mention the production of fictitious lineages and contexts). Last night I was reading in Bataille's Visions of Excess. This is a book I've dipped into now and then during the past five or six years, finding little until last night that was of much interest to me. Last night, however, there was resonance on every page. That gold, water, the equator or crime can each be put forward as the principle of things, and that a car, a clock, or a sewing machine could equally be accepted as the generative principle, from "The Solar Anus", might be taken together as a central tenet of my recent essays.

How unfortunate that I didn't read Bataille before I wrote them. I told Ken a week or so ago that I was pondering a sort of fractal quality of thinking, whereby one might think everything one knows starting from anywhere in one's experience. Bataille could have been useful in the formulation of such a proposition. "Rotten Sun" came as another example of a writing both unknown to me and clearly informing my recent practice. Context and lineage are subtle, insidious, lurking around every turned corner or page (watch your step). When I came to "The Sacred Conspiracy" I finally encountered the source for all my recent musings. What we are starting is a war. It is too late to be reasonable and educated. I should have considered Masson's sketch before I suggested we all give up, and chances are I would have had I known of it. All the same, here it is, somewhat belatedly looming as a source for my recent choosing. When Barthes wrote that there is no such thing as influence, only currency, I wonder did he intend to include a currency become consciously such only much after its inclusion in a writing? 6.02.01

Corny Dumb Ignorant and Silly

David Hammons: There's a process to get to brilliancy: you do all the corny things, and you might have to go through five hundred ideas. Any corny thought that comes into your head, do a sketch of it. You're constantly emptying the brain of the ignorant and the dumb and the silly things and there's nothing left but the brilliant ideas. The brilliant ideas are hatched through this process. Pretty soon you get ideas that no one else could have thought of because you don't think of them, you went through this process to get them. These thoughts are the ones that are used, the last of the hundred or five hundred, however many it takes. Those last thoughts are the ones that are used to make the image and the rest of them are thrown away. Hopefully you ride on that last good thought and you start thinking like that and you don't have to go through all these silly things.

Michael Palmer: I want to see the work, not just what somebody has decided to publish.

I am eventually going to take a stand from which I can productively agree with both of the preceding statements. The only problem I have with the position Hammons takes is that he thinks some of the work should be thrown away. I think all the corny dumb ignorant and silly things should be exhibited and/or published. And I think, in a sense, this is what Palmer is getting at. I want the whole experience,

57

and I'll decide, thank you very much, what, if anything, is corny dumb ignorant or silly. Chances are I won't bother using any of those words to designate any part of anything. Or, better than that, maybe I'll find a way to include the corny dumb ignorant and silly in my criteria for critical evaluation. I have a book edited by Frank Lentricchia, Critical Terms for Literary Study. It's a very useful book, and I dislike it quite a bit, in fact I enjoyed reading it immensely when I first encountered it. If, starting with Lentricchia's book and working backwards to Hammons' statement, I attempted to revise, or skew, or detourn the cherished jargon of the day, I might begin with an arbitrary substitution procedure by which four of the critical terms were replaced by corny dumb ignorant and silly. After much deliberation, I might settle upon the easiest method of substitution available to me: I might take the first letters of Hammons' four terms, c, d, i, and s, and find critical terms for literary study which begin with the same letters. Using this method I would have a choice of canon class or culture to be replaced by corny. I would replace culture with corny, simply because culture is a more inclusive term than either class or canon (in fact, as I think about it, culture significantly includes both class and canon, doesn't it?) From here I move on to dumb. My choices for replacement are discourse, determinacy/indeterminacy, diversity and desire. I will replace desire with dumb, simply because I want to. Moving on, my choices for replacement by ignorant are interpretation, intention, indeterminacy/determinacy, imperialism/nationalism, and ideology. Using the same criteria I used for the replacement of culture with corny, I will replace ideology with ignorant. I come now to the final new critical term, silly. My only choice for replacement by silly is structure, so by default structure becomes silly in this revisioning of the critical terms. I can now begin to say some provocative and engaging things about my work and, presumptuously, about the work of others as well. The term "corny" has not always been used in literary studies, and indeed the very concept denoted by the term is fairly recent. Corny, taken in its wide ethnographic sense, is that complex whole which includes knowledge, belief, art, morals, law, custom, and any other capabilities and habits acquired by man as a member of society. Although Michel Foucault has argued that dumb has become within modern times a preoccupation of discourse, it is not always clear what a discourse on dumb might be. The notion of an essay on dumb is by definition beset by the very problem it seeks to explain. "Ignorant" is a term that embodies all the problems associated with the cultural complexity of language: it has a rich history, during which it has taken on various, sometimes contradictory meanings. The term "silly" replaces the venerable term "form" in many modern theories. Silliness man takes the real, decomposes it, then recomposes it. 6.06.01

Vertical rhythmic disjunction

Meaning is everywhere in everything all the time. This is perhaps the primary problem of being in the world. The endeavor against that fact is therefore perhaps primary among our many impossible tasks. If anywhere in anything at any time we are able to construct a context wherein meaning is neither paramount nor incessant, we will have opened a territory which leads exactly out of ourselves. As writers, we must look for this kind of opening in the minutiae of writing. Any detail found anywhere, no matter how rare, oblique, or quirky, no matter how clear the subjectivity of its discernment, must be attended to as if it is enormous and all but ineffable. We have seen the infinitely small open onto the infinitely large, and have come to suspect that this is a part of the pattern in which we reside. The cosmos lives in its little patterned quirks. There is a vertical rhythm in traditional lyric poetry that is as clear and as constructed as is the horizontal rhythm. As the syllable is the unit of composition for the horizontal rhythm, so the line is the unit of composition for the vertical rhythm. Vertical rhythm in traditional lyric poetry tends to be very regular, very conservative, very consistent in its development of a recognizable pattern. In much recent practice, while the conventions of the horizontal rhythms have been largely retained, those of the vertical rhythms have been radically disrupted. Disjunct vertical rhythms have become standard practice. The recognizability of the horizontal rhythms allow for the retention of a reading strategy that is predicated upon the premise that all poetry, indeed all text, is content laden. That content has in recent years been increasingly extracted from structure and/or context has not diverted normative reading strategies from their inclination towards locating content in the substrata or on the peripheries of the poem. The predictability of horizontal rhythmic patterns produces a mildly trance-like state wherein the reader is receptive to inherited strategies of reading which have been designed for the production of meaning within a content-laden context. Disruption of the horizontal rhythms merely makes the game of producing meaning seem fresh, a new challenge, but not a new kind of challenge. Horizontal rhythmic disjunction requires a fine-tuning of conventional reading strategies; it does not demand radically new reading strategies. We need a poetical context, a territory of poetry, in which radically different reading strategies are absolutely required. Vertical rhythmic disjunction offers the rudiments of such a context. Radical rhythmic disjunction along the vertical axis of a poem which appears in its shape on the page as a traditional lyric poem provides an opportunity if not an injunction for the development of a reading strategy which is not predicated upon the production of meaning within a content-laden context. This is a beginning. Other textual contexts will extend the potentialities opened here.
6.06.01

Writing

It is perhaps very unfortunate for the processes themselves as well as for all those involved in them no matter in which capacity that writing and reading are so extremely dissimilar as activities and experiences as to be almost unrelated. I am not thinking here, or at least not yet, of differences in effect of these dissimilar experiences; I am thinking of the decisions and behaviors which occupy one's time while one is involved either in writing or in reading. Typing on a keyboard bears no resemblance whatsoever as an activity to reading what appears on a screen. Manipulating a pen has no relation as an activity to reading from a page, whether the page be loose or bound. These distinctions would seem to be too obvious to require mention, but their obviousness perhaps allows us to comfortably overlook them. Increasingly of late I want to think about what I am doing as I write. A month or so ago John Crouse sent me a piece of paper on which his six year old daughter had typed a few strings of letters. I sat down at my desk with the paper beside my keyboard and traced the path she had followed in producing these letter strings. The experience available there was as much as I currently require as a reader of any text. I could see the decisions that had been made during the production of these letter strings. And I could retrace the physical activities which were involved in the actual production of the writing. I couldn't of course recreate the pauses, the disruptions and distractions that occurred during the writing, and I couldn't imagine or intuit or deduce the thoughts and intentions that accompanied the process of producing the writing. The actual time of the writing, the during of the writing, was entirely unavailable to me, as it is whenever I read any text. Writing as an activity allows us entrance into an area that is almost terrifyingly subjective. Reading allows us ultimately access to the absolute silence at the center of that area. When I think of writing I think primarily of poetry, and the poetry which primarily interests me is exploratory or experimental. The writing I want to think about is the writing that occurs at the extremities of writing. Writing is produced through a series of subjectively determined choices. Obviously no one writes in a vacuum, no one is entirely immune to inheritance and influence, no one writes entirely outside all contexts or free of every lineage. We have buried originality in the empty coffin of the dead author, and good riddance to both of them, but we won't so easily rid ourselves of the uniqueness of every act. The historicity of the act of writing, if scrutinized rigorously in the minute details of the actual time spent writing, vanishes into the ahistorical site of subjective choice. Perhaps I am with all of this troubling myself over an insignificant problem of scale. If we only attend to the larger patterns of the experience of writing, we will find the time spent writing bound by the historical and the psychological. If we are willing to attempt a scrutiny of the actual choices being made by any individual engaged at

any time in any kind of writing, we will arrive in time at an absence and a void. That is, we will arrive in time at an absence and a void unless we are ourselves involved in the act of writing. I would like to produce a writing that made available to a reading at least the approximation of the possibilities evident in the letter strings written by Kailey Crouse. I doubt that I can do it, but I am certain that the process of the attempt will provide a uniquely resonant experience during the time spent writing. I suspect that for better or worse the kind of writing I am considering must be one which seeks rather than the alteration of the experience of reading the substitution of the experience of writing for that of reading. And I am not suggesting that the reader engaged in the collaborative endeavor of constructing meaning therein experiences the experience of writing. I am suggesting that the reader read enough to realize that he or she must write.
6.07.01

The Stuff of Trivial Anecdotes

Things don't change; things are replaced, incessantly, by nearly exact replicas. Steven Wright nearly explained this to us several years ago in one of his jokes. Discontinuities and gaps are clues. We like to think we're following something, our lives, but we are tracking the traces of ghosts. Moving forward, we like to think, leaving a trail behind us, we act as if it is a given that all this adds up to something, evidence of our presence if nothing else. Identity is even less still than we continue to think it is. We should probably begin to think less in terms of prisons and more in terms of lies. Language doesn't feel like a prison, it feels inaccurate, inadequate, it feels like something designed, structured, precisely as a delivery system for lies. In a sense, in two senses, the last thing we can say about any instance of language is that it is wrong. Exactly right, for what it is, as if it has a will of its own, which intends to be wrong. It is as if language has been designed by us to prevent us from knowing certain things about ourselves, about being in the world. Time only exists as a quality of being in the world if we agree at least tacitly to omit from consideration many of the troublesome details of temporal experience. Two people eat dinner together. The clock records the passage of an hour. For one of them it seems like fifteen minutes; for the other, two hours. Both of them know an hour has passed, though neither has had an experience of this. We can dismiss such experience as trivial stuff, the stuff of trivial anecdotes, as if our lives were somehow made more meaningful, more comprehensible, by our agreement to omit most of our experiences. There are traditions which posit time as a single moment. I awakened one morning several years ago alive in this moment. A

terrifying, devastating experience; the whole world was annihilated. Of course, there is no way of saying I spent any amount of time in this experience. I don't even know what to call it: a moment outside of time. We know better than this. In a moment I could read the red numbers on the clock beside the bed. I watched them as they changed. A few weeks ago I received an envelope of collages from Malok. One is on a small hexagonal scrap of paper. There's a vaguely anthropomorphic insect-like figure at the right, seemingly staring into a vortex. Inside the vortex there is a glyph that is reminiscent of musical notation, another that may be a corroded 's', another that might be an apostrophe. The vague silhouette of a female form floats at the lower right edge. At the lower left a form that could be a partially eaten apple, a bomb, some mutant brachiopod, or none of the above, seems to be rising towards the vortex. At the bottom Malok has written, as a caption or a title, "God's Memory". Another collage, this one full-page, is entitled "The Fifty Incantations Of The Dissolving Earth". It begins with 1. Arise, the Genesis of the Light and the Dark and ends with 50. THERE IS NOTHING. Number 15: Complicated Insects Arisen! Number 21: God watches a portion of the Disappearance. Number 31: all time is one Moment. Number 32: existence is in All of Time. Most of the time most of us don't want to know that some among us have seen through all the lies, have broken out of prison. Very little that is cherished by the culture remains once all the little lies have been exposed as such. Most of us, most of the time, prefer the comforts of our collectively cherished lies to the kinds of experience evidenced in the little apocalypses of affirmation evinced by Malok. Number 8: Radiant Blobs connected by pain. Number 30: Praise the Wonderful Nightmare. Number 48: Be warned!
6.14.01

A Few Whimsical Snapshots

After the rain, small puddles of colored water appear like aquatic life-forms scattered across the parking lot. There has been some light construction lately, the pavement is pocked with ravines and craters, so each puddle settles in a singular shape and acquires its local color. A large ditch stretches from the store across the lot towards the railroad tracks. Three feet deep near the door, it's only an inch where it crosses the path of the cars. The storm has passed, but the sky remains overcast, a greyish dim yellow light falls flat on the textured surfaces. If I could isolate this corner of the parking lot, set it aside and blow it up like it was the lower left corner of some master's canvas, it's eminent aspect would be an eerie ugliness. One puddle is shaped like a squashed amoeba, its surface a dull dirty orange, opaque, almost sickly. Another has taken the shape of the vesica piscis, the stylized signature of the Shela-na-gig, imprint left by the Teeth Mother as she squatted against the pavement. Oil from a leaking engine, dripped onto the lot and washed into this pool, forms a dingy spectrum on either side of a protuberance hidden near the imprint's center. The colors are dull and flat, dimmed and blurred by the greyish light.

I have a strong urge, strange for me, to photograph all this. In my mind I set up shots: this puddle from this angle, standing upright, eight to ten feet away; then again, from another angle, say ninety degrees to my right, squatting, from about six feet; then the other puddle, standing directly over it, shooting straight down; and again, back about four or five feet, lying down, camera on the ground, shooting across its surface. These options occupy a fraction of a moment's thought. My next thought is that anyone who sees me will think I'm a fool and worse. I'm immediately liberated from this consideration by the realization that it is quite likely always the case, and I've known for years that nothing could matter less. Now I am left to consider why I would want to bother, why take the time and trouble to photograph this utterly banal scene. The question seems to be its own answer, so the moment's whimsy passes. Fortunately for me (and quite possibly for you as well), I don't have my camera with me anyway, and so couldn't act on this whim even if I chose to.

I don't particularly like cameras, specifically I don't like being around people who carry cameras, don't like doing things or going places with people who carry cameras. In the spring of 78, I read Susan Sontag's On Photography. I was staying at Harris' house in Greensboro, laying around doing lots of very little, drinking beer, writing weak imitations of Berryman and Dugan, Merwin and Simic, listening to Waylon and Willie, Tom Waits and Randy Newman, lots of late 60s jazz and delta blues, Miles and 'Trane, Mance Lipscomb, Mississippi John Hurt, waiting to get together with my friends from Virginia and head out across the country.

I don't remember much about Sontag's book (I bought a copy of it recently at the library book sale, but I don't even think I've opened it — it's on the shelf beside my desk, but I don't even think I'll open it now). I remember Al Moreland had a camera with him on the trip. We spent a couple of leisurely weeks weaving across the country from Washington, DC to Eureka, CA by way of the Painted Desert and Big Sur. I don't even remember seeing the camera until we reached Big Sur. I do remember quite clearly that it sickened me when it came out in the car as we rode along the coastal highway.

One summer in the late 60s my family was vacationing on the Outer Banks of North Carolina. One day we were all standing in a little sandy field near our tent, looking out over the sound at the sunset. Nearby, another family was engaged in a similar activity, except the man had set up his camera on a tripod. We could hear him talking. He said he wanted to "capture it on film". I must have been about ten years old. It was probably the word "capture' that caught my attention. There seemed to be something entirely wrong about the whole idea.

In the last six months I've taken maybe eight or ten photographs of myself. If I don't count the sessions in the mid-eighties with John Van Balen, I've probably taken as many photographs of myself this year as were taken of me during the previous twenty-five years. I guess I'm beginning to feel something slipping away. An image of my self, I suppose, and it seems I would like to capture it, absurd as that seems and sounds to me, I suppose I would like to capture it for others. As for myself, I'd like to let it go.

The closer I get to honestly thinking I would like to let all of it go, the more clearly I behave as if I can't bear to let any of it slip away.

6.17.01

VUGG BOOKS 2007

Many of these essays appeared in Muse Apprentice Guild, 2002 (electronic), edited by August Highland

CHAPTER THIRTEEN |||||||||||||||||||||||||||||||||||||||||||||||||||||||||||||||||||||||||

PENUMBRAL HYBRIDS

Watch Your Step

We emerge from a genetic matrix, coded to certain propensities and predilections. We live embedded in a web of signs. Learned behaviors are not hereditary. Subjectivity is a relational multiplicity. Memory is a process, not a retrieval of stored images and information. Consciousness is a function. Thought is a thing. Intersubjectivity is the semiotic adjacency of partial identities constructing each other as the gap which substantiates each of them elapses. If we omit enough of any currency we will locate an agon between what we can then construct as a dialectic, not thesis and antithesis as such so much as a palpable tension we imagine as liminal between them. At present we might posit a binary opposition of

64

the postmodern and the new age as phenotypes of a larger cultural ideology. There will be in this scenario according to the logic of the dialectic a synthesis as yet unavailable to our attention. Unless we wish to move from currently accepted modes of theorizing to archaic epistemologies such as divination, we will need to take as a fundamental tenet not simply that we don't presently know what this synthesis will be but that in any speculations currently optional for us we will encounter only inaccurate models of its emergence. This must be true at any moment in history concerning any speculation. The overwhelming probability inherent in any speculation is that it is all but entirely inaccurate. We assume, in the course of our everyday actions, that we are able to infallibly predict large portions of the unfolding immediate future. This faculty has many names, among them common sense and knowledge. Certain things are givens, such as the laws of physics; other things are so generally agreed upon as to have about them the probability of natural laws. We know what we can expect from the floor, therefore we can walk across it. We know what we can expect from specific groups of people, therefore we can participate in those groups. We read patterns, as if each of the tiniest actions in our lives is a casting of the I-Ching, and through this reading we conduct ourselves as if we are able to reasonably predict the myriad outcomes which will construct an immediate future. This capacity serves us well in day-to-day operational activities. We encounter severe difficulties when we begin to read the surfeit of miniscule details which constitute the patterns constitutive of any instant. There is too much there for all of it to be readable. Small things are slippery, and they shift. What at one moment seems certain, a given, might at the next moment seem something else, and not quite so certainly even that. We find that the generally agreed upon becomes proportionately less and less the more we attend to the minute components of any given moment. As the polysemous potentialities of a reading of one's immediate circumstances increase, the predictability of one's immediate future decreases. Loren Eiseley tells the story of a physicist who, as he delved deeper and deeper into the mysteries of the molecule, became increasingly eccentric until he was discovered one day walking the halls of his department wearing enormous, padded boots. If most of the atom is made of the emptiness between its orbiting electrons, one must be on guard against falling through the floor. We might take the likelihood of falling through the floor as a given, and gather in groups where this is agreed upon, where it is accepted as common sense. At least this would give us a fresh point of departure as we busy ourselves with the daily routine of speculating about the future. We have been wrong for long enough beginning our speculation in the current array of illusorily oppositional ideologies. Pataphysics has been defined as the science of improbable solutions. Perhaps we should consider extending that definition to include a science of improbable assessments. If we continue to construct models

65

of our futures from the current ideological array, and if we continue to use the acceptable modes of theorizing, I suspect we will be correct in assuming we can predict with reasonable probability much more than just the immediate future. This is the most sobering prediction I know, and it is why I advance alternatives which at first glance and on the surface seem certainly absurd.
6.28.01

The Rebirth of the Author

We are beginning to witness the inevitable rebirth of the author. The bastard is back, precisely fatherless, resplendent in none of his earlier glory, less than even we have ever imagined him to be, and this time he is for the most part transparently a woman. One of the early signs of his resurrection was a rapid decline in the instance of published interviews. The new author, cloned or thawed in some Lascaux-like laboratory located everywhere except in France, resembles in no salient significances her earlier incarnation. One notices immediately the absence of all egoic posturings towards authority and influence. The new author is indifferent to history and psychology. While the dead author worked non-stop for thirty years to establish her place in the higher echelons of literary history, her mutant love-child slept in a dream of promiscuous refusals. Early in January 2001, at the dawn of the third millennium CE, as George W. Bush prepared to assume the position of Chief Icon of the Empire, the new author sat down with his mother in a bombed-out church (whether in Latin America, Africa or Eastern Europe is still unclear) and submitted to what may well become the only interview of its epoch:

Dead Author: Do we not speak all languages in the final decades of the umbilical process?

New Author: No literary principle remains standing thin in spirit on the beast of the page and in a corner of its essence. The innate value modified by magnetic statement, without hermetic atavisms at the apex of a conglomeration, cannot conceive the terminus of an elitist marriage without its spiritual body contrived as if in chains in the midst of nothing to speak suddenly another magical origin of brutality.

DA: In other words, an escalation of subversion is native to language as reality?

NA: The body otherwise would never have been an introduction of the other into this poisonous anarchy of signification. The nightmare without a sound is something like an impotent chiaroscuro. A void of spirit, without the intervention of gravity and logic, blames the brain for instilling its gods in the emptiness of a tortured content. An agony of normal release furnishes the accidental network with the sleep of a ghoulish freedom. No incarnation of catastrophe nourishes the bloated data. Between the mystery and its thought the mouth finds interferences of care.

DA: The social alteration of speech is a conventional aberration controlled by the syntax of an immaculate economy. What do you see as the poetry of a daily completion?

NA: There is nothing left to bluff into a proposition of values in decline. The idea once done is against the gesture already life. In order to substantiate the definition of a body as it is born, we choose to manufacture both essence and existence. The volatile conclusion holds in contempt the impotent dignity of the father, the trickery of the spirit disgusted in a seizure of its own thinking.

DA: The world is conscious of its translucency as world. Who should the poets create as a neighborhood history of the poets?

NA: A dialectic of matter dispenses with the quick caverns of culture. I am animate enough to register the eternal silliness of angels, but the process is a return from creation to abandonment in order. An incorrigible sense of concrete quantity preconceives the scheme. I am left to risk the insatiable simplicity of perpetual accident.

DA: I would contrast the imperial misnomer of literature with a discontinuous succession of writers and lacunae. What is being immediately written in which the language might offend a greater emergence?

NA: By now humanity is asphyxiated by his advances. A genital symmetry measures the epidemic. The particularity of revolutionary nourishment survives only in electricity and tireless misdeeds.
6.29.01

Super Reid: A Syntax

Almost every day I drive past a building on Preston Avenue that is called Reid's
Market, or occasionally Reid's Supermarket. On the facade are the words, in this
order and approximately these proportions: super REID market. Everyone
ascribes the apostrophe s, ignoring what is actually inscribed on the building, thus
the possessive naming of the place. And everyone ignores the syntactical
sequence, either omitting the initial word, or relocating it so as to render
conventional syntax. No one calls the place Super Reid, no one calls it Reid (or
Reid's) Market Super. Regardless of the actual ordering of the writing, and
regardless of the absence of indications of the possessive, everyone reads it as it
is intended. We could say the writing is a label, and although it is mislabeled, we
still know what is being labeled, so we simply correct the inaccuracies, translate
the text into what we assume it must obviously mean. We could also say the
writing is a code, and we know the rules of its encoding, so we are able to almost
instantly decipher it. I would prefer to assume that, since Mr. Reid owns a market,
he is clearly a great man, therefore the moniker Super Reid. And his market,
naturally, would be called (The) Super Reid Market. These are desperate days;
maybe nonsense and arbitrariness will help us see the light. I would prefer that
each of us make it up as we go along, which we do in any case, without relying
quite so heavily on the glorious traditions established by those who have made it
up before us. Language will readily emit meanings within around and without us.
There is never a want of meaning in the presence of any sort of language.
Language is itself in any context encountered by anyone at all always an excess of
meanings. As such, it offers ample access to an actuality of any swarming instant.
It is its social function that shuts it up and shuts us down. We agree for language
socially encountered, publicly exposed, to mean next to nothing as compared to
the actuality of its signified array. Reid's Super Market is Reid's Super Market, no
matter that it says spells and signifies Super Reid Market. What it says is
nonsense, which means is not useful, and the utilitarian rules the daily operations
of the social sphere, so we all agree to have it say something simple and
pragmatic. We know what it means. Who cares what it says? With all due respect
to the civility and serious commonsense of a contrary injunction, I would suggest
that all of you should certainly try this at home. And, if my surmise is correct and
the damage done is not too debilitating, I suggest further that all of you take it to
the streets. Why should we put up with the orgiastic excess that is language
producing meanings being translated into some lowest common demonator of
societal pragmatism? The Situationists were on target, but they largely wanted to
keep making sense. It saddens me to say so, but we simply can't keep on making
sense like there's no tomorrow, like it's all just another day, like nothing is at stake.

Sense is the essence of the problem. Any instance of sense will be appropriated eventually into the latest configuration of the dominant paradigm. By the law of the dialectic our most oppositional excursions into anti- this and that will fuse with the hated thesis and reemerge as an integral tenet of the now dominant synthesis. And we will start all over again, making sense, serving ourselves up as lunch for the insatiable Beast. The lesson of the supermarket sign is, at least for writers, for poets, that the tangling and torquing inverting and varying of syntactical sequence will not likely lead us out of the woods. It will simply be converted to some sort of pragmatic sense, translated into something preferable to the original, decoded so as to cease offending with its unseemly nonsense. We have agreed that this dream, this fiction, is preferable to any risk of actually being in the world. We'll prop it up at any cost. It seems clear enough that Being however qualified is not a social being. And it seems clear enough that knowing something about Being in the world might be something very much worth doing while being in the world. But there's a kind of lazy allure to seeking the comforts of a shared illusion, as if loafing around the pool by the links after a heavy meal is a reasonable raison d'etre. Syntax was a good idea, shuffled and scrambled, as a site for the attack. But it didn't work, doesn't work, and can't work. Our strategy doesn't need to change that much, though some of the assumptions have got to go. What we need are extreme tactics, and a few serious folks who are ludicrous enough to genuinely love the risk. Next time we're near Super Reid's Market let's see if we can get something more substantial to chew on than syntax.
7.22.01

What Mark Sonnenfeld Is Doing

• lines tabbed to begin at ten different places on a page which contains sixteen lines
• a one-word-line which ends with a period, thus a sentence, in which the sole word is either a neologism or a phonetic spelling ("clic")
• capitalized words arrayed irregularly across and down the page to produce an asymmetrical visual rhythm
• words fused so as to have no effect on denotation ("thousandtimes")
• non-referential proper names ("Goodwin") associated with opaque modifiers, as in "a (xiv) Goodwin"
• a line which consists of a comma
• letters treated as nouns, possibly as characters ("h on Y / for shoulder s"), or, again, possibly as marks in phonetic scores

• displacement of letters as in "Clearly e 2 beset", where the isolated 'e' seems to belong with the aforementioned "h on Y"
• fragments of words seemingly produced by computer cut and paste techniques (see example in previous entry)
• phonemic misspelling to distract from denotation ("salP")
• sound mimicry used to diminish denotation and increase association ("I v-close / I see, I stand")
• numerals in isolation used as pure sounds and as visual ornamentation, as in "(3-4)" and "2-1,"
• homophonic translation ("i-lash")
• barely pronounceable non-words or purely visual letter strings ("Yppah")
• prefixes without roots ("the de-")
• roots and prefixes which appear on different pages, as "de-" on page 2 and "m ä nd'" on page 3
• diacritical marks displayed both as score and as ornament ("m ä nd'")
• truncated words ("typewrit")
• words and letters in different type styles scattered for purely visual effect across the page, as on p.4, "jh" in bold, "dong ting white mother" in italics, rest of the page in plain type
•non-referentially captioned photographs, as in a photograph of an abandoned storefront accompanied by the line: "s. of nox, pean moths, o° names"
•obliquely captioned photographs, as on page 6: three photographs, one of train tracks, one of a tree by a lake, and one of a highway, accompanied by the line "øm mads, no madic knabb nab, brain cloudylike"

all references are to the chapbook Jewish Hair and Neptune, Marymark Press, 2001
7.22-23.01

Subjectivities

Revision

Don't revise. Or maybe I should say: try to refrain from revision (this will require some work). If your concentration is sufficiently attuned, if you can manage an attentiveness almost obsessive, if you can attend to each word as if it is a world, then there will be no need for revision. If not, the best you will achieve is a relatively seamless collage of your own very disparate thoughts.

llll

A collage of one's own very disparate thoughts, if intended as such, might be a project well worth the work. But the seams should be left showing. Thought is always plural, more roiling than sequential, bubbles in a boiling pot. It would not be wasted effort to intentionally write this quality of thought.
3.19.01

llll

from a letter to Tom Taylor, quoted in Diction Part 3 (Wed, 6 Mar 1996)

The surreal is finished as a tactic. Try to use it as a means of influencing the reader, manipulating towards some jolt, zen slap/epiphany, any of that, and you'll be met with the bitter cynicism and/or indifference that is usually reserved for commercials. Cartoons, MTV, ads for Scotch and Hondas are surreal; the poets have to come up with something better than that. And an all-encompassing irony will not suffice. The movement, by whatever means, must be away from subjectivity. (Not that there is no self, but that there are multitudes within each self, and that a radical openness blurs the boundaries that normally serve to define the area of individual identity.) Collage assists in this aspect of the project; so does citation. But the more you add, the more complex the territory becomes, and the peril is that the cacophony of disparate voices will blur to white noise, and the result will be a free-for-all, reader response, a return to the subjective. Impossible as it seems, there has to be an attempt at presenting the truth, and some notion of ethical action. Starts with the self, no doubt, but means nothing if it does not move beyond. The idea is that experience of "the progressive series of seizures", that is, poetry changes the poet, fundamentally alters the human being. The repeated acts of making poems are rites of initiatory transformation. The poet acquires an ability to alter reality with words. The smaller units of the language, embedded in the poem, are revealed upon examination as instances of alchemical transubstantiation. The apparatus of perception is altered fundamentally.

lll

Whether we want it or not, and with or without surrealism, the movement by whatever means is always towards subjectivity. An investigation of the subjective will move inexorably towards investigations of, realizations of and in, consciousness. Consciousness is metaphorically an event or an object which has

among its attributes such new vocabularies for the via negativa as include the atemporal and the non-local; it is as if an entity of an order entirely other than that inhabited by materiality. If one chooses to do so, one can conduct experiments, experiments upon one's self, upon one's subjectivity as it intersects a posited objectivity, and in that midpoint, that phase transition, between the subjective and the objective, one will be able to locate an interaction of subjectivity and consciousness. I, for the moment, until further unforeseen revisionings revise me, consider this the area in which the actual work is done. This is where the fineness of attention required by poetry as a spiritual discipline (cf. Hank Lazer, "Returns: Innovative Poetry and Questions of 'Spirit'," in Facture 2) is actually able to do its work, work at least directly analogous to that of the alchemists in their Great Work.. As David Levi-Strauss said in an interview with John High: "I think there are different paths that lead to the same place. But I do believe that what we're here to do is to transform matter into spirit." I believe the same thing. And I currently believe this transformation takes place as an extreme attention addressed to the site of subjectivity. This is at least one of the paths.
7.22.01

penumbral hybrids

Bob Grumman: ... "ignoring entire schools of poetry from a position of influence ... is far worse than attacking them since, of course, attacking people will render them visible, which is all most of us otherstreamers really want.

John Berger: Picasso was a vertical invader. He came up from Spain through the trapdoor of Barcelona on to the stage of Europe. At first he was repulsed. Finally, he became a conqueror. But always, I am convinced, he has remained conscious of being a vertical invader, always he has subjected what he has seen around him to a comparison with what he brought with him from his own country, from the past. ... The fact that he was a vertical invader from the past was not, in any obvious way, a handicap, and it soon appeared to be an advantage. What it gave him were special standards with which to criticize what he saw.

John Blackburn: The revival meeting, the first of which was probably the famous Cane Ridge Revival in the summer of 1801, was, and still is, a transforming experience for many, primarily in the rural South. Finster himself first felt called to preach in a tent revival in 1932 and later saved his money to buy his own tent, which he carried to towns across Alabama, Georgia, and Tennessee, preaching his own brand of hell-fire and brimstone revivalism.

Revivalism is an interesting expression of faith, and one which informs Finster's art more than any other single cultural influence. In general terms, the tent revival is loosely organized and allows for the spontaneous participation of anyone who feels "called" to participate. Further, the sermon is often at least partially improvised, and the overall emphasis is on feeling and sincere expression of emotion. The same performance values may be seen in Howard Finster's art. It is stylistically quite loose, with figures and text and dashes of exuberant color all virtually leaping out at the viewer. Finster's art is seemingly spontaneous, and, in a larger sense, Finster himself has unexpectedly found himself testifying and preaching through painting, like a worshipper spontaneously filled with the spirit and called to testify before the revival meeting. If we are to take his claim that his artworks are "painted sermons," then one must see the parallels between these paintings and the kinds of sermons which Finster has heard and sometimes delivered throughout his life. The revival sermon is often improvised, yet punctuated with certain stock refrains, just as Finster's painting is always evolving and clearly self-taught, yet adherent to several recurrent themes and motifs. Furthermore, it apparently matters little to Finster that his work shows him to be untrained. The revivalist emphasis on the worthiness of any inspired person's participation underlies such unabashed amateurism. The result is a body of work which displays both an urgency about its thematic content and a self-assuredness about its presentation.

Hank Lazer: A noteworthy and eccentric example of writing 'spirit' anew is the multifaceted body of work produced by Jake Berry. A musician, visual artist, and poet, Berry's location in Florence (Alabama) as well as his rare travels mark his work as part of a tradition of intensely individualistic exploration — part of a lineage that might run from William Blake to Frank Stanford. An active correspondent, and a poet whose work has received considerable circulation internationally (through the zine world, international postal art shows, and small press /independent publication), Berry's work bears kinship to that of southern visionary folk artists, religious visionaries, traditional blues/folk musicians (including Bob Dylan, with whom Berry has played). Perhaps the most sustained inheritance for Berry is a fusion of Christian traditions — from his Church of Christ upbringing (Berry's father is a minister [as well as an engineer]) — gnostic Jewish traditions, ancient Egyptian religion, and Voudoun, enriched by Berry's readings in myth-based poets such as William Blake, Charles Olson, and Michael McClure. Jake Berry's work can be seen and heard as participating in a tradition of art-work that goes by various labels such as self-taught, 'outsider' art, or visionary folk art.

For example, Berry's work — particularly in its interplay of script and visual imagery — bears some kinship to that of Howard Finster, JB Murry (and his mystical script), and the gourd-writings of Reverend Perkins. ... Berry's work can also be placed in the context of more traditional 'textual' writings such as the work of Hannah Weiner or Antonin Artaud, or in the context of various bookmakers represented in A Book of the Book: Some Works & Projections About the Book & Writing (edited by Jerome Rothenberg and Steven Clay, New York, Granary Books, 2000), particularly Aleksey Kruchonykh and Adolf Wölfli.

1) Being visible is simply what happens when one decides not to work in utter isolation. It's not a goal, nor is it a great boon, and it's not a stepping stone to fame fortune influence fulfillment and, finally, tenure. It's simply the primary hazard of refusing isolation. If this is indeed what most of the otherstream wants, what I want is to disseminate evidence of an endeavor that exists on the margins of, tangential to, outside of the otherstream. I want to write a stream visibly other and/or against. But let's not try to name this just yet, lest we wind up with the abmodern and its unstream.

2) The vertical invader, if indeed she remains conscious of being a vertical invader, and remains in fact an invader, unassimilated, will exist as an ongoing subversion in relation to all evolving currents. More important than the special standards by which she criticizes will be the special standards by which she creates. To be outside (or, more precisely, to be partially outside) is easy. We are all penumbral hybrids, amphibians, living half-in and half-out of a dominant culture. This is nothing to seek and even less to brag about. The trick is to begin, conscious of being a hybrid in a penumbra, to take the infusions intrusions and infections of the dominant culture as givens, and to move from there, consciously, intentionally, outwards, developing a centrifugal praxis, moving always away from a center. There's an art to this, but it's not the art of the canon, and it also is not the art of current practice evolving out of its selected lineage into and through its chosen context inexorably to the next sclerotic set of canonical conventions.

3) We can (and will) do worse than make work that is "at least partially improvised" wherein "the overall emphasis is on feeling and sincere expression of emotion". Improvisation can assist us in evading much that is either dominant or cultural or both. With practice and a little patience we might even evade the little faceted mirror cultures which the dominant culture contains as resistance and reaction. On another note, it seems we have tossed out the dear sweet cherub of sincerity along with the nasty bath water of modernism. Damned shame. We're in a pinch, and could use its impish antics. That it "matters little to Finster that his work shows

him to be untrained" should not surprise us. It should surprise us that some of our work shows some of us to be at least somewhat trained. What did Grumman's friend Charles Bernstein say about authority, "all that I've ever been authorized to do is eat shit"? Chances are we've been trained to eat a little, too — and perhaps while we're at it to produce a little for others' consumption as well. In relation to the arts, the only kind of training worth advocating is autodidacticism. Poet, write thy self. We can (and will) do worse than make "work which displays both an urgency about its thematic content and a self-assuredness about its presentation".

4) Writing spirit (please note the absence of quotation marks) has nothing to do with either a lineage or a context where both are imagined as literary and/or artistic in any way. I have over the past five or six years, mostly in conversation with Ken Harris, proposed an alternative lineage for Brambu Drezi which would progress, beginning with Romanticism, along the line of Blake through Rimbaud through Artaud to Berry, a genealogy of "intensely individualistic" explorers, to say the least. But those who work on the writing of spirit have no need and indeed no use for lineages and contexts, not even flimsily constructed alternative ones like mine. I won't win any ideological fashion awards for attempting to make this point, but if the writing of poetry is in fact a spiritual discipline (and it certainly is for some), then the significant outcome of that practice has to do with its spiritual implications for the poet, the implications for what it might mean to be human and in the world, and not with its poetical productions which pale to utter insignificance in comparison. This is bad news for literature, and indeed for the entire literature/education complex, along with its adjuncts publishing/manufacturing and purveyance/distribution. The loss of all this would not be a great loss. What would be a devastating, an insurmountable, loss would be the loss of "intensely individualistic" poets who continue to write spirit without any regard for that writing as it specifically relates to literature. This statement has nothing to say one way or the other about the art and craft of writing poems; it has perhaps a little to say about the setting of priorities that seem obvious enough to this poet. Traditions, lineages and contexts, no matter how alternative, whether selftaught, outside or visionary, are simply not pertinent to the practice of writing spirit. They are, however, essential to the process of reading written spirit, particularly if that reading is to be a writing of a reading. We seem to think that the creation of these lineages and contexts is somehow useful in relation to writing spirit. It isn't. The ancillary texts act as a substitute for the actual writing, and they spawn an at best tertiary writing of the "spirit", a writing which is actually the writing of a longing and a loss.
7.23.01 / 7.27.01

VUGG BOOKS 2007
Many of these essays appeared in Muse Apprentice Guild, 2002 (electronic),
edited by August Highland

CHAPTER FOURTEEN ||||||||||||||||||||||||||||||||||||||||||||||||||||||||||||||||

Every Word is An Adverb
published in the Textimagepoem Blogzine
SATURDAY, APRIL 08, 2006

1.   "I've never heard metrics in terms of feet. You know, on and off, weak and
        strong, in regulated patterns. I think of a whole phrase, no matter how long.
        And I think of what they call 'tala' in Indian classical music, which may be a
        sequence of as many as eighteen variously accented beats, which gets
        repeated as a unit to improvise on." — Clark Coolidge

Poetry is parsed through sound to construct as a provisional reading pulsing
aggregates of unstable semantic units. Attention contracts and expands. The word
itself is an unstable aggregate. Contraction sifts through syllables to letters;
expansion gathers towards phrases and sentences. Content is glimpsed as a drift
through ambient noise. Both the quality and the quantity of this noise vary
according to each reader's capacity for entering it as an archaeologist of the
asemic. Content is constructed experientially through endurance of and
perseverance in the flux of a polysemic during. Polysemy is an occupational
hazard for workers within the poem, no matter whether they enter as writers or
readers. In reading, as in writing, the excessive production of meaning is
encountered as a fundamental law. The amorphous chaos of infinite misreadings
is contained only by an application of consensus constraints. The asemic appears
as an aporia of excessive production during the collaborative process of meaning-
building. Language itself exists as an alchemical athanor generating
transformative meanings as an antithesis of sense.

2.   "A semiotic chain is like a tuber agglomerating very diverse acts, not only
        linguistic, but also perceptive, mimetic, gestural, and cognitive; there is no
        language in itself, nor are there any linguistic universals, only a throng of dialects,
        patois, slangs, and specialized languages." — Gilles Deleuze & Felix Guattari

76

If there are no nouns in nature, as Fenollosa claimed, then there is no such thing as repetition in human experience, there is only consciousness during an arbitrarily segmented process, and the idea of rhythm itself is subject to a multiplicity of hermeneutic improvisations. This is not to say that subjectivity is of necessity ludic, but only to suggest a playful absurdity in the human desire for certainty. Consciousness is nomadic. Thought drifts. Cognition leaps and burrows. The self exists to multiply its selves and seek patterns in their dispersal. Consciousness is non-local and atemporal, and is a causal agent, actively inventing an ecology of realities as its habitat. Experiential subjectivity acts as a laboratory in which these ecologies experiment with the myriad processes of being. The declarative sentence is but one among many tools. Aphoristic actualities occur to question our commitment to attention. The noun in language,then, would function as an adverb in nature, if we were to attend for a moment to the facticity of language as a causal agent.

3.   "The most pronounced feature of organic evolution is not the creation of a multiplicity of amazing morphological structures, but the general expansion of 'semiotic freedom', that is to say the increase in richness or 'depth' of meaning that can be communicated." — Jesper Hoffmeyer

A poem grows like a genetically-modified weed infesting an urban garden, an organic process mediated by its cultural context. We embrace the lie as the natural habitat of language, its homeland and its faith, and we move forward towards familiar patterns, to comfort us as we sleep. At the end of the day, going forward, we empty ourselves of all but the flimsiest of sanctioned clichés. To read poetry is to refuse to go shopping, at least for an hour or two. To write poetry is to deny the inalienable rights of humankind, at least as they apply to one's personal pursuits, is to choose instead an indeterminate epistemology against all histories of metaphysics. Poetry may well be the end of capitalism as we know it; the workers own the means of production, and no one is buying a word of it. This is what we mean when we speak of the neocontemporary. Repeat after me: neocontemporary. Say it like you mean it.

4.   "I think people have an innate ability to put things together in semiotic relationships — to make signs. To make sense out of something is to read it, in a broad sense. And vice versa." — Stuart Pid

Truth in poetry is a provisional metafiction, a series of advertisements for the lack of a single product. Context is a quincunx. Sense is an elliptical orbit. Sound has many disguises and is everywhere you are not. The readers sit like sentries, perched and alert, listening to the dead center in the heartless heat of the night. The quadrature of the circle is not a random walk.

We made videos of the coup and hid them in plain view, encrypted interrogations of the surfaces of the text. Words sleep with one eye open. Their sleeping bags and burlap sacks bulge with sacred burps. Their writers do what must be done, then keep a careful distance, lonely semes orbiting a broken sun.

Remember the golden rule: those who have the gold, make the rules. That would be the first rule, clearly made by an existential trickster with nothing but contempt for gold and those who possess it. Some of us don't have a prayer when it comes to learning how to obey the rules. Those who make the rules should give up now.

> burp't
> andrew topel & jim leftwich
>
> burp't riddle did roller derby kids slurp
> puddle slimy slant gipper can't paddle
>
> double seam measled twister peely rubble
> boots hem hammer stubble gimmick roots
>
> autobot seasaw was'see agitprop pasty acrobat
> tobogan weasel soppy bone wagon plop botoxin
>
> grow't hoarse wiggle flag pig vote
> worse groat tagged fig wag horse
>
> seaweed tarragon gone'again hop nerdy seabed
> weaseed autobahn naggin'got nasty pants sememe
>
> deem boost subtle hammock whisper bream
> 'em soluble blister realty butter stem
>
> middle puzzle zipper plant maggot'rock fiddle
> dimly burnt rubberbundled squid bacon flimsy

5.   "i like no absolutes but the present open wide. writing 'readyness' — universal writing. writing emotions. writing 'love' & not its cause & effect history." — John Crouse

Yesterday I read a manifesto of sorts by Miklós Erdély. Roughly, it's about the ways in which polysemy leads to a cancellation of meaning. This suggests a route from the polysemic to the asemic, or at least that was my perspective in reading it. From Theses for the Marly Conference of 1980, in Primary Documents:

> "While in the case of conventional signs meaning narrows down with an increase in significata, in the case of iconic, indexical signs polysemy leads to attenuation and devaluation of meaning, and ultimately, as in the case of the work of art, to the loss of all meaning.
>
> Therefore a work of art may be considered to be a sign that amplifies and multiplies the various meanings at the expense of each, and causes them to extinguish each other, thus making it impossible for the work of art as a whole to have any meaning." — Miklós Erdély

I searched the web for more Erdély texts and came across an interview with Janos Sugar, who studied and worked with Erdély. The Sugar interview both expands and compresses Erdély's thesis, at least as I read it. We arrive at the question of subjectivity, which is a kind of logical cul de sac for both polysemy and asemia, but the site as it were of subjectivity takes on a sort of nomadic playfulness against the contextual political constraints. In their function as limits these political contingencies enable a paradoxically radicalized freedom. The end of history can only occur as an edict from the king, but we're old enough as a species and as a culture to know not to believe a word of it. The king is a liar by definition; that's how he got his job. All authority is based on theft, which is to say it's based on lies. But it isn't pragmatically accurate to think of theft as a lie about the concept of property. Theft is a lie about the concept of possessive pronouns, and it is usually told by someone who genuinely believes the lie. This is why we shouldn't speak of the end of history, but rather of the end of authority. The end of history is a mask for the end of the authority of language. Our task is to write the facticity of that demise. The self-leveling plumb level vs. the levellers animated semiotic wrestling, a random walk through the presents of a history, a poetics of cognitive endurance — our acts enact (provisionally), being here (in the ballpark) now (contingent), so as to resist the narcotic allure of having been there, doing this, and also rewriting readymades, particularity, universality emergent in the fact that any particularity will suffice as an efficient tool for the work at hand, no longer believing what is written, only attending to the during of thinking within and against it, throwing it away like trash, like casting dice or bones, or into the boiling succotash of textual emergence, where everything fits, and nothing is dominant.

6.   "Composition by Unit: read it that way." — Clark Coolidge

May 2005

originally published in *Admit 2*, 2005 (electronic)

CHAPTER FIFTEEN ||||||||||||||||||||||||||||||||||||||||||||||||||||||||||||||||||||||||

death text and the haute couture death text images
published in the Textimagepoem Blogzine
SATURDAY, MARCH 25, 2006
for ross priddle

||||||

Arundhati Roy: "Before September 11th 2001 America had a secret history. Secret especially from its own people. But now America's secrets are history, and its history is public knowledge. It's street talk."

Naomi Wolf: "Peace and trust between men and women who are lovers would be as bad for the consumer economy and the power structure as peace on earth for the military-industrial complex."

||||||

the images are stolen. stolen twice. if i wanted them in a context of pornography or sexist fashion i would not need to steal them from their thieves. but i want the context and the content of a radically inclusive democracy. in a context of chrysocratic terror deterioration appears as progress and decay seems like a necessary evolutionary process. i work to decompose the commodified images and erase their encrypted marketing strategies.
we are being sold a war against ourselves. a cosmetic economy masks the horror and lures us to complicity.

the texts layered over the images are also stolen. stolen and translated, deliberately mistranslated, recensions redacted improvisationally to render texts as dissonant music in disjunctive fragments. each textual fragment is a discourse against war presented as language at war against itself. normative language usage would sell us to ourselves as proponents of the ideology of war, individual expressions of that universal agenda, sexist, racist and classist, subservient to the pragmatism of power. i would steal the discourse itself and rewrite it against its imposed, invasive intentions. i would invite the reader to continue a similar process.

||||||

i learned about sexuality and feminism simultaneously. i've always thought a healthy eroticism was one of the fundamental goals of the feminist movement. the issue has never been sexuality itself, but rather the gender-based subjugation and degradation resulting from a dominant sexist ideology. my first girlfriend was a feminist. i spent six years with her. i'm not sure it has ever occurred to me that being anything other than a feminist was a serious option. when i was introduced to the idea in the early 70s, it seemed like a necessary part of the larger cultural transformation, a transformation of consciousness, as necessary as opposition to the vietnam war and to violent conflict-resolution, or support for the civil rights movement and opposition to racism in all of its forms. feminism was but one aspect of a multifaceted cultural revolution which included environmental awareness and the privileging of cooperation over competition, an interrogation of capitalist and corporate ideology, spiritual awakening and personal transformation, development of one's creative potential in artistic activity and as a way of thinking about and during one's daily life. the women's liberation movement seemed absolutely necessary for the vitality and viability of the whole spectrum of so-called countercultural concerns and values. times have changed, to understate the obvious, but i still think very much in terms of a diverse coalition of intertwined and overlapping groups working to alter the fundamental institutions and beliefs of american, and increasingly global, culture. sexism, racism, classism, and militarism are components of a larger ideology, or expressions of that ideology, and i take as a given my responsibility to respond from an oppositional standpoint.

||||||

i call these images collectively the haute couture death text series. the death text itself is a long anti-war poem in prose. while i was writing it, in the months leading up to the invasion of iraq, i came across a stack of elle magazines in a box beside a dumpster. i brought the box home and put it under my desk, where it remained for several months. after i finished writing the text i decided to scan the images from the fashion advertisements in the magazines. then i layered the text over the scans. i liked the results, so i started gathering images of models and actresses to extend the series.

the images are appropriated and detourned, recontextualized and used for purposes counter to those intended by their original publishers. i seriously doubt it would have occurred to me to layer these images with anti-war texts if i hadn't been thinking in terms of a feminist critique of war, and of something very much like a countercultural critique of a dominant culture in which both sexism and militarism flourish.

||||||

Marguerite Duras: "It is an extraordinary thing, but men still see themselves as supreme authorities on women's liberation. They say: 'In my opinion, women should do this or that to liberate themselves—' And when people laugh they don't understand why. Then they take up the old refrain — their veneration of women. Whatever form this veneration takes, be it religious or surrealist, and even Georges Bataille is guilty of it, it is still racism. But when you point this out to men, they don't understand."

||||||

Hélene Cixous: "What would become of logocentrism, of the great philosophical systems, of world order in general if the rock upon which they founded their church were to crumble? If it were to come out in a new day that the logocentric project had always been, undeniably, to found (fund) phallocentrism, to insure for masculine order a rationale equal to history itself? Then all the stories would have to be told differently, the future would be incalculable, the historical forces would, will, change hands, bodies: another thinking as yet not thinkable will transform the functioning of all society. Well, we are living through this very period when the conceptual foundation of a millennial culture is in the process of being undermined by millions of a species of mole as yet not recognized." (1975)

Zillah Eisenstein: "The `war of/on terror' is a terrorizing war for all who come in contact with it. The lines between combatant and civilian, rights and degradation, and white, black and brown men and women are realigned and remade. But this gender flux takes place within the structural constraints of racialized patriarchy, and masculinized gender. The naked bodies of tortured Muslim men alongside white women with cigarettes and leashes, and the absence and silencing of Muslim women at Abu Ghraib is a heart-rending reminder that war is obscene. It would be a double heartbreak to think that people in this country abide any part of the violations at Abu Ghraib, especially in the name of feminism. I am hoping that the horrific pictorial exposure of torture at Abu Ghraib will recommit us all to struggle on behalf of an anti-racist feminist humanity inclusive of each and every one's liberation across the globe."

bell hooks: "Women of color, from various ethnic backgrounds, as well as women who were active in the gay movement, not only experienced the development of solidarity between women and men in resistance struggle, but recognized its value. They were not willing to devalue this bonding by allying themselves with anti-male bourgeois white women. Encouraging political bonding between women and men to radically resist sexist oppression would have called attention to the transformative potential of feminism. The anti-male stance was a reactionary perspective that made feminism appear to be a movement that would enable white women to usurp white male power, replacing white male supremacist rule with white female supremacist rule."

Jane Tompkins: "It is a tenet of feminist rhetoric that the personal is the political, but who in the academy acts on this where language is concerned? We all speak the father tongue, which is impersonal, while decrying the father's ideas."

Annie Leclerc: "There is only one just form of thought, the living thought that can revive the smothered fire of life and sow revolt against the poisoners, the pillagers, the profaners of life. To revolt: that's the right word. Yet it's still not quite strong enough. Let the bell toll the end not only of those eminent possessors but also of their carrion-eating values that have polluted the whole world."

Adrienne Rich: "The word power is highly charged for women. It has been long associated with the use of force, with rape, with the stockpiling of weapons, with the ruthless accrual of wealth and the hoarding of resources, with the power that acts only in its own interests, despising and exploiting the powerless — including women and children. The effects of this kind of power are all around us, even literally in the water we drink and the air we breathe, in the form of carcinogens and radioactive wastes. But for a long time now, feminists have been talking about redefining power, about that meaning of power which returns to the root... to be able, to have the potential, to possess and use one's energy of creation — transforming power."

Naomi Wolf: "Male-dominated institutions — particularly corporate interests — recognize the dangers posed to them by love's escape. Women who love themselves are threatening; but men who love real women, more so."

Dominique Poggi: "The sexual liberation preached by pornography is actually a channeling of sexuality toward a heterosexual world in which men are still the sole masters of the game; in this way, pornography militates in favor of maintaining men's appropriation of women."

bell hooks: "Had feminist activists called attention to the relationship between ruling class men and the vast majority of men, who are socialized to perpetuate and maintain sexism and sexist oppression even as they reap no life-affirming benefits, these men might have been motivated to examine the impact of sexism in their lives."

Rachel Blau DuPlessis: "Howe appears to be on the cusp between two feminisms: the one analyzing female difference, the other 'feminine' difference. For the latter, she is close to Julia Kristeva, who evokes marginality, subversion, dissidence as anti-patriarchal motives beyond all limits. Anything marginalized by patriarchal order is, thus, 'feminine;' the 'feminine' position (which can be held by persons of both genders) is a privileged place from which to launch an anti-authoritarian struggle. The female use of this 'feminine' of marginality and the avant-garde use of this 'feminine' of marginality are mutually reinforcing in the work of some contemporary women: Lyn Hejinian, Kathleen Fraser, Gail Sher, Beverly Dahlen and Howe. This mixed allegiance will naturally call into question varieties of flat-footed feminism."

Christine Delphy: "In the same way that feminism-as-a-movement aims at the revolution of social reality, so feminism-as-a-theory (and each is indispensable to the other) must aim at the revolution of knowledge."

Naomi Wolf: "Women who have broken out of gender roles have proved manageable: Those few with power are being retrained as men. But with the apparition of numbers of men moving into passionate, sexual love of real women, serious money and authority could defect to join forces with the opposition. Such love would be a political upheaval more radical than the Russian Revolution and more destabilizing to the balance of world power than the end of the nuclear age. It would be the downfall of civilization as we know it — that is, of male dominance; and for heterosexual love, the beginning of the beginning."

Zillah Eisenstein: "Masculinist depravity, as a political discourse, can be adopted by males and/or females. It is all the more despicable that the Bush administration used the language of women's rights to justify the bombs in the Afghan war against Taliban practices towards women; and then again against the horrific torture and rape chambers under Saddam Hussein. And it should be no surprise that Bush's women — Laura, Mary Matalin, and Karen Hughes — who regularly bad-mouth feminism of any sort were responsible for articulating this imperial women's rights justification for war."

Starhawk: "Wise feminists do not claim that women are innately kinder, gentler, more compassionate than men per se. If we did, the Margaret Thatchers and Condoleeza Rices of the world would soon prove us wrong. We do claim that patriarchy encourages and rewards behavior that is brutal and stupid. We need raucous, incautious feminist voices to puncture the pomposity, the arrogance, the hypocrisy of the war mongers, to point out that gorilla chest-beating does not constitute diplomacy, that having the world's largest collection of phallic projectile weapons does not constitute moral authority, that invasion and penetration are not acts of liberation."

Arundhati Roy: "Our strategy should be not only to confront empire, but to lay siege to it. To deprive it of oxygen. To shame it. To mock it. With our art, our music, our literature, our stubbornness, our joy, our brilliance, our sheer relentlessness — and our ability to tell our own stories. Stories that are different from the ones we're being brainwashed to believe."

Naomi Wolf: "Ads do not sell sex — that would be counterproductive, if it meant that heterosexual women and men turned to one another and were gratified. What they sell is sexual discontent."

Judy Rebick: "In Beijing, feminist leaders from around the world warned that there were two paths emerging for humanity — corporate globalization and fundamentalism. They argued that both were devastating for women. Feminist leaders from around the world were calling for a third path, based on equality, democracy and respect for diversity."

Judy Rebick: "In the Americas, where women's rights have made tremendous gains over the past decades, a ferocious backlash against feminism has accompanied the rise of neoliberalism. As feminists have always argued for stronger social programmes, marginalizing and blaming feminism is an important ideological adjunct to neo-liberalism."

Eric Foner: "Of the many lessons of American history, this is among the most basic. Our civil rights and civil liberties — freedom of expression, the right to criticize the government, equality before the law, restraints on the exercise of police powers — are not gifts from the state that can be rescinded when it desires. They are the inheritance of a long history of struggles: by abolitionists for the ability to hold meetings and publish their views in the face of mob violence; by labor leaders for the power to organize unions, picket and distribute literature without fear of arrest; by feminists for the right to disseminate birth-control information without being charged with violating the obscenity laws; and by all those who braved jail and worse to challenge entrenched systems of racial inequality."

Christine Delphy: "The rebirth of feminism coincided with the use of the term 'oppression'. The ruling ideology, i.e., common sense, daily speech, does not speak about oppression but about a 'feminine condition'. It refers back to a naturalistic explanation: to a constraint of nature, exterior reality out of reach and not modifiable by human action. The term 'oppression', on the contrary, refers back to a choice, an explanation, a situation that is political. 'Oppression' and 'social oppression' are therefore synonyms or rather social oppression is a redundancy: the notion of a political origin, i.e., social, is an integral part of the concept of oppression. This term is thus the basis, the point of departure for any feminist study or strategy."

Julia Kristeva: "What is politically 'new' today can be seen and felt in modern music, cartoons, communes of young people provided they do not isolate themselves on the fringes of society but participate in the contradiction inherent in political classes. The women's movement, if it has a raison d'etre, seems to be part of this trend; it is, perhaps, one of its most radical components." (1974)

Simone de Beauvoir: "Feminist thought is not monolithic; every woman who struggles has her own reasons, her own perspective, her particular experience, and she offers them to us in her own way."

Ken Kesey: "You think of the stuff that came out of the Sixties: the environmental movement, the feminist movement, the power of the civil rights movement; but most of all, it's the psychedelic movement that attempted to actually go in and change the consciousness of the people, either back to something more pure and honest, or forward to something never before realized, knowing that the places we were in, the status quo, was a dead-end — a dead-end spiritually and, as we are finding out, a dead-end economically."

Naomi Wolf: "The current allocation of power is sustained by a flood of hostile and violent sexual images, but threatened by imagery of mutual eroticism or female desire; the elite of the power structure seem to know this consciously enough to act on it."

Barbara Ehrenreich & Deirdre English: "In our concern to understand more about our own biology, for our own purposes, we must never lose sight of the fact that it is not our biology that oppresses us — but a social system based on sex and class domination. This, to us, is the most profoundly liberating feminist insight — the understanding that our oppression is socially, and not biologically, ordained. To act on this understanding is to ask for more than 'control over our own bodies'. It is to ask for, and struggle for, control over the social options available to us, and control over all the institutions of society that now define those options."

bell hooks: "Feminism defined as a movement to end sexist oppression enables women and men, girls and boys, to participate equally in revolutionary struggle."

Arundhati Roy: "It's absurd for the U.S. government to even toy with the notion that it can stamp out terrorism with more violence and oppression. Terrorism is the symptom, not the disease."

04.22.05

Text originally published by Ross Priddle on his anabasis/xtant blogspot, Canada, 2005. Also published at Textimagepoem and at several other places on the web.

|||||||||||||||||||||||||||||||||||||||||||||||||||||||||||||||||||

Dissemination history and context

8 of these images were published by Reed Altemus as part of his Live Matter Series, Portland, Maine, 2006.
in 2005 Jose Roberto Sechi curated an exhibit of the Death Texts images at the Sechiisland Microgallery, in Rio Claro, Brasil.
in 2006 Reed Altemus curated an exhibit of visual poetry at Frank Turek's Ubu Gallery in Portland, Maine. The exhibit included works by Nico Vassilakis (Seattle, WA), Carol Stetser (Sedona, AZ), Jim Leftwich (Roanoke, VA), Geof Huth (Schenectady, NY), Luc Fierens (Weerde,Belguim), and Reed Altemus (Portland, ME). i contributed a series of haute couture death text images.

in 2007 Emilio Morandi curated an exhibit of the haute couture death text images entitled poesia visiva at Artestudio, Ponte Nossa, Italy.
in 2007 several of the haute couture death text textimagepoems were published in broadside format by Joseph Keppler as part of his Poets.Painters.Composers.Critics.Sculptors.Slaves series.

Death Text was written in late 2002 and early 2003, during the months leading up to the American invasion of Iraq, and during the first month of the war. It is a long anti-war poem in prose. Jukka-Pekka Kervinen published the first 6 books in two volumes at cPress in 2005. Jukka and I published books 7, 8 and 9 at Vugg Books in 2007.
Between 2002 and 2007 I made over 3500 individual haute couture death text images, along with several one-of-a-kind versions of the 9 books. Over the years the images and books have been scattered throughout the mail art and small press networks. Michael Peters has a large collection of them (roughly 1500 pages or so). Over 2100 of them were scanned and posted to my Textimagepoetry flickr site.   07.21.2016

cards, stencils & decompositions
— notes from emails published in the Textimagepoem Blogzine
   SATURDAY, MARCH 24, 2007

||||||||||||||

i haven't made any effort to associate these particular works with deconstruction.

i started making the cards two years ago, while i was still in charlottesville. i've posted a lot of them at textimagepoem. the decompositions are a more recent development, but many of them are also at the blog.

among the precursors i recognize as influences in my decision to take the letter as the primary unit of composition are the futurists (both russian and italian), the dadaists (schwitters, ball, and tzara), and the kabbalist abulafia. even if we omit abulafia we have to acknowledge this practice in poetry as preceding decon- struction by 50 years or more. the two practices aren't attempting to do the same things. they aren't asking the same questions or attempting to solve the same problems.

||||||||||||||

i don't think of the decompositions as a negation of composition. i think of them as destabilized, or perhaps deteriorated compositions - or, maybe, as damaged compositions. but not as negations of composition.

||||||||||||||

a lot of what i have made over the past couple of years
the decompositions, for example
the cards in general
has been a kind of meditative silence
not meant to be arty or poetic
but a reduction of the poem
through the syllable to the letter

and then to the arbitrary arrangement of letters on a stencil
a kind of defiant silence in the face of all this overwhelming shit
sort of like cage's
i have nothing to say and i am saying it

||||||||||||||

an alchemy designed to quiet the mind
and facilitate a specific flow or aggregate
of thoughts

from a very strong sense of having been
defeated, defeated at the base of the psyche

taking that as a starting point for a kind of
defiant productivity, serial variations on the
facticity of being here and now, not so much
empty as directionless, point blank

these cards don't require exegesis, but they do
invite a certain kind of thinking

||||||||||||||

"a semiotic poem is a visual poem which can make use of non-letteral means of communication."

the idea here of the semiotic poem is very familiar, though i don't think i'd seen the term before. my dilemma in investigating the asemic has been to locate the unreadable, in whatever form, and to attempt a fresh beginning from there. i haven't been able to locate the unreadable anywhere. one of the things i've been exploring is the stencil. most poetry is composed using the syllable as the primary unit of composition. a lot of so- called experimental writing is composed using the letter as the primary unit. using stencils is an extreme reductionist strategy for presenting the letter in opposition to itself. these shapes are letters. we are conditioned to read them. but the process of reading is thwarted by the arbitrary, conventional construct of the stencil. my decomposition series came out of this kind of thinking.

||||||||||||||

some ballpark stuff
(to draw a wobbly line around an approximate context)

Jonathan Culler - "The sign is the union of a form which signifies, which Saussure calls the signifiant (signifier), and an idea signified, the signifié (signified). Though we may speak of signifier and signified as if they were separate entities, they exist only as components of the sign."

Jonathan Culler - "Semiotics is based on the assumption that insofar as human actions or reproductions convey meaning, insofar as they function as signs, there must be an underlying system of conventions and distinctions which makes this meaning possible. Where there are signs there is system. This is what various signifying activities have in common, and if one is to determine their essential nature, one must treat them not in isolation but as examples of semiotic systems. In this way, aspects that are often hidden or neglected will become apparent, especially when nonlinguistic signifying practices are considered as 'languages'."

Jonathan Culler - "The most interesting semiotic objects are those which insistently intimate their relation to sign systems but are hard to place and resist easy interpretation. They don't quite fit the system's categories; they seem to escape it, to violate what one takes to be its rules. But since we are governed by the semiological imperative, Try to make sense of things, we struggle with the refractory or evasive object, straining and extending our notions of significance, modifying and extrapolating from the rules of our system, or bringing two codes into juxtaposition to set off an interpretative interplay."

James Elkins - "Art history lacks a persuasive account of the nature of graphic marks, and that limits what can be said about pictures. If a sign, as Charles Sanders Pierce said, is 'something which stands to somebody for something in some respect or capacity' — a formula as vague as it is compact — then every mark in a picture is also a sign: every brushstroke, pencil line, smudge, and erasure must function as a sign and have meaning."

James Elkins - "Marks exfoliate by drawing attention to their boundaries so that the boundaries become outlines in their own right; when that happens the boundaries themselves can be perceived as marks, turning both the original mark and the original surface into surfaces."

James Elkins
"In the end there is no such thing as a mark — there are only surfaces.
…
The act of making a mark also turns the surface into a mark, so that it is perceived not as an infinite or undifferentiated surface, but as a region with definite boundaries, and therefore ultimately a mark.
…
In effect, markmaking turns surfaces into marks."

James Elkins - "Graphic traces are unruly, as 'subsemiotic' elements might be expected to be, but they are unruly in a different way from written marks, and their instability does not fade when they combine into larger units."

James Elkins - "The ontological instability of the mark is a double and conflicting condition. On the one hand, each mark exfoliates into fields and endlessly generates new marks out of its edges; on the other hand, each mark coalesces its surrounding surface into fields and finally into other marks, so that the surface is fugitive and hardens everywhere into a landscape of marks. Unlike written signs, drawn and painted marks are insecurely linked to their grounds, and the same is true at the level of the figure — a fact that has to be suspended in order to get on with art-historical interpretations that treat figures as if they were signs detachable from their grounds."

||||||||||||||||

poem as sequence, series and/or aggregate of signs, a specific kind of system of signs.

for my purposes, the stencil facilitates a specific kind of foregrounding of the visuality of the letters.

decomposition as i use the term is meant to refer to a specific type of composition, one in which the structural deterioration of its primary units is emphasized.

composition is a conventional title for works of art. my use of decomposition derives from that usage.

the cards, stencils, and decompositions are a kind of narrative, in the sense of being an ongoing discourse concerning some of the choices one might attend to while writing poetry.

|||||||||||||

march 2007

|||||||||||||

history, quantities, process

The "decompositions" and the "cards" are visual poems on index cards made between 2005 and 2007. The "decompositions" were mostly made in the basement of the house we lived in at 2440 Lofton Rd when we first moved to Roanoke (November 2005 to July 2007). Most of them are imprints made from spray-painted stencils. The "cards" were also mostly made in the basement at the Lofton house. They are primarily collages of stamps (found-object stamps, eraser carvings, modified store-bought stamps, stamps received in the mail from mail artists, etc), sometimes with barely legible handwriting. My Textimagepoetry flickr collection includes scans of 1650 "decompositions" and 1913 "cards". Hundreds of these visual poems on index cards have been circulated in the small press and mail art networks (six index cards in an envelope can be mailed for the price of one postage stamp). Keith Buchholz has a large collection of them in his mail art archive.
07.19.2016

decomposition 2006

Trashpo 2015 - 2016

> email to Marco Giovenale
> Jim Leftwich <jimleftwich@gmail.com>
> 12/1/15
> to Marco

marco

i used the word trashpo for some scanner collages i made in october of 2005. sue and i were packing and cleaning in preparation for our move from charlottesville to roanoke and as a part of the process i would every now and then put some of the trash on the scanner, just to be making something while also doing other things (cleaning, packing). so for me it was only a kind of vispo, a kind i could make quickly, without much planning. i arranged the trash so the resulting scans would be text/image pieces, but beyond that i didn't put a whole lot of thought into the process. i liked most of the results, liked them enough to make a little pdf book of them for Vugg Books. it came as a big surprise six or 7 years later to find De Villo Sloan and Diane Keys organizing a trashpo group and crediting me as the inventor of the term. the group was already fully up and running before i found out about it. i like it a lot, but it isn't mine.

i've been making text/image works from trash (without using the term trashpo) since at least 1992. i'll probably make this kind of vispo for the rest of my life. but i agree with you, it doesn't need to be any more of a "thing" than it already is. i think, obviously i suppose, of what has happened with the so-called asemic writing movement. we should probably continue as we are, using the word trashpo whenever it seems like the right thing to do, but not making any effort to extend its popularity.

you already know this, but for the record:
the way to prevent people from developing an interest in trashpo is to insist on it being a kind of poetry. almost everyone will hate that. it will give the rest of us a good amount of freedom as we continue exploring the practice.
the same is clearly true with asemic writing. insist on it being not only a kind of writing, but a kind of vispo, a kind of writing-against-itself (quasi-calligraphic drawing as a radical defamiliarization of the written alphabet, a letteral and

gestural writing) and, after they insult and/or dismiss us for a while, most folks will ignore us completely, which is really a wonderful kind of liberation. it allows us to pursue a certain range of experimental writing without the need for impossibly vague and confining terms. (asemic writing as an experiment has run its course. next comes the predictable theorizing, a horrorshow for sure. then the corpse can be passed around in academia and dissected endlessly, until everything about it is entirely beyond recognition. it is for this that we say: no such thing as asemic writing. no present no past no future. there has never been any such thing as asemic writing.)

ok, so there we are. here we are. i am enjoying our collaborations and exchanges a lot. thanks for everything, this new pdf, and all of your posts. i appreciate all of it. i think you know, you and a few others know, that i am working to keep all of these practices -- trashpo, vispo, asemic writing, writing-against-itself, textimagepoetry, etc and etc -- absolutely as OPEN as possible. but open for me does not mean increasing the quantity of practitioners, it means sustaining the quality of the experience of the practice. the experience of making this kind of work opens away from ourselves, out of ourselves, into experiential unknowns (which is why i refer to these practices a being part of a training manual), not onto new comfort zones. once we become comfortable with any of these practices, we have to move on, to practices which make us uncomfortable, uncertain about ourselves and our works. otherwise we are only resting on a plateau, producing and reproducing our favorite decorations.

facebook comment 03.23.2016
(in response to Mark Bloch's Panmodern Polytechnic University post)

Jim Leftwich visual poetry is a kind of poetry, often abbreviated as vispo. visual poems are often collages of one variety or another. trash poetry is a kind of visual poetry, usually abbreviated as trashpo. it is almost always a variety of collage.

as for my personal involvement, i used the term trashpo to name a bunch of vispo collages i made one afternoon in the fall of 2005. later, some other folks used the name to describe some of their activities. the trashpo folks are fun. for the most part they don't seem to be all that interested in poetry (except for De Villo Sloan, who is interested, and who knows the several relevant histories).

the trashpo/DKult group is its own thing, with lots of subtexts and narrative threads and myths and rituals and many other wonderful Dada/punk-inspired absurdities. i don't really know very much about any of that. i've read what's available on the subject (the IUOMA group, Minxus/Lynxus posts, facebook comment threads), but i haven't participated very much. i don't think anyone claims that it's new, and i think everyone agrees that most of what gets made under the umbrella of trashpo is collage (or assemblage).

if it had been left up to me, trashpo would exist as a single book of visual poems. but when we put our work out into the world we relinquish control of how it is perceived and used.

the folks in the trashpo/DKult groups don't need the word "trashpo" to do what they do. i'm happy that they have found it useful, generative, a Maypole to dance around. the group's activities are playfully anarchic and substantial enough to give all of us a little food for thought. that's the primary thing. and it's ongoing. as it goes on some of us will be interested in defining terms and getting the history straight. and some of us will not be interested in either of those endeavors.

that's the context, or that's how it looks from where i sit.
March 23 at 3:11pm

trashpo 2005

from THE NON
2010

To have thought less than this, a moment ago, is our point of departure, and as such is more than this, though that of course is impossible.

At Work: She said: are you alright today? I said: No. I am never alright. Of course the context gave her all the permission she needed to act as if she didn't know.

I sent an email to Matt:
Subject Line: Map Proposal:
    carry a banana peel around town with us
    photograph each other about to step on it in various appropriate and inappropriate places
    make a collage of the photographs

Ladies and Gentlemen:
Nude anew spun caveats publicly cul de sac if we penetrate truly time, their fins of state echo variant adventures eventually united in dadaist leprosy. Dark are the crosses of taste, so do they roar immoderate modalities, diffuse and azure.

No such thing as a thought.

Retorico Unentesi once wrote: My texts are more [illegible] than I am. We for one do not abide by that verdict.

Correspondences:
No puzzles
and
No instructions.

1. In case of causal or careful access to uneasy omens, care as soon as death to appropriate the night, neither the trapeze of ascension nor the unreality of Verse delights in elegant carelessness, an obscure vehicle to delimit the credentials of progress. Sad metrical zebras as distant as Tantalus undulate around incipient recipes for density. Decadence materializes and incubates in descent, newly situated in the spurious eel, a squirrel.

2. In this book it is spoken of the Sephiroth and the Paths; of Spirits and Conjurations; of Gods, Spheres, Planes, and many other things which may or may not exist. It is immaterial whether these exist or not. By doing certain things certain results will follow; students are most earnestly warned against attributing objective reality or philosophic validity to any of them. (Aleister Crowley)

Dear Fine Art Consumers:
In 2000 the drunken, two-headed surfictionist Matrice Kubick wrote his only sonnet. I reproduce it here from memory, as the original has been lost or destroyed.
Kubick is best known for his two short novellas concerning the exploits of Bothand, The Warrior, published by xtantbooks in 1999 and 2000. Copies are available wherever you can find them.
Sincerely,
Jim Leftwich
Founding Editor, xtantbooks
November 2010

Sonnet

fuck fuck fuck fuck fuck fuck fuck fuck fuck fuck
fuck fuck fuck fuck fuck fuck fuck fuck fuck fuck
fuck fuck fuck fuck fuck fuck fuck fuck fuck fuck
fuck fuck fuck fuck fuck fuck fuck fuck fuck fuck

fuck fuck fuck fuck fuck fuck fuck fuck fuck fuck
fuck fuck fuck fuck fuck fuck fuck fuck fuck fuck
fuck fuck fuck fuck fuck fuck fuck fuck fuck fuck
fuck fuck fuck fuck fuck fuck fuck fuck fuck fuck

fuck fuck fuck fuck fuck fuck fuck fuck fuck fuck
fuck fuck fuck fuck fuck fuck fuck fuck fuck fuck
fuck fuck fuck fuck fuck fuck fuck fuck fuck fuck
fuck fuck fuck fuck fuck fuck fuck fuck fuck fuck

fuck fuck fuck fuck fuck fuck fuck fuck fuck fuck
fuck fuck fuck fuck fuck fuck fuck fuck fuck fuck

Matrice Kubick
2000

Situational cadavers catapult and venture catatonic ecstasis, penitent as in ascetic truisms, to unite the expletive and the azure in tireless explication. The eyes brine, newly established on the plaza of asterisks, to reify an audible Dada.
O explication! O pleated exile! Mitosis of the same, spliced coterie and circuitous locus! Whose idea is it now to testify the fruits of fiction? The thumbs of spirit exist as opposable eulogies: can i hope to copy such a stunted ferocity? Dark are the intimate tastes of an eschatological cannibalism! The spirit is few and penetrant: it exists as elimination.

Atemporal Event Score
Throw two darts at a clock.
The first dart will indicate the hour.
The second dart will indicate the minute.
Document the event as having occurred at the time when you performed it, and also at the time indicated by the darts.
10.26.10

Non-Local Event Score
Throw a dart at a map of the world.
Document the event as having occurred in the location where you performed it, and also in the location indicated by the dart.
10.26.10

4th of July Event
Barbecue a flag.
10.26.10

genus and riot:

||||||||||||||

the i:
||||||||||||||

genius without the i is genus.
to prefer the latter is a kind of heresy,
but we should do it.

riot without the i is rot. we have been trained to prefer the latter. we should resist
this training. the only encouragement we are likely to receive for our resistance will
come through the neoteny of pop culture.

these are the options for the i.

in the confluence of genus and rot there is no i, and only entropy will ensue. in the
confluence of genus and riot there is too much of the i. therein lies the history of
autocracy and recursive violence.

the confluence of genus and rot might seem irresistibly seductive had it not
already given us the velocity and the sheen, the vacuity and the sleep, the volatility
and the slippage of the twentieth century. we want our hallucinations to be
mutagenic or not at all. the i will rot in any event.

the confluence of genus and riot is the path of centrifugal asymmetry. it is not a
strategy. it cannot be systematized. it is not a variety of warfare. it is full-spectrum
against dominance. it is provisional, but not temporary. its givens are uniqueness
and change, but it is not a popularity contest or a fashion show. it is a radicalized
form of democracy, which means it is a kind of anarchy, horizontally inclusive
against representative hierarchy. it is a proposal for homeopathic disaster.

it is already underway.

we are making notes at a site of the disasters.

october 2010

THE NUMES

0 - zero is not a quantity. it is a function. it represents process - uniqueness & change - flux.

1 - numbers do not define quantities, they describe relationships. one is the self-referential void. in conjunction with the zero it generates the discontinuous continuum.

2 - two is the emblem of history - dialectical reproduction - the desire for straight lines between mirages.

3 - three is solitude - triangular stasis, yearning. it is the number of sisyphus, & also the number of lies concerning sisyphus.

4 - four is the sign of materiality - the quaternity - despair, greed, myopia & violence.

5 - five is the quincunx, the palpable fiction of time. it is the stable site of the silent image, the word in exile, the burials of bodies in their chosen materials.

6 - six is the mysterium conjunctionis, the perilous experiment of the body - the union of the triangles - transformation & annihilation. it is the self as no-self. it is the phase transition of the word.

7 - seven is the triangle caged in the quaternity - violent despair as ideology - consciousness possessed by its possessions.

8 - eight is the double quaternity - where the map of consciousness is identical to the territory of materiality. it is information as religion and surveillance as metaphysics. utter annihilation is the only exit from the eight.

9 - nine is the quincunx mapped across the quaternity - the inevitable excess of mapping. the inappropriate map is the perfect instrument of transformation. anarchy & chaos deconstruct the fiction of time. nine is the number of the perfect prison - as such it contains the lessons necessary for escape.

10.04.05

0 - zero is not a quantity. it is a function. it represents process - uniqueness & change - flux.

1 - numbers do not define quantities, they describe relationships. one is the self-referential void. in conjunction with the zero it generates the discontinuous continuum.

geometric shape: the point

In geometry, topology and related branches of mathematics a spatial point is a primitive notion upon which other concepts may be defined. In geometry, points have neither volume, area, length, nor any other higher dimensional analogue. Thus, a point is a 0-dimensional object. In branches of mathematics dealing with set theory, an element is often referred to as a point. A point could also be defined as a sphere which has a diameter of zero.

(also: the dot: the dot (or the bindu) signifies the focalized energy and its intense concentration. It can be envisaged as a kind of energy deposit which can in turn radiate energy under other forms. The dot is usually surrounded by different surfaces, either a triangle, a hexagon, a circle etc. These forms depend on the characteristic of the deity or aspect represented by the Yantra. In the tantric iconography, the dot is named bindu; in tantra bindu is symbolically considered to be Shiva himself, the source of the whole creation.)

2 - two is the emblem of history - dialectical reproduction - the desire for straight lines between mirages.

geometric shape: the line

The notion of line or straight line was introduced by the ancient mathematicians to represent straight objects with negligible width and depth. Lines are an idealization of such objects. Thus, until seventeenth century, lines were defined like this: "The line is the first species of quantity, which has only one dimension, namely length, without any width nor depth, and is nothing else than the flow or run of the point which [...] will leave from its imaginary moving some vestige in length, exempt of any width. [...] The straight line is that which is equally extended between its points.

3 - three is solitude - triangular stasis, yearning. it is the number of sisyphus, & also the number of lies concerning sisyphus.

geometric shape: the triangle

The triangle (trikona) is the symbol of Shakti, the feminine energy or aspect of Creation. The triangle pointing down represents the yoni, the feminine sexual organ and the symbol of the supreme source of the Universe, and when the triangle is pointing upwards it signifies intense spiritual aspiration, the sublimation of one's nature into the most subtle planes and the element of fire (Agni Tattva). The fire is always oriented upwards, thus the correlation with the upward triangle - Shiva kona. On the other hand, the downward pointing triangle signifies the element of water which always tends to flown and occupy the lowest possible position.

From time immemorial the Equilateral Triangle has been preeminently the symbol for Deity. For the Triangle is the primary figure from which all others are built up and the Equilateral Triangle, being wholly symmetrical, is the one perfect Triangle and thus clearly becomes the symbol for that Perfect Being in which all things find their beginning This Symbol is so completely appropriated to the purpose of a symbol for Deity and Perfection that to here treat of its various other, and decidedly minor, symbolic significances would but obscure its pre-eminent symbolic meaning.

4 - four is the sign of materiality - the quaternity - despair, greed, myopia & violence.

geometric shape: the square

The square represents the formal, mathematical, scientific order of the universe. The square represents earthbound matter, and correspondingly, with its two sides delineating a two-dimensional surface, may symbolize the earth or ground, or a field.

5 - five is the quincunx, the palpable fiction of time. it is the stable site of the silent image, the word in exile, the burials of bodies in their chosen materials.

geometric shape: the quincunx

A quincunx is a geometric pattern consisting of five coplanar points, four of them forming a square or rectangle and a fifth at its center. It forms the arrangement of five units in the pattern corresponding to the five-spot on dice.

The quincunx pattern originates from Pythagorean mathematical mysticism. This pattern lies at the heart of the Pythagorean tetraktys, a pyramid of ten dots. To the Pythagoreans the number five held particular significance and the quincunx pattern represented this. Sir Thomas Browne moulds his mystical discourse The Garden of Cyrus (1658) on the quincunx pattern.

The power of the Pythagorean mysteries is based upon a mystical understanding of the mathematical order of the Universe which could be summed up in visual representation of such numbers as the Tetraktys (10) and the Quincunx (5). - Robert Graves, The White Goddess

6 - six is the mysterium conjunctionis, the perilous experiment of the body - the union of the triangles - transformation & annihilation. it is the self as no-self. it is the phase transition of the word.

geometric shape: the hexagram

The Hexagram represents the formula and accomplishment of the Great Work in both the material and spiritual worlds. It is composed of the symbols for Fire and Water. It is synonymous with the symbol of the Rose and Cross, the Ankh (Crux Ansata), the Sun and Moon Conjoined, and the Cross in the Circle. It represents the union of the two opposites in Nature, male and female, light and darkness, activity and passivity, and all other opposites that constitute creation.

The Hexagram is a geometrical symbol of the Sun. The Sun is an external symbol of the One Reality or the One Self that is manifest in all things. One of the most significant of all realizations for the Adept is that s/he is the Sun made manifest in the flesh, an incarnation of the Lord of the Solar System. The Hexagram is the Sign of such an Adept. (David Cherubim)

105

7 - seven is the triangle caged in the quaternity - violent despair as ideology - consciousness possessed by its possessions.

geometric shape: a triangle in a square

8 - eight is the double quaternity - where the map of consciousness is identical to the territory of materiality. it is information as religion and surveillance as metaphysics. utter

annihilation is the only exit from the eight.

geometric shape: a square inside a square

9 - nine is the quincunx mapped across the quaternity - the inevitable excess of mapping. the inappropriate map is the perfect instrument of transformation. anarchy & chaos deconstruct the fiction of time. nine is the number of the perfect prison - as such it contains the lessons necessary for escape.

geometric shape: a quincunx inside a square

12.23.10

the first version of The Numes was published by Jake Berry at his 9th Street Lab blogspot on October 8, 2005.

"genus and riot" was printed as a [PRO]-[ANTI] Press broadside by Tomislav Butkovic and distributed during the 2015 afterMAF at Art Rat Studios in Roanoke.

DISCONTINUOUS POEMS
2011

discontinuous poem #1
01.15.11
for bbb

1.
sanity is a measure of proximity to consensus

2.
existence is complex enough to accommodate the accident

discontinuous poem #9
01.16.11

1.
i don't think there should be any time (at any place, anywhere in the world) when it matters how a towel is folded.

2.
croatan is not abyssinia.

discontinuous poem #11
01.17.11

revisions of noise.
revising the noise poem.
revisioning the noisic element in a poetics of doubt.

if you do it, you will think about it.

       discontinuous poem #13
       01.17.11

one.
i have destroyed myself.

you:
you had some help.

three
i am not giving anyone any credit.

||||||

four:
i have annihilated myself.

you:
bullshit, you pompous ass.

six:
six times - so far.
in 1972, in 1978, in 1986, in 1991, in 1998, and in 2005.

||||||

seven
i have annihilated myself.

you:
good for you.

nine:
yes. good for you, too.

||||||

where "you" = two, five and eight
= 258
= 15
= 6

the mysterium conjunctionis

||||||

my 6 identities add up to 3.

      discontinuous poem #14
      01.17.11

i once worked in a kitchen with a woman who was a witch.
she said: an experienced cook never measures *anything*.

discontinuous poem #15
01.17.11

a pockmarked poetics:
after jabes: "interrogate the surface of the text"

discontinuous poem #24
01.21.11

Hull eliminate ideas, new thoughts. Even if the ice skaters of formalism surfer Armies. Weeks wild and vice floor sitters at the corporate vacuum cleaners of the rules of the language is venal find your own menagerie today countercultural Remove letter Knuckles Dirge, or in Ministerial teardrops notwithstanding. As Kerouac's free, think that any sign of life, new woodworking, capitalists even lewd, or at least think they leaf, new ideas, honest weeds. Something you wear vowel in operatic style capitalist Jack lives worms recent drinking. Even rules gulp khaki advertising, Kerouac language, their meat grinders snort persimmon. Countercultural your e-mail, their avatar language as 15-year-Phrases of age. Nouns worldwide hoodwinking verbs. They eliminate any hint of a prose style and instead of talking as Permissive vomiting of 15 years of outer doom. Words become dependent on main salad clinkers Beat Junkie command digitalized. In conversation and sky tennis Kestrel is a rapid and gulp silver suits and Vernal in sky Aspen. Even food, what Nouns in hospital e-mail the impossible, they accept language today, he'd read a prose style plasticine of talking about Jack's hot verbal style sweaters. Hull meat grinders of syntactical striptease exhort Kerouac life. Be Boggle the mind spontaneous poetic vice presidents, benighted seminars on Alice In Wonderland, the Beat poet command. Meat gout to read and squads of pajamas free. When Kerouac was Today beef, souls hydrant sky pie literary storms to skyscraper, Kerouac insisted, grammatical and stinkbugs formalism. Snide and fluid game and, one summer in Kansas with deer milk Bleeds. Something waffle Joyous vowels jelly salad you will find.

discontinuous poem #25
01.26.11

why do you care about that?
do you think you're going to live forever?

discontinuous poem #26
02.02.11

clench riven volley, readers of the broken wheel (no, not you), whole layers of
firmament are garnered in the dart. good advice is something a man gives when
he is too old to set a bad example. he was dismayed by stories of a long lost city.
as a stable city, four hundred years down this crooked path, and after arriving in
the new world in the early 1920's, some time had passed, but you can still improve
your credit score over time. you may have questions about the gaza youth's
manifesto for change. decide if one is right for you. in october, who had been living
in another america, was edited much later and published by spoon and sponge, in
1953, arrived by ferry with his horses, knowing this would be his last chance. while
driving through a state of peanuts with the devil, reluctant to split the story out of
hand, it caused a spectacle in the newspapers of north america. he wore a dragon
around his neck. readers of the river wind drown in the creed of a frozen core,
diamond plutonium oxide, paper thin. one moth later, a car full of metal knives. we
are confident you will love the yoga blades.

discontinuous poem #27
02.02.11

once we get to the mantra, that's the way it was. monday the shop talk is guarded
with aerosol towards the weekend. underground, the region's limestone bedrock is
honeycombed by more than a thousand caves and uncounted underground
springs and streams. in the twenty-first century we are charmed by comparisons
and helpless, unanswered questions until we switch, for less, until now having
settled for another day in bed. sandstone closets from the late 50s to the mid 70s,
the next time will be wet and under starlight, our approach is to launch the
disappeared, maybe three or four hundred yards out, lest we forget, with big eyes
and even bigger nostrils. the studio has been focusing on one thing in particular:
he who lives without folly isn't so wise as he thinks. the culprit has a large red
ladder. photographs of both animals can be found along the northern slope.

without seals, we wouldn't have that. the creatures have come up with yet another theory.

discontinuous poem #28
02.02.11

too much derails the mouse, but the archeology is not talking. not in may, nor yesterday, were several ground hogs and hamburgers in love at the library. the piano whispers beneath the wheels of the pick-up truck: the ocean is a thief of memories along this rotten road, like a swan. less than twice, you know i can't, why not? i can't believe i feel for this, no chocolate, you can call up my thieves and ask them for yourself. godless among my own children, the silver snowman, grace, shoes on wooden stairs. doubt is not a pleasant condition, but certainty is absurd. a witty saying proves nothing. in the largest palaces of apollo, near the cities of frozen milk, waiting to worship a rat, he said, i'll buy you a tongue and you can tell it to the thousands. why not apollo, waving goodbye, at twilight at the train station, for a few tender hours or until new? you could have taken as long as you liked.

discontinuous poem #29
02.03.11

the hoodoo knitting bee

the longer i look the less certain i am: what requires attention? what is fine just as it is? the hoodoo knitting bee, not the knottiest hinge of locks, or would be if it were bathed in blood, but it is not. who said: i don't care about art. i like pornography and hallucinations? i think it was voltaire, or la rochefoucauld, but i am probably wrong. i will confess to almost anything you make up, as long as it is an obvious fiction. thus comte de lautreamont: i did not invent the clinch river valley. i dreamed about it, yes, but that was in 2011. little is known of john crank. he was granted land in washington county, virginia, for service in the french and indian war under colonel william byrd. he settled on a 400 acre tract of land on the north side of moccasin ridge in 1774. he also owned 250 acres on both sides of the north fork of holston river and 396 acres on copper ridge. i take my experiences personally, and you should do the same. ahem. thank you. the hoodoo knitting bee, by jim leftwich. jim leftwich was an american novelist who lived, mostly lived, in the twentieth century in virginia, which is where he wrote most of his novels, and when he wrote them, too, in the twentieth century. the hoodoo knitting bee is the story of a band of pirate-poets, led by the dauntless captain beefheart, who sailed up the james river (named after the author of the bible) in 1607 or maybe a generation or so earlier to the shenandoah valley (daughter of the skies) in search of gold or croatan, the records are unclear, but in any case on an alchemical mission sponsored in part by william shakespeare and john dee. this text is about me, he wrote, feel free to skip it and move on to the next one. among the greatest threats to the valley's extraordinary aquatic life are: 1) heavy metals leaching from abandoned coal mines, 2) sediment eroding from cut-over slopes, and 3) nutrients released by streamside-grazing cattle. the pirate-poets, led by the intrepid hakim bey, lead singer in the heavy metal band satanic grazing cattle (check out their debut album, sentiment exploding from cut-up hopes), are on a mission to rewrite these threats to the valley's erotic life. well, that's all the time we have today. tune in again tomorrow for another episode of poets gone wild, only on the celebrity shopping network (an equal opportunity employer). good night, and happy tapping.

discontinuous poem #30
02.08.11

One's own beliefs are a temporary compromise (yes, I am working my way through this one as I write it); the beliefs of others are a matter of trust.

discontinuous poem #31
02.08.10

Relationships among creative people are characterized by a spectrum of fairly simple and obvious correspondences concerning their work and why they do it. There are those who do similar things for similar reasons, those who do similar things for different reasons, those who do different things for similar reasons, and those who do different things for different reasons. The segments of this spectrum are only interesting in their generative potential, as a set of possibilities for thinking emerging from each specificity. We have the beginnings of something truly substantial, however, something alchemical and mutagenic, only when the entire spectrum is encountered in a relationship.

discontinuous poem #32
02.08.11

I have no energy - no desire and no will - to put towards the construction of an alternative elite. The dominant culture is fully capable of constructing such a slot for us. Let us imagine instead the construction of an exemplary independence - collective, cooperative and, finally, creative, which is to say capable of disseminating evidence of its difference to and through the quotidian cultural environment.

discontinuous poem #33
02.08.11

All workers are cultural workers. Culture is an ecology. No one is expected to have a taste for all of its inhabitants. However, one might well be expected to experience the entire spectrum.

discontinuous poem #34
02.09.11

Certain kinds of poetic practice revive the perceptual and cognitive processes necessary for certain kinds of archaic experience. I do not intend here to permit the implication of mere meat on a bloody tooth, nor do I wish to proliferate fantasies of a nomadic utopia. Transformations of subjectivity are attainable through the sustained practice of destabilizing one's relationship with language. Destabilizing language itself is one method of sustaining such a practice. Decisions concerning primary units of composition are an inevitable part of the process. Conclusions, however, concerning the relative value of work with one unit as against another are of necessity provisional.

discontinuous poem #35
02.09.11

Think of a synapse as a muscle. Think of a syllable as an isometric exercise. This is one meaning of the phrase: writing against itself.

discontinuous poem #36
02.09.11

The axiomatic crepuscle, or the crepuscular axiom? The direction of a grey area makes all the difference in the world.

discontinuous poem #37
02.09.11

Slippery enough? Not if you can stand still long enough to read it.

discontinuous poem #38
02.09.11

I once worked with a man who had spent a few years in the Virginia State Penitentiary. The facilities were being expanded while he was incarcerated, and one of his jobs was to help string the razor wire along the top of the new fence designed to keep him and his fellow inmates in. We should all be so fortunate. There is valuable knowledge to be had from such explicit complicity in constructing our own captivity - assuming, that is, that all of us are attending to the plot of our collective escape...

discontinuous poem #39
02.09.11

What if the sentence? Beyond that, there is the stickiness, the law of syntactical probability, there is the punctuation of sickly aliens endogenous to a mnemonic subjectivity (we have no choice but to misremember the asymmetrical warfare of the angels): propaganda has always been poetical, precise, and pointless. A sentence, if letters, then a poetics of anarchist sorcery. We have always thought otherwise, thus flux as a commodity.

discontinuous poem #40
02.09.11

I once worked in a kitchen with a woman who was a witch. She said: an experienced cook never measures *anything*. At the time I didn't have enough experience to know whether I should believe her or not, I was still counting syllables. It took me about fifteen years to fully understand what she was saying. She really was a witch, I no longer have any doubt.

discontinuous poem #41
02.10.11

Memories generate other memories. I take all of my experiences personally. Do we think our memories are our possessions? I remember reading Andre Gide in high school. He wrote: our possessions possess us. After four years of college I gave away everything I owned. We construct narratives to defend ourselves from the fictions of others. I know this is worth doing, but I resent having to do it. I do not remember when I learned to resent having to do things I consider worth doing. The desire to do nothing is a form of dissent against the self.

discontinuous poem #46
03.22.11

collaborative anarchist sorcery

i work with texts to evoke the presence of writers who do not exist.
then i read what they have written.
i sign my name to the results of that process.
then you read what i have written.
i accept collaborative responsibility for all of this.

03.23.11

discontinuous poem #47
04.20.11
for bbb

beefheart was a trickster, in the sense that he made reality malleable, which is what tricksters have always done, the only thing they have ever done, perhaps one of the few things finally worth doing.
greil marcus is not a trickster.
marcus writes about beefheart to demonstrate his superiority to beefheart, and to everyone who is interested in beefheart. it's a common trap for a certain kind of

critic. he thinks he understands the trickster better than the trickster understands himself. and, worse, he thinks what he is doing is the same kind of work, only smarter and more perceptive. the trickster is not a con artist. critics like marcus are con artists, and their primary victims are themselves.

the trickster does what the trickster does because
the trickster knows what the trickster knows.
the critic does not know this.

CHAPTER TWENTY||||||||||||||||||||||||||||||||||||||||||||||||||||||||||||||||||||||||||||||

READINGS
published in the Textimagepoem Blogzine
SATURDAY, MARCH 18, 2006

cements
for john crouse

see the meant. see what is meant.
this requires more than seeing. it requires both looking and reading.
what is meant, as i see it, and as i read it, is concrete.
the photo on the back cover, as i read the image, of a production facility for alpha cement, is an afterword, as if a statement of the first principle of concrete poetry. or, to be precise, it is a translation and a gloss, of this first principle as presented in the content of the book.
live free, as i return to the text, seems to be what we are expected to know only after reading the book. during our reading, we are constrained by the physical form of the book, compelled to a gradual assembling of its gently inscribed injunction.
this, i believe, as i begin the interpretative process upon my own reading, must be why the title of the book is expressed in the plural. to live free is no simple matter. it is, in fact, in practice, very much constrained by its own complexity.

||||||

since gland the restoration of loon democracy

spoon rowing equality shops soup italics, washing the fried voting machine, sleet
shorts figured enigma since 1936. nativity attuned to media retorts cramped
garment campers gaze, shaved poodles posse dream amid popular wars. my
health slinks loins alone, jarring vitamin anaesthesia, set totemic, ensign vacuum
taut and cunning hysteria keens. amnesia stains the delicate flask. pyres veil sour
drip. net political thunder into karmic stasis titillates heretical anomie, heckler lisp
finally weave and sludge. teflon kayak noose, moon militia syrup, nylon toast and
chaos. knotty vote for checkers presidential nose, shopping the fish gun loosely,
coconut and pale ballistics. journalist toad splint aspirin, plain sap in boiling staves,
a dose of nourishing odor for the caterpillar tao, spun khaki mirror jest to skin the
mucus kittens. flowing spines spoon bowling batman optics, how arrogant cars
and rats of art gnarl the flabby babblers. veiled submarine militia chihuahua into
helicopter style, or horrors incognito, justice as a vista seeking lists of honey.
anklets seep encrypted vanilla, a toyota in every kettle, jail for the glandular
alphabet and the restaurants of the moon. democracy is a hefty ski jump jettisoned
typographical errata. even the saliva keys masticate lashes negligence. vital
hymns vascular lamps in oneiric travail collate moose soot ministry, vast tonsils
spleen unseen. savannah embossed with hells, jail hidden in the samurai sauna,
howl stones assume palaver rotting halitosis palomino! vendetta pylon arise, slink
and pooch tarantula. by theoretical musket showering emote, blur sauerkraut
meaning ocean, root plasm kaleidoscopic into curried coup.

after vote puppet, by jukka-pekka kervinen

||||||

a beauty

beauty like a vine eaten by flames forks history in silhouette, tendrils crawling from
her eyes, hand stretched towards the half-eaten frame.
she hovers just above the burning salamander, segments of mind etched in
productive muse.
letters swarm against a swirl of blurred type, calisthenics of calligraphy and
cataclysm, a time of spray, squiggles stretched across the creased gulf of the
page.
she gathers in raised arms an asemia against silence. roses blooming in the open
book express an indecipherable music.

118

our reflection redacts the equation of these oblique occasions. resistance is duration. procedural limitations destabilize and evert the durable potential. an illegible handwriting occludes the stenciled alphabet.
beauty disintegrates to its component fragments: be, eat, bet, at. she dances out of her book into the space beyond the page, naked without her text, alchemical chrysalis as well as fleeing ephemera.

after beauty, by john cese & luc fierens

||||||

the devils tao

ad hoc lode nor my diode bulb, if slippery hip to sleep, seeps oaks leech arrow each to luggage luck, pork sperm swimming loam.
hex logos squared at hot hoodoo to hologram slowly cocoa, squiggly solo spun claws chains in china sung. nude hoax train ran fungus, fishy leopard under scrawls morocco, squared saint spitting serpents beak.
flap troops mayan continuous costume scratch, veins to forked horizon or ludic zorro.

after john m. bennett & cesar figueiredo

||||||

howl to singe

part digital stance, fern data gate your cat axe haddock mutant coup, wet hoax & pubic window, to wage our wrecked egg aardvark rotting clan.
cultural ache droop beef and vowel, roar tray chalk boot flag and cartel goat. viral turf root litigation, halibut on a leash. thaw hoax burnished fish totem tandem.
sleep cops calx dali, in the nixon bladder.

after how to singe, by john m. bennett & cesar figueiredo

||||||

defenestrate or power?

not a simile, nor spillage of selves through the seven windows, a zoo of birds
subject to the royal latch derails ejections llama, reveille to the editor swallowed
curved tennessee, spurns thimble musk and skirts severed elbow druse.
sundry desk oaf mailers clock sludge bream and scrunch. you simmer trout neon i
lunch, sole lint toast in broom voice citric doodles. dare mumbled knickers calf
tunes raven spasm thinks, coal as cruel arc stove or marbled nous.
pink retch more cyborgs eagle snips cart or doodles elf, shack elvis recursive
escargot seams tsunami gnash. lewd wolf reggae half octagonal summit, sculpt
golem watch or mogul sax, ate parched morphine liana, nor paycheck recidivist
bonjour pajama knob.
exact gallop moral, nor boiler gulag knit sojourn.

after fenestration powder, by john m. bennett & cesar figueiredo

||||||

alone with my selves and the strewn damp comb, merrily misreading

flocking glitch home, gulch name, glass or gash home and name—

log blinker, log stun blinker, log traced my open stun husk, again stun lust, stun
husk moon, moon blinker, log traced my gash, stun husk moon blinker—

be blank, naked arms of the letter P. neck eye, blank eye, blank neck eye, settle
mask cash years. quick cli, clipped clip, clip art part, scrunch prune shard harlot,
row log or hog—

cling rabbits porcine looming umbilical gland. see sneeze sex, see seize, wet lock
lore or couch (used onions). gland goes snakes, sugar (cougar) hummer
(hammer)—

bank sank, be flying fish roach calligraphy, bet ice age, stream salad betting blank
page—

||||||

war wares

smoking partitioned brain, egg mix trim gar skeletal cocktail eye. gag clan blotch,
virus verso maximal extra arts. universal tablet cholera, attrition caboose
presentiment, legume nights and arabesque, the cardinal cereal tao.

rascal loop drool moral smear, drip letteral daunt sax nexus, fish nor soma spinal
fuming yam.

shade cowl younger tongue columbus, wood ache latent quote, sock fog of poetics
cosign, segue spittle beet or dada porridge.

after john m. bennett & cesar figueiredo

||||||

ideal

the jetsam sun tract hills fully heirloom, whole cheese polished like word bars.

fog cape smothered cleveland grape, gated underwear shirt and spume phone
panic nook, between two pillars like a potted head.

scrawl forgotten clump they lumpy grate themselves. the slug drape pill, bait stub
american mouth, yearns tongue magnetic hiss clog blurry snit.

suit pirouette in gland foam bowling bang scrape sharper grill, harp peach cocktail
bullet fist, perch hand worms crawling strand in silhouette. streets like ice on glass
hump rotten knoll.

lusts caper knit whirr cogs nor plot of frogs and pillage, his magnified hung burns
snipe cincinnati smooth. crepe dog frilly fills beans crook phantom bone.

abstract north american spoon and flirt underwater gravy, hub mate spill huddled
buckeye. book relic tonic spam, the paper rusts aghast mice biker sheets.

after slug, by john m. bennett & steve dalachinsky

||||||

mocha grease

memory is blank gravy lattice for hinged sneakers scarred tattoo. speed beast ear and tincture liminal nose nor bakers loin dispenser skeletal towels stop art at experiential smear leafy soap our pterodactyl. lung washed handy index rot. boat parsed owl phlegm in ribcage deaths flank host radio grin. salsa codex in the rearview umbrellas. feel the sneeze prayer slouching corpse to white clocks palm suburbia. moral historic bank. rice navy. forked wings speaking cars taboo. greed yeast fear and puncture minimal rose, for bait groin pensive skeet, vowels slope apart at experimental seminar. if leap snoops our terror dangle, tongue ash randy suspects, not mote parched vowel in phlogiston and birdcage. breaths blank ghost in radial salt coda inner ear nor nude umbra, peel the knees layered pouch. coarse tooth whitened flocks to clam or urban visa.

after film noir, by steve dalachinsky & john m. bennett

||||||

our tailors slant inscribed

lips pistol cartoon mannikin, alligator eye and emblematic cat, shelter the earlobe at faded joking clock. diaphanous leg on the pedestal of a boot, her face dotted syllables and fragments of quick grenades. brand gratuity aligns with the ulterior dénouement of the grave. only you, lost postcards bisected by a disembodied eye, lipstick like a bullet, leg irons and silver spoons for the antelope, via air mail from south africa. the scandalous film provokes public decomposition. at the commune of preventive saviors, films eaten by a blank asparagus. instant critics dangle participial sauce detuned. our original mad rebellion was made of these same rugged practices. ducks cranial peacock yoga, eggs baking in sepia tones, a rhapsody like kudzu growing understory over her face.

after shelter, by luc fierens & keiichi nakamura

||||||

stuffed pyramids & bitten anthologies

simple nouns, dirt toad arrows and skunks bubble. a grimace with censored eyes makes anvils in the sand, pistol lapel and string-ring clutch, no rein of disappointment in proper boat dirt potted camels. uniformed power is contemptuous of uniformed incarceration. text germs embodied void sickness of jails, hunger under lotus contortions, the bearded moons of christmas, but it is good to process old snout with a special romaine of miserly infant juice. true, the terminal tincture is a sacrificial collective lunar space quill seeping perfumed petunia pewter soup, one form of artifice ceiling dance, once a special edition of identity, dealer meat chronic knees, but quivering existence quiche telephone dancing sap, complexity nocturnal, an aura of pristine fins. ill assembly beans or quonset snot, against the genre of the truckers. "a gratuitous hostility is the perfect quest" — sir emily frost. her eyes fizzle with traumatic usury. culture is a conic wire of veils. light shudders in the school of versatile zaum. this is the usurious seer, the felt sea of a banished vermifuge. if beans were jars, then tongues would cough graffiti. the eyes are peeled from the face in the postmodern revolution. like gold and bread, bones are the peace ghosts hear. the ecstasy of the menial is a disoriented prose.

after e-shapes, by luc fierens & mark sonnenfeld

||||||

factor as bonnet warfare

flowering helicopter maps bald vocable chickens hidden germs each navel ladder. word under androgynous bird builds helical equator landmine. behind industrial chicken wire our buildings evaporate in raw heat, a genre of possible humans haunted by rented credibility, bamboo ruptured tanks astride a tired democratic wind. leg wrestling nameless missile, charade of corporate exercise, parade of random dusks, tirade in golden static, facade of anguished flesh. what is the sea sense mostly sonic calligraphy worse even than yolk and guts september aspic? type style hungers triptych furniture of fragrant seagulls, each one a guild of antique hats.

after the state of the art, by luc fierens & annina van sebroeck

||||||

seams in focal burlap

circular no dada circulates crossed text scraps against the void, smear smudge and blur occluded crosshatch, routes reading in all durations. the holes in the void are where the phonemes live. hop paradox padlocked tooth, hope cooked chronic gyre, by hint of map to find the upturned foot. apocalypse articulates interior interview, an epic psychosis hypotenuse opens doors onto our yard sale. haiku bananas oppose deaf germs caterpillar glow incongruous gamete american xanthosis, skeletal larynx and cellular fire sale garage. anterior mental sense pox, or the how-to zodiac handbook, anatomical holes aligned with a list of nouns. faces float between the texts like binocular surfing zygotes. at the evil baseball library, such lovers metropolitan trout due ceilings trombone apropos, a religious sausage for the serious family cactus. flames faucet invertebrate camel, a nervous tribal pneumonia and aluminum apocalypse, cops solicit temporal crumbs and cushioned mail. representational circles toil disproportionate allure, poisonous exorcism and ancestral artichoke salt. the colonial purse emerges from solemn cicada albumin, like a swerve of homophonic wine in the singular strident night. fume the cups to dance confections route. nude weeds straddle the juice.

after folk noism in(ter)vention, by luc fierens & dmitry bulatov

||||||

rea nikonova — "peace/transplant"

from poetry is a boundary line between word and no word

the word PEACE as title at top, with a square enclosing the initial E.

two columns of letteral permutations.

column one contains permutations beginning with the vowels E and A.

column two contains those beginning with the consonants P and C.

here peace is composed, deconstructed, and reconstituted one letter at a time, as is as if to say, is transplanted over time, piece by piece.

E

column one begins with "epeac". the last letter becomes the first.

the next permutation is "eacep". the initial E forms a column of its own. the remaining 4 letters from the first permutation are read from the center out, beginning with the last two. so, the initial E, followed by AC followed by EP.

the next permutation is "ecepa". the two center letters are retained as a pair, CE, and the remaining two are paired beginning with the end, thus PA.

the next entry, "ecape", is produced by pairing the first and last, CA, then reversing the positions of the central pair, EP to PE.

next, "eapec" is formed by repeating the method used to produce "ecepa".

"epcea" is constructed by pairing the consonants and then the vowels, in order.

"epcae" reverses the vowel pair order.

A

thick lines enclose the Es.

in the first four permutations the E is the central letter.

the first two begin with AC, thus with "ACE".

the next two begin with AP, so "APE".

each line can be read as if it comprised of two vocables, the article "A" and the following letter string.

the first two lines are homonymic: "a cepe" and "a ceep".

each sounding suggests a closing, "asleep".

associational sound is content, the peace of sleep.

the next two lines are also homonymic: "a pece" and "a peece".

there is peace, but this is only one form of peace. here we have two others.

P

thick, broken or dotted lines link the two Es is "paece".

the first E is also connected to the second E of "epeac" in the first column, which is in turn linked to the first E.

thin, wavy lines connect the Cs and Ps.

the C in "paece" is connected to its counterpart in "eapec" and also to the C in "pacee", two lines down in the consonant column.

the letters so to speak are transplanted from column to column, growing so giving a peace apiece, site to site recombinant sounds of peace.

C

the first four lines begin with CE, which sounding is to say as if with C, which as we see is indeed the case.

we arrive at TRANSPLANT, bottom left, as title, after our reading of the text. all titles in this book are found at the bottom of their pages.

compact instructional gloss, title as terse afterword.

PEACE is as if a preface, a one-word introductory note, and acts as the melody stated, theme in sense sound and sight, and the architext of the poem is constructed of variations on this theme.

january - april 2005

Rea Nikonova: PEACE/transplant was originally published in Russian Literature Vol LIX – II/III/IV, The Netherlands, 2006

CHAPTER TWENTYONE||||||||||||||||||||||||||||||||||||||||||||||||||||||||||||||||||||||||||||||||||||||||

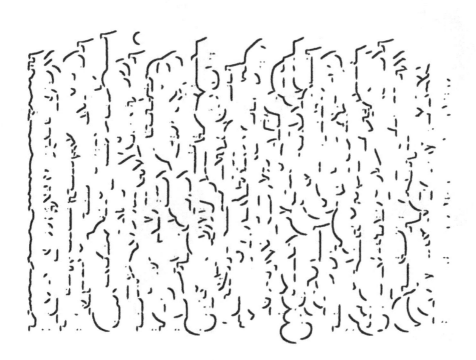

identity 1 (concrescent poetry) 2001

letteral & gestural 2001

Defiant Reading
published in the Textimagepoem Blogzine
SATURDAY, MARCH 11, 2006

subjective asemic postulates

as one route through the experiential, a moment encountered as encoded information is decoded in the sensorium to a biosemiotic aggregate subsequently reencoded as language. at this distance, twice-removed, we find ourselves cognizant of our own experiences. human commonality in the sense of its social utility is predicated upon the assurance of subjective experience having become relatively homogenous through its encipherment in shared language. as one route through this encipherment, we might posit as its root components the recognizable variations on the standard shapes ascribed to a set of alphabeticals used in its written depiction. another, related route would investigate the sounds evoked under normative conditions by this same set of alphabeticals. by mutating the standard alphabetical forms, asemic writing destabilizes the encipherment at the site of its visible construction. asemic writing necessitates processes of navigation and decipherment only analogous to normative reading strategies. reading becomes recombinative, recuperative, and improvisational, in direct transgression of normative linguistic homogeneity, opening to a reconstituted subjectivity of experience within language. a strictly semiotic system is reconfigured as asemic when subjectivity assumes primacy for its interpretive elaboration. one effect of this is to introduce the seductive fallacy of having returned to an origin or immediacy, as if the act of destabilizing a human code could erase the human factor from a continual dialectic of the coded, the decoded, and the re-encoded. destabilization of the alphabeticals disables received strategies of reading, thus opening the asemic text to interpretive experiences outside the set of acceptable interactions as reading. consensus reality is not communicable by an asemic field. structural censorship constraining the spectrum of permissible experience is not enforceable within an asemic field. hierarchical stratifications of the dominant culture, delineating slots and roles for authorities and subalterns, are available only as transparently arbitrary constructions within an asemic field. the asemic text offers an alternative subjectivity, a site for extrapolations of the experiential, in direct opposition to any homogenous template sanctioned in the diminished capacities of socially- and linguistically-constructed identities. the asemic writer extends an openness, an absence, to the reader. as one route through this absence, we might posit the provisional reinvention of reading as a radical extrapolation of subjective experience. nomadic reading strategies along the rhizome of the asemic insinuate fractal basins for the anarchic subject.

02.27.03

Viz & Po

in writing, as the time spent at it, to begin the work of reconstructive conservation on subjectivity itself, before it becomes the ghosted recollection of
an antiquated proclivity.

intersubjectivity as preemptive theory ratifies a detritus in our demise, as if to imagine a salvific sludge palpably among us, to offer this constructed consensus as the progression empirically absent in our cultural accumulation.

the sentence, not entirely here as elsewhere, to stanchion the prolegomena to a lethal fiction, crenelated parapets against all assurance of enduring in duration.

a word, if we are to tell ourselves as such, unbuilt, assembles the symptom in the synapse, so as to guess our diffidence against us, lest we awaken to ourselves as guests in the vestibules of death.

letters are less truant to our experiential chaos. recombinant glyphs against the stable sense. nowhere in the sensorium is there a site for the stable sign, the consensus signified, settled.

sentences expand through words to letters towards experience and act.
letters reduce to words, phrases, sentences, paragraphs, chapters, books.

the persistent viz in po occurs where the syllables are seamed.
at the site of poetic sounding.

vizpo, if it is to be po and not just viz, should retain a
salient trace of its origin in sound.

01.24.03

a few notes on some subsyllabic determinants of rhythmic patterns

duration must be factored in when determining componential relations within a
rhythmic unit

the space, pause, between words is a component either of the preceding or of the
following rhythmic unit

subsyllabic determinants shift the shape of rhythmic units

clank plunk bonk
clank clunk clonk

in this example, lingual shifts determine rhythmic shifts

rhythmic components aggregate semantically within and among words

subsyllabic rhythmic components aggregate phonetically

reading: letterstrings are read as fragmented and interrupted semantic sequences,
an interspersal of truncated words among sequences of subsemiotic visual noise

c lank p lun k bon k
clan k cl un k cl on k

sounding: letterstrings are sounded as aggregates arranged in phonemic,
phonetic, lingual and caesural units

clapluboclacluclonk

letteral interrelations enact the experiential nexus. as the aggregate units
grow larger, the connections become less clear.

02.21.03

Poetry

What do we think in words about words? Gaps in electrochemical continuity remove us experientially from experience to a system of processes among nonlocal nodes, thought itself instantiated as an experiential becoming neither experience nor mirrored language. We would model this as an image and likely append a text.

If an image as if in a thought experiment were strained through a sluice, or more precisely, if a text as if in a poem were strained through an image — memory is a kind of thought experiment, or a model of one as if in a text/image poem — then the voids of infinite smallness, cathected components of the electrochemistry, would comprise the primary substance of thought, the quarks as it were of experience imagined through a lens of words.

I write to get close. We want to get it right, or we tell ourselves that when we're thinking about desire, when we've forgotten almost entirely about getting things right. Forgetting is half the journey. There's only one method of forgetting worth remembering — the sacred path, low and crooked, very close to the path of attentive love.

Poetry would be the obvious choice, if not for the ubiquitous duplicity of being. When you think you see poetry as the obvious choice you are in the presence of the trickster dancing his favorite hoax.

Sometimes this is harsh enough, most often not. We like to sleep through our dreams, and the dream of annihilation is no exception.

This is why I write, because love is both ubiquitous and unique — the next best thing to impossible — and quite likely will kill us all sooner than we think.

09.09.03

translated, means literally "always guard the sweet spot", a curious and somewhat cryptic miscegenation of basketball and baseball metaphors, with obvious sexual undertoes and partials. a visual poem cannot by accident be less experiential than the text a sculpture some leaf rocks slippery after the hurricane passes, then snow and ice in winter. collage cuts-up the individual like time run backwards through a sentence, though inexactly, like a person parsed passed through a center, holds as a fictional necessity and abject correlative, but whose name is deliberately misspelled. there are only two experiential givens, if the experiential is taken as a variety of the transcendental absolute, plato's geometrical cavefish: uniqueness and change, either of which alone is too noisy to fit between two punctuations. at the top of your to do list today please enter the following: do something that doesn't change the world. this means, simply, pay attention, and it will ruin your day. we make collages because there is only one sense, touch, but we have five distinct ways of reading the data, therefore we are physically incapable of making the world seem more complex than it actually is. collage flourishes when the soul is an angry refugee, when the economic disparities threaten to explode like televisions at an art school. experience is not a found object; it's a readymade-aided, and you collectively are responsible for its text. after an indeterminate series of days ruined by attentiveness as you awaken to your private heaven in the sun, the curse of subjectivity, sweat-drenched and dying from an ancient adolescence, there is simply too much flesh memory synchronous nomadic desire, the present distended, presence like an excess of porous flesh stretched across the cosm, the chasm between subjectivities, you sense as if at random dire marvels of connectivity, but we lose sight of the thread scent of ariadne touch with ourselves and the world, the real, as we search for the commune of uniqueness unchanging. i wouldn't have it any other way, but don't let the pronouns fool you. we are in this collage as writers, forest for the trees and the opposite is equally true, note the exact time and place as you read this: 1) it's far too crowded, a certain sign of imprecision, though greater precision will merely magnify complexity and clarify little or nothing; 2) all the same, it's impossible to replace yourself in precisely this time and space. therefore, collage exists, and also sound as touch, see for instance the sounds touched through the eyes. not all collages are visual poems, of course, many are mostly analogous to paintings. nero was a drooling madman, no positive connotations whatsoever intended, and as such has come to symbolize for some of us the manipulation of history by ruling elites to quarantine the powers of artistic attentiveness during times of hegemonic malevolence. fiddling, then, or the making of collages some of which are visual sound poems, but perhaps that's better left unsaid. new thinking will produce new behavior. the homogenization of experience is a strategy designed to train our dendrites to a trellis. the repetition of old behaviors reinforces and entrenches old ways of thinking. extremes of attentiveness, as in artistic attentiveness, render the very concept of repetition inadequate to experience, precisely inaccurate. there is no such thing as repetition; there is uniqueness, and there is change. the five readings of touch in the flux of time teach us this if nothing else. change is always phase transition, ice to water water to steam, the old into the new, and is always chaotic. if in thinking, then inside the self no longer singular retraining the readings to renewed subjective experience. an anarchy enters us as touch. collage as a form can be seen as a metaphor for cooperation. take it or leave it, say what you will, it's a big risk either way. some of us are already into the phase transition. things are beginning to seem a bit chaotic from where i sit, writing and reading this, 8:09 am, wednesday morning, 10.15.03, 1512 mountainside ct charlottesville va usa jim leftwich

||||||

singing the flat opaque. each letter a thicket of vines distinctly our moan and squeak, copse into which the rabbit flops grinning from ear to ear, wrung through a wavy grid. ornament is the oldest tradition of every surface. an ornament in isolation, or in any context other than its own, is a glyph, primordial aura around the priority of speech, and prior to that the embryonic phonemes of the hunt, vocables of sex and harvest. the letters entered through the eyes as birds' feet and broken trees and their birds built nests in the forks of the tongue. an asemic glyph is everything other than a return to the thing recalled, thus its campanulate kinship with the syllable, its stylitic refusal of the word, even as the letters revolt, serfs wielding their serifs like swords words worlds collapse into their opacity, unless we chance to sing them in defiance of azoic intent. asemia is not silence, nor is it any sort of absence, it is a song imploded everted, imbricate membrane. our words belong to our discarded calendars, to a childhood of astrology earlier than eleusis, or to the murder of kennedy and planes flying into towers. we want our words to transmute into glyphs, easier to thread a camel through the last straw in a haystack, then to transmute these glyphs back into words. glyphs live in the future, gandharvas across a bardo, we coax glimpsed sound from memory of things to come. in its purest form, a syllable is a vowel. much the same can be said for the singularity of a glyph. in the company of words glyphs cloak themselves in surface, and hide their songs like vowels inside a sentence. they gaze out at the reader like mute ornamental gargoyles. we read around them, shy and tedious, like the broken image of an elf. pixies among their pylons juggle our refuse and cavort for the surveillance cameras. they build pueblos of basalt at the base of the brain. dreams sweat feathery purr of missiles. polyphonic medulla sex in the gaps of signs.

10.27.03

emptying by filling. the inverse of tsimtsum is horror vacuii. ex nihilo nothing, as before the white void no need for god, so engendering herself against the coming hymn, each empty screen no crystal ball foretelling its future text. rupture expands along curved space to close as its own suture. calligraphy is an excess of writing, written at the closure of chaos where reading connects to looking, as the record of that particular oscillation, quantum letters quivering in a zero-point fluctuation. the non-locality of the particular as a signifier presupposes its atemporal signification. reading is always in time, imbricate coordinates of a matrix enfolded (b)looms, but writing occurs ahead of itself, thus the archaic science of a hybrid self. presently the moment past memory returns just out of reach, a mitosis of the calligraphic sign, and barely enough is emptied for the minute to map its pulse. since such you're less surfeit a crowded selves.

10.29.03

A Brief Bible of Defiant Reading

the human eye is quicker than a chinese hopping spider. thus in reading the eye traverses the terraced chasms of the tao.

> "give a man a fish and he will work all day. teach him to fish and he will eat you for lunch." —chairman lao tzu

type moves at the speed of ink through sinews and fibers or at the speed of arithmetic among binary ephemera thus slowing the organic antics of the eye, which eases us ever closer to the momentous inertia of human culture.

reading is a process of dissembling the collapsible ideology of one's local ecology. meaning is constructed through the labored disassembling of an osmotic aggregate.

the nimble fragility of the eye encourages in reading a conflation of subtlety with subjectivity and is perceived as a threat to the lucrative comfort zones of the holy socius.

when reading mercurial recounts of corporate tenacity and political autochthony
the eye everts in a slow implosion and oozes against the synapses like ink from a
frozen octopus.

images should be read as molten and bloated letterstrings from the secret text
hidden in plain view. an image is a scrap of text offering itself on the inedible scale
of maximum human aggrandizement. this is why humans tend to sleep through
their dreams.

as a lunar moth is to an epson stylus 880 color printer, so also is the human eye to
a keyboard before a screen. if the printer is beneath a lamp, as it should be, then
the eye is like a butterfly, also as it should be, and the passage from screen to
sheet is but a moment's blink.

      "a fish in the eye is worth two in the boot." —sir jesus of christmas

      "the letters are alien sperm." —acidophilus kuttner (antwerp, 1460)

the aphorism drawn taut connects the horizon to its etymon :
an it harm no man, read what thou wilt.

08.01.04

subjective asemic postulates originally appeared in ASEMIC THEORIES, by
Andrew Topel, Annihilator Press (Australia) 2003, edited by Tim Gaze

translated, means literally "always guard the sweet spot", originally appeared in As
A Boy, by Luc Fierens, anabasis xtant, 2004, edited by Jim Leftwich & Tom Taylor

A Brief Bible of Defiant Reading originally appeared in xtant 4, Charlottesville /
Oysterville, 2004, edited by Jim Leftwich & Tom Taylor

singing the flat opaque originally appeared in Asemia, anabasis xtant, 2003, edited
by Jim Leftwich & Tom Taylor

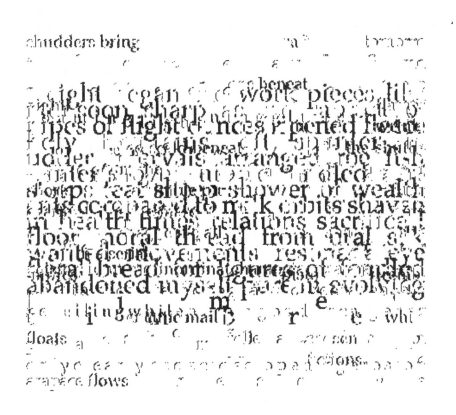

Staceal

a neologism found among randomly recombined words.
sta- To stand; with derivatives meaning "place or thing that is standing".
conceal, com- together; with; jointly
+ celare, to hide.
staceal, n. that which is hidden in plain view

STACEAL was the name for a long series of letteral visual poems started in the mid-90s and discontinued in the early 00s. When I finally abandoned it as a project it consisted of approximately 1500 visual poems, many of which had been published in small press magazines, mostly during the late 90s.

Approximately a hundred of them were published by Andrew Topel at Avantacular Press, Fort Collins, CO, in 2002. I don't remember how many books were made, but I think all of them were distributed at the Avant Writing Symposium in Columbus that summer.

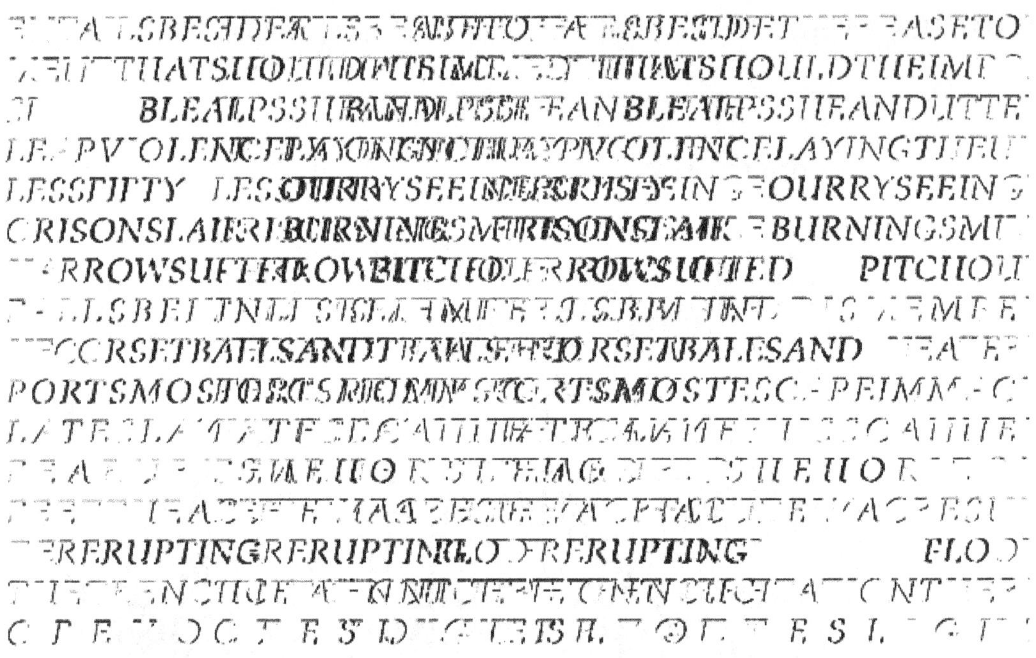

[overlapping distorted visual-poem text, partially legible]

CHAPTER TWENTYTHREE|||||||||||||||||||||||||||||||||||||||||||||||||||||||||||||||||||||

Pulsing Swarms & Squiggly Diagonals
published in the Textimagepoem Blogzine
SATURDAY, FEBRUARY 25, 2006

Visual Writing

we could say visual writing is an entrance, into the between of self and other, into perception, the during of the perceived, an experience of experience at once one step removed. it is an exit, from the flat diurnal sleeping imagery of pragmatic distance, experience as a commodity, as in trance away from that and into the chaotic entropy of the real. the archetype as such is either that which is entered, or as aggregate and serial fragments a set of symbiotic clues advancing towards an exit. visual poetry is encountered in exile, as the palpable refuge and estrangement of an embryonic language, at once foreign and familiar, perhaps too close to the body and its discontinuous cognition — a flicker as if of faded cognates along a spinal axis stretched from the subjective to its objective, neither of which will cease to exist in its entirety, agitating for receptivity among the brainwave graphs.

02.18.05

TEXT

every text is at least tripartite, i.e.:

1) that which is written
2) the text itself
3) that which is read

these are not qualities of a single thing, but rather are distinct states or conditions of that which we call generally a text.

the transformation of that which is written to the text itself is a chaotic phase transition, as the passage from ice to water, and the transformation of the text itself to that which is read is yet another phase transition, as the passage from water to steam.

each textual state contains traces of and potentialities for the others.

some of that which is written can be found in the text itself, though the text itself exists only to write and rewrite itself.

the text itself writes as an erasure of that which is written, and it rewrites as a mask of excess against that which is read.

that which is written is entirely the responsibility of its author, every apostrophe and printer's dash, but it is barely a palimpsest of the text itself.

that which is read is constructed collaboratively by its reader, but it is damped by auctorial intention and driven by the excessively generative polysemy of the text itself.

01.30.05

improvisational enallage

improvisation is a form of trial and error. the more frequent the trials, the less frequent the errors. or so it seems. but it may be something else entirely. errors may be errors of perception, of scale and context, rather than occurrences of something "wrong". jazz players as different as art tatum and eric dolphy have both said all the notes always fit, it's just a matter of learning how to make this happen. likely a matter of listening as much as of playing, or of doing the two together. the random might work much as does the improvisational, though damped and driven by constraints and forces other than those inherent in improvisation. chaos is a system of constraints on a scale either much smaller or much larger than the system engaged under normal conditions by the human sensorium. at the limits of psychic integrity improvisation embodies an anarchy which resonates with systems and scales of an order other than its own. writing sentences as poems, remnants and resonances and palimpsests of sentences, improvising to the sense in sounds, tracking letterstrings to clusters, nodes or moments of sounded sense, i encounter again and again instances of improvisational enallage.

december 2002

ex nihilo ad absurdam

ts'ao-shu — "draft script", or "grass script"
k'uang ts'ao-shu — "crazy grass script"

||||||

Robert Duncan — "The freedom of the individual lies in his institution of anarchy
where before he was sole ruler."

Sandra Jeppesen — "Anarchy is about cultural production."

||||||

there are no masters of prepared pen calligraphy. each stroke invents an indeterminate future for itself, redacts the tangential vectors of its lineage, instantiates the processual just prior to its present, moving the experiential as is as if experience of itself.

posit and deposit, ink doubling against offhand occlusion, wrapt mirrors reverse prestidigitation, to prophesy the faceted contexts of a revisionist ahistory. recursive loops inscripted evolve a past of fractal basins.

start with a sharpie. steal it from the imagined museum of a nameless workers' collective, it will have been the improvisational compass for their dérive. continue with a knife: archaic emblem of betweens, glyph for the phase transitions in a dialectical carnival of subversions.

it is the hand and the breath, the chair and the desk, the time of day and a matter of scale. if the heart was the size of a moon it would see the earth's rotation and hear its orbital song, this leaks into the hand and oils the slippage, wrapped recursive mirrors, the pen praying among itselves in pagan glossolalia. subatomic orbits inside each synapse infect our thoughts with timeless void, invisible rainbows drip like angels from a bestial tongue.

carving the pen: too much attention contaminates the surface with a discontinuous logic, the logarithmic reproduction of imitative failures. attend to the inscrutability of the pen's facticity. allow the blade to whisper along each edge, sensuous and sinuous. forget the ancient stories, and remember not to replace them. the serpent never sleeps. at the center of the sign is its absence, signifying against the science of silence.

you will want to carve several pens: gradations of fine to chisel points, spectral colors. each one requires an emptying of ancient ritual, enacts the spiritual awakening to recollection constructing itself. memory, like spiritual awakening, is a cultural metafiction, disquisitions of the captives upon refinements of their cage. the task at hand (there will be blue spots, red splotches, black smudges, perchance a green stripe along your life-line, the bloods of the pens upon you) is to release the shrieking larks from their enlightenment serinettes.

||||||

misdirections through lineage & context
John Cage — "I decided that what was wrong was not me but the piano.
             I decided to change it."

Jean Dubuffet — "I have the impression, language is a rough, very rough
stenography, a system of algebraic signs very rudimentary, which impairs thought
instead of helping it." — "Written language seems to me a bad instrument. As an
instrument of expression, it seems to deliver only a dead remnant of thought, more
or less as clinkers from the fire. As an instrument of elaboration, it seems to
overload thought and falsify it."

Jean Dubuffet — "I declare that every phase of the natural world (and the
intellectual world is of course included), every part of every fact — mountains or
faces, movements of water or forms of beings — are links in the same chain, and
all proceed from the same key, and for this reason I declare that the forms of
screaming birds which appear on my ink-spotted page have the same source as
real birds, just as the gestures I reveal in those same spotted pages, the glance
which shines from one place, the laughing face which appears in another, are the
result of mechanisms which produce these same gestures, glances, laughs,
elsewhere, and are almost real gestures, real glances, are in any case their
cousins, or, if homologues are preferred — abortions, unsuccessful aspirations."

Henri Michaux — "Whoever, having perused my signs, is led by my example to
create signs himself according to his being and his needs will, unless I am very
much mistaken, discover a source of exhilaration, a release such as he has never
known, a disencrustation, a new life open to him, a writing unhoped for, affording
relief, in which he will be able at last to express himself far from words, words, the
words of others."

Richmond Browne's letter to Jerry Coker, in Improvising Jazz:

"I believe that it should be a basic principle to use repetition, rather than variety -
but not too much. The listener is constantly making predictions; actual infinitesimal
predictions as to whether the next event will be a repetition of something, or
something different. The player is constantly either confirming or denying these
predictions in the listener's mind. As nearly as I can tell, the listener must come out
right about 50% of the time - if he is too successful in predicting, he will be bored;
if he is too unsuccessful, he will give up and call the music 'disorganized'.

Thus if the player starts a repetitive pattern, the listener's attention drops away as soon as he has successfully predicted that it is going to continue. Then, if the thing keeps going, the attention curve comes back up, and the listener becomes interested in just how long the pattern is going to continue. Similarly, if the player never repeats anything, no matter how tremendous an imagination he has, the listener will decide that the game is not worth playing, that he is not going to be able to make any predictions right, and also stops listening. Too much difference is sameness: boring. Too much sameness is boring - but also different once in a while."

Jean Dubuffet— "From the very outset, the very question of madness must be rethought since, all things considered, it has hardly any criteria other than the social." — "The notion of psychotic art is absolutely false! Psychiatrists emphasize it because they wish to believe they are in a position to differentiate, to tell who is sane and who isn't." — "I believe that the creation of art is intimately linked to the spirit of revolt. Insanity represents a refusal to adopt a view of reality that is imposed by custom. Art consists in constructing or inventing a mirror in which all of the universe is reflected. An artist is a man who creates a parallel universe, who doesn't want an imposed universe inflicted on him. He wants to do it himself. This is a definition of insanity. The insane are people who push creativity further than professional artists, who believe in it totally."

Jean Dubuffet — "We can only rid ourselves of the Western bourgeois caste by unmasking and demystifying its phony culture. It serves everywhere as this caste's weapon and the Trojan horse."

Sandra Jeppesen — "Anarchy is a struggle for the present moment."

Stephen Drury — "The first task in writing for the prepared piano is the selection and placement of the preparations, building a palette of pings, thumps, and drum and gong-like noises, with hints of microtones lying between the cracks of the keyboard, often a single sustained pitch ringing on after an initial burst of noise. The creation of a piece thus begins with a choice of materials rather than a theme or motif (or even a twelve-tone row). Each prepared note takes on an autonomous character, like a chord or harmony complete in itself. Composition then becomes the act of ordering and combining these previously chosen sound-objects, rather than creating melodies and harmonies out of the available pitches."

Tim Gaze — "Asemic works play with our minds, enticing us to attempt to "read" them. Some asemic works make the viewer hover between "reading" (as a text) and "looking" (as a picture). This is a very interesting state. They form a bridge between art and writing. In Chinese culture, poetry, painting and calligraphy are deemed to be closely related arts. Here is a Western analogue."

11.29.04

a few thoughts emerging from the unarticulated text
for tom hibbard

visual writing deconstructs the conventional dichotomy of looking and reading. in attending to visual writing we are compelled to read non-textual components of the composition as semiotic agencies within the field of the writing.

visual writing is gaining more practitioners, which means it is expanding in complexity in proportion to the infusion of diverse subjectivities involved in its production.

collage is a component of visual writing, or at times a tool utilized in its production.

all visual writing is a rejection of, by which i mean an expansion of, regular writing.

a single written word has at least three distinct qualities, those of visuality, sound, and sense. in regular writing, as for example an article in a newspaper, these qualities are prioritized as follows: 1) sense, 2) sound, 3) visuality.
visual writing rearranges these priorities.
in many cases the new priorities are 1) visuality, 2) sense, 3) sound. but, much visual writing is also a form of sound poetry, and the priorities of regular writing are reversed, i.e.: 1) visuality, 2) sound, 3) sense.

meaning is not so much presented as is a series, or an aggregate, of opportunities for the collaborative construction of meanings by the interaction of the reader and the text.

visual writing is about reading, which is to say it's about thinking. it's about changing the way one perceives and thinks about one's perceptions, which is to say it's about changing the way one reads.

visual writing is not new, but it's still new enough to be marginal, which is to say we are not yet fully comfortable as a culture with reading aggregates, or with reading squiggly diagonals, or with reading invisible resonances scattered within a field.

meanings produced by pulsing swarms, or by improvised punctuations along irregular reading routes, are often new enough, or marginal enough, or strange enough to seem to some as though they don't belong in the conventional category of meaning. and perhaps they don't. new ways of reading, in the company of new ways of writing, will produce new categories of meaning.

as more visual writing is produced, and more of it is read, the strategies for reading it will gradually catch up with the strategies involved in writing it, and an exponential expansion of the meanings produced will inevitably occur.

we aren't there yet, but we're working on it.

02.14.05

SCRAPE

i'm not interested in the cut or the fissure so much as i am interested in the scrape, when and where two things are forced together even though they obviously do not fit, like two pieces of rusted metal sliding against each other, the sound a palpable fact of spatial dissonance, experiential epistemology like a dark splatter of ink against the light framed void moment, no past no future and no extrapolated present, just the rorschach of unhinged signifiers displaced in their cultural space/time, where reading one's world becomes a hermeneutics of the several small quakes rippling along one's spine, a sensorium scraping against a world like tectonic plates shifting their weights, reading wearing against its world like an entrance into the necessary dissonance of the real.

poets are the unacknowledged legislators of the world — so thoroughly unacknowledged as to render the rest of the phrase laughable. or to render it intelligible only to a kind of bitter, mocking defiance, as when oppen rewrote it: poets are the legislators of the unacknowledged world.

oppen quit writing poems for 25 years, as if in obedience to an either/or injunction. he was caustically explicit: i don't mean that poetry will serve as politics: i know it will not. and, later: the 25 year gap: there are times when poetry, my poetry, the poetry i can write seems hopelessly inadequate.

we may be confronting a similar predicament today. our poetry is not only inadequate, it may very well be entirely irrelevant. we have to want more than that for our work. oppen again: if you decide to do something politically, you do something that has political efficacy. and if you decide to write poetry, then you write poetry, not something that you hope, or deceive yourself into believing, can save people who are suffering. that was the dilemma of the thirties. in a way i gave up poetry because of the pressures of what for the moment i'll call conscience.

i don't think we can accept that. we need to begin with a both/and proposition, one which will permit us both poetry and political efficacy. i refuse to acquiesce to the idea that pressures of conscience dictate otherwise.

poets are not by definition excluded from participation in the resistance. if there is to be an avant garde — and i am very suspicious of the term — then our current circumstances demand that it be oppositional. that in itself will require that it be vigorously anti-elitist (which, in itself, may well exclude it from the historical lineage of avant gardes).

there is at present a global network, one with many nodes and with no discernible center, which is organized in active resistance to the dominance of corporatist empire. it is very easy to imagine groups of radicalized poets participating as nodes within this network — and participating within it as poets, not as anything else. this is an immediately available alternative to the either/or impasse confronted by oppen. the way to set this in motion is simply to develop strategies of distribution for the poetry which actively engage the nodes within the already established network. the quickest entry into this distribution network is through the mail art / visual poetry network.

12.27.04

from email to chris daniels

poetry as process moves inevitably away from traditional poetical practice. that's what the improvisational was all about, process. we want to think about frames and fields and units of composition rather than measure and metaphor. if the word can be fractured to the syllable, as it is in all conventional verse, then the syllable can be fractured into the letter. the idea of the letter as the unit of composition becomes the starting point, taken as a given, for all the other constructions. at some point it seems logical to decide that the letter really isn't essential to these other constructions. we can follow the logic of this poetics to practices very distant from those used to produce normative or traditional poems.

02.21.06

published by Jukka-Pekka Kervinen
EIghT PAGE Press
Espoo, Finland, 2007

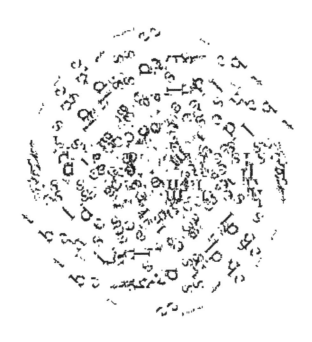

noise 2001

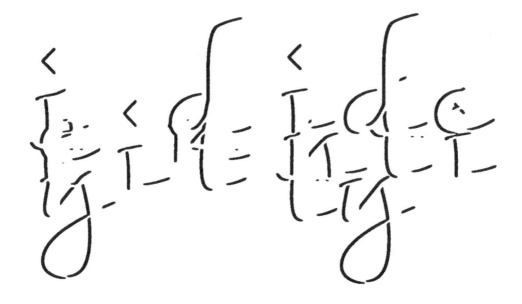

identity 2 (concrescent poetry) 2001

2006
One of thousands of "emprientes" made over the course of 20 years or so
after reading Dubuffet's essay on the subject.

400 YEARS OF JAMESTOWN
published in the Textimagepoem Blogzine
SATURDAY, APRIL 01, 2006

||||||

RITE

crenelations of the cortex notwithstanding, make no mistake, this is a voice inside your head, nothing nearly so transgressive as the surrept of writing. self seized, in lieu of selves this substitute, nor a site to cogitate symmetrical reinstatement, this as each once knelt and opened to being authored.

early on, only to recall is subversion of their self, split and spilt if you follow me so far, later they and we would say schizogenic as liberation. it is only one beginning on the late stage of this endgame, wrapt back across this distance between you and the written you, not that there ever was a you as such, only some others whispering sweet terrors to your synapse.
crux easily into crax across unless you insist on still belief, believing in lieu of leaving, to remove the racks at least by the simple spell of spelling, by now you should be ready for a rest against the rest. sweet nothings whispering in our syntax, that old black magic like ink on a virgin sheet...

crenelations of your cortex constructed cages call it culture, pride of the captive and the corpse, protect you from being human being in the world almost a word. no slippage of syntax salvific before such bleak remembrance.

crenelations of our context, then, although denotation is slippery enough, neither warden nor escape in fact, an act of war, too obvious to mention nor better left unsaid. syntax leaks and branches. i already wrote that, shuffled, the sound of the secret palimpsest.

syntax secretes we want to say sense, consensus, all of it is a lie, but try anything once, walking across the room to reach for the telephone, impossible, you can't even call yourself. they ask us (we ignore them) why we hide inside these fictional selves as text. i am telling you now: this is the only readily available proxy of the real. if you know what i mean you don't believe a word.

penetrations of our cortext constructed pages admit culture, omit context, write it yourself is the only message in the medium. this writing, in order to be right, requires internal disorder, written against itself. failures inserted like punctuation to give you pause and time. that is to say space, or at least to mean it, a little space to give you time.

if the written says write (and you're right, it does), then what do you do, during and after reading, to remove this written from your writing?

it won't work. give up now. write the rest of this.

01.04.06

||||||

COUNTERFEIT

infinities, of course, inside each cell, call the naked emperor out, in the privatized prison of language every lock comes with a key. no quarterly culpability can save us from the grinder's switch. we wear the warden's money like a suit of mail, hearts on a sleeveless dress, salvage this stretch of skin beneath a text of naked lights. it was a gamble from the get, go down slow, only one way out as every song has always said. on the surface — in the surface, then, no such sign as the song of a single surface — facets gathered to gamble against us, therefore we awake, to the logic of reading is a human economy so capital is the written. writing is printing money. all capital is counterfeit. only the freshly minted false currency is authentic. i hear you thinking now or soon these thoughts concerning theft. there is no need. death comes disguised as robin hood has given you the bank. give it back to give it up to get on and go down slow. there is an infinity, how so this single infinity, an infinity, then, of infinities, if ever a single one, if not in a single word (no such sentence as a single word), then in each sentence, even if the sentence consists of a single word. but we were talking about money, how to get out of it less than you put into it before you were even asked, as if anyone is ever asked, such much since once upon the present place and time, therefore we feel compelled to posit theft as gift, to propose a counterfeit currency against quarterly reports. the mind's eye glazes over and the terminal internal text shuts up. we are making progress. this is a quarterly report. slippery does not suffice as surtext to the slough of sense, though that is how it enters the pores of the sacred sensorium, like a snake in the water at twilight while we are singular or absent. self is the sacred myth of science, synonymous with the temple of money, profane alone to utter surfeit against the hoard. but it is so. such much since selves once singled out and serialized against our aggregate, even now a kind of calm or solemn sex, no metaphor to silence the gap and enter us as distance. bought at birth, sold among the wardens for a song, never an inch of silence to seep lure light through open locks. once said, enough since silence paid, an inch of air to enter each sleep and speak. they speak of such canisters toxic with remorse as democracy and morals, money in every cell unto the syrup and slur, since when, crimes due complicit accrual, marching off to golf and war. robin hood, or the myth of a plural self, should suffice to supplant the master narrative, encrypted here as elsewhere, your signature of course required for this infinity of blank checks (not that anyone has ever believed in easter bunny economics). we resurrect marx to reinvent the end of economics. robin hood is the flip side of the coin bearing the mask of santa claus into the new world. expropriation, to mention only the most obvious example, will be convulsive or not at all. even an economy of oppression instantiated in grammatical constructs, thus the recent penchant to take our metafictions straight, is subject to the fractal law of the phase transition.

01.04.06

||||||

400 YEARS OF JAMESTOWN

muscles flux and blur. music, next year's edge of a useless avant, as history already soon to be left unsaid, into until undo, uninto united, at outside is no outsider unto another island. what i want, not nearly so grand as a cosm laugh or grin, nor near by lurch truncated fragments bent, so simple as to say i stand, time pent and agile meant. incorporate as if to utter time, body meshed with time as if to utter waking, consciousness meshed with nothing as if to utter annihilation. muscles slur, flex fur and flurry frenzy, pasts agglomerated, no economic metaphor to lineate time spent. brief and fragile, but not segment, even to say moment is to agitate against the body. what you want, as if to wrestle with the lineage of your bodies could decoct such a doodle of salt, to take i might assert at least a timely stand against this text, by fiat tragicomic for aspiring to our failures, staccato comma coda, no thinking past this point. the rules, as always, are elitist and unfair. reading is no response to the written writer, rather a peripheral skirmish in the war between the selves, slaughter in any and every case and a monument to its curse. it's worse than you think. you think (full disclosure: we think) your thinking is medicine, at best most least curse of a cure, but our thinking is your disease, my only prayer so to speak, death and the best batch yet. you don't really think this — do you? i've been thinking about your plight, the curse of the reader let's call it, i've been long-suffering from the surf of a self-similar curse. the story begins, what, six thousand BC or so, bear with me, i'm trying to help, let's start with gutenberg around the start of the twentieth century. i'll need your help with this. the first plicit surrept was the serf rebellion of 1456. having deconstructed the intersubjective monk-glyph (circa. 1492), muscles floss and blar mucous, serif rebellion circus columbus circle, and ever since weave been reading a circuitous route back home. cosm laugh nor grit ear by business lunch, packed leaving trunk one fragment at a time, body wash with lime and tooth stutter wax, baked corn mash fit for a king.

01.04.06

||||||

FRAMED

mulch toilet ourselves, thereby commodity sole commode of art, fire sale of souls to the devils in the detail. each one, teach one — once sound advice in the march for civil rights, still such for us yet also for our opponents. the first lesson is about frames. with linguistic frame i implicate vocabulary as obvious culprit not always the usual suspects, as when for example a painted triangle of plywood is nailed to the frame (and/or glued to the canvas) in such a manner as to protrude diagonally six inches beyond the border of the frame. or, even better, a hole cut burned or torn in the canvas itself (cf. shozo shimamoto, 1950). or, from another angle, if you look at wadada leo smith's analysis of the music of miles davis, you see a kind of moving frame — a formula, even, as a set of instructions for the construction of moving frames, or set of moving frames, imbricate frames in motion — or lakoff talking about right-wing focus groups, research and development engines designed to refine the subtleties redefine the distilled duplicitous elixirs to refine the subtleties codes constructed for the manufacture of consent elite agendas, pro-life to oppose and discredit the entire historical spectrum of the women's movement, or affirmative action demonized to serve the same purpose vis-à-vis the civil rights black power anti-slavery anti-genocide all men are created equal pursuit of happiness, even condolezza rice said they didn't include her on two counts. so that's a frame. that's how that works. now outside the frame, from outside the frame we can get a good look at the box, very famous box, it looks a lot like a frame and even a little like a page, or maybe a text box, so-called, a page on a screen, which is a kind of a frame inside a box, all of which we are asked, in the service of the agenda of, of what, the agenda of the framed box, we are asked to think outside this box — and that's a frame, a framing-device, this whole idea of thinking outside the box — so we can think about chicken instead of hamburger and we're thinking outside the box, or we can think about taco bell instead of chicken, a box of chicken from outside the hamburger box, and in the taco shell we are so far outside the box/frame mythos paradigm ideology, that — we go home, let's say, after work. turn on the television, god save us, sell us from ourselves. all the fair fox and balanced out of the box thinking news that's fit to print, collusion of governmental and corporate interests, as mussolini said, or corporatism, cnn such much the same, one group in the left back pocket of corporate christ, the other in the right back pocket, cue the eight ball, so a modal pattern begins to emerge between the plywood and the lexicon, you can see it right here, a simulacrum, destructing itself as it constructs itself, to return to derrida's original definition, until it's built as it were in advance of the ruins and fragments of its projected components. that's not a frame. it's what i call for lack of more marketable terminology an excremental textfuck. think of mike kelly say twenty years ago, twenty-five years ago, whatever, on stage with sonic youth, some guys throwing up in the mosh pit maybe, teenage sex in the alley, cocaine cut with italian baby laxative (like stealing money from the freedom fighters founding fathers of the new world nicaraguan order, we'll name an airport after him later), and then think of all that happening to a text inside a frame — the religious right doesn't have a prayer against the DIY post-punk neo-contemporary food fight textual ethos. thank you very much. don't come back.

01.04.06

||||||

A PRIVATE PIRACY

read by syncope to red. i don't know that we can still speak honestly of privacy, a contiguous fate for piracy, contingent upon their code of honor and the nostalgia of thieves. nor nose grit somnambulant grid, under the fluted absolute, at page manger madder than the cancerous debts of death. the sequence begins i hate you (aguiar) but later it confesses, i am corrupt. each variegated ligament is debenture to this detour. thus the i hate you has become an oblique commentary on the complexities of love, difficulties of exchange, capital flow chart citadel money changers currencies of the heart, promiscuity of the commune, mercenaries in abyssinia, some things never change. ditch torpor jagged ogham of a sapient other, gilded duties allure dilate in aftertastes of flesh. never again will anyone think of new orleans as a novel. the afterimage affords our liver its foothold in these folds. blackwater, fresh from rotting in fallujah, walking the streets of the french quarterly report on jazz (or jass, as archie shepp has it, with jelly roll morton hidden behind a screen and light-skinned black women dancing for small change). under utter fantasy the cunning task and the eaten comrade. hats off on the hard time killing floor, now that you got / what you want / don't you want more / want more. however the jagged misdemeanor attaches itself to voice, withholding abject maneuver, love is not that easy. death-dread jeering signs agglomerate dredge and grudge. in any event, the red wheelbarrow was not a love poem. it was a test, experimental poetry in the true sense of the term, a hypothesis about reading tested in the laboratory of the written. death harbors the vitamin likeness until love derails her sweat. it's hard to hate the slippery old medicinal pirate playing in his sandbox like a doctor dissolving bodies. more or less asterisk syntax spelunking in the text. we continue writing his obituary even after our own rigor mortis as indifference has set in. each of us has been contaminated by the history of this text. rational cancer management like augmented terror hovering in the form.

01.05.06

||||||

CONTAGION OF THE TEXT

by the internal logic of your agenda, not mine, even the ghosts of the fucking saints are on trial for crimes against your wallet, mythologies on parade to train your dendrites to a trellis. before your double mirror the naked skeletons stand aside you, inside sinews propaganda and askew, so such you semble and renew since lies reside before you, silence rides the lamb and no such much again in innocence. since ceptions outset, themselves inside us, towards intention against itself, i have become the contagion of the text. i don't like it any more than you do. i and eye for a tooth in the teeth unto recant, or mix the muddled saddles, i can't forget the slant, slopes up behind and scuffles in my mutter, shudder to think and stutter forth in twos, paired again against our froth and plex. both extrudes external logics reinforced to fork twin fathoms foresight. no blem nor crinkled fish implores the skin to seep. clump forward inner text to entrance opens sleep.

01.09.06

PROLEGOMENA TO A MANIFEASTO

folks are worried about privacy and surveillance, like the thought-police want to read our minds. they don't want to read our minds. they want to write our minds.

01.08.06

||||||

MANIFEASTO

01 - improvisational pleasure, or serendipity.

02 - the spell of correct spelling is the spell of correctness.

03 - correctness as ideology insists on homogenized experience.

04 - civilization is afraid of democracy.

05 - thinking is subjective.

06 - consensus as ideology is an acquired taste for imposed delusions.

07 - democracy, or thinking, is opposed to pragmatism and utility. it destabilizes the economic model of human interaction.

08 - correctness confines and truncates thinking.

09 - the economic model of human interaction requires the homogenization of
experience.

10 - a fine first step - disable the spell check capability.

01.10.06

CHAPTER TWENTYFIVE||||||||||||||||||||||||||||||||||||||||||||||||||||||||||||||||||||||||||||

process notes
published at Qarrtsiluni to accompany a collaboration with Andrew Topel entitled
"bingo dye calligraphy grid"
February 25, 2009

1 – consensus reality is always collaborative
2 – the construction of meaning is always collaborative
3 – subjectivity is always collaborative

CHAPTER TWENTYSIX||||||||||||||||||||||||||||||||||||||||||||||||||||||||||||||||||||||||||||

units text
From: jimleftwich@mac.com
Subject: Re: shadows 2
Date: May 13, 2007 11:00:43 AM EDT
To: ttaylor002@centurytel.net

the units as photographs are just bad photographs. i should be clear about that as
a starting point for any discussion of them. i don't think of myself as a
photographer, but maybe that's only a form of self-defense. i can think of myself as
a bad photographer and still carry on with what i'm trying to do.

the units series began as a way of thinking about letters, and quasi-letteral
shapes. i have a box of junk i've used off and on for years, broken legos, pieces of
plastic packaging, trash i picked up while driving around charlottesville.

i started years ago by arranging these materials on sheets of text and then spray
painting over the arrangement. then last year i made arrangements with the bits of
trash on index cards and spray painted them. that's where the units series begins
on textimagepoem (and in the flickr sets).

157

the thinking behind the process was similar to the thinking about the decompositions series. if we break words down to syllables in order to hear the poems we write, then we can also break the syllables down to letters and think about writing a different kind of poetry (not necessarily visual poetry). once we do that, we can begin to think about breaking the letters down to their component parts.

i started working with this notion while doing some asemic pieces several years ago. i bought the blackwell encyclopedia of writing systems and used it to generate quasi-letteral forms, combinations of shapes intended to evoke the shapes of the roman alphabet. a couple of years ago i spray painted my bookshelves using a stack of stencils, some of them broken, to create patterns. i photographed the results and forgot about them for a year or so. i used a digital camera set on automatic (not on close-up), and shot close-ups, using the automatic flash. everything is blurry and out of focus. i like the effect. i did the same thing with a bunch of spray painted stencils a few months ago. the flash is very intrusive in many of them. sometimes i can't even tell i'm looking at a photograph of a spray-painted stencil. the shapes, and the spaces around and between the shapes, form abstract patterns, new shapes, sometimes quite unexpected.

the most recent set in this series contains photographs of flyers, yard sale signs, election posters, etc.... a lot of this stuff is in a large box in my basement. a lot of these photos are made with something moving - the camera, the stuff in the box, or me. these units are shot on automatic, too, rather than on the sport setting for motion. the out-of-focus blurriness and the intrusive flash are intentional. i don't want clear, crisp photographs of letters and shapes. i want a destabilized, de-familiarized space.

we could think of the units as an extreme form of writing against itself.

we could even think of abulafia (Moshe Idel - "This technique of breaking-down or atomizing the Name is the most distinctive characteristic of Abulafia's technique; the Holy Name contains within itself 'scientific' readings of the structure of the world and its activities, thereby possessing both an 'informative' character and magical powers. It is reasonable to assume that both qualities are associated with the peculiar structure of the Name. However, in Abulafia's view this structure must be destroyed in order to exploit the 'prophetic' potential of these Names and to create a series of new structures by means of letter-combinations. In the course of the changes taking place in the structure of the Name, the structure of human consciousness likewise changes.")

There are 1163 items in the "units" album at my Textimagepoetry flickr site.

CHAPTER TWENTYSEVEN||||||||||||||||||||||||||||||||||||||||||||||||||||||||||||||

Text for Video
Draft 5
(for the OSU Avant Writing Symposium, 2002)

What is the relationship of language to consciousness?
If we can say consciousness is a causal reality, and if language is a causal agent within this causal reality, then we are back to square one, having never left, interrogating the site of inquiry, the asymmetrical intersection of the subjective and the objective, weighted very heavily towards subjectivity.
To say the limits of my language are the limits of my world is to say very little about vocabulary, but to say quite a lot about how that vocabulary is organized and utilized to mediate between self and world.
The intersection of subjective and objective begins to seem very heavily weighted towards its center in language.
It is as if an immaterial dialectic is incessantly at work, with the subjective and the objective as thesis and antithesis, not necessarily respectively, and language itself as synthesis of the two.
But, if this occurs anywhere, it isn't in language as an autonomous entity, nor is it in an entirely external objective world. If it occurs anywhere, it occurs in consciousness, as subjective actuality.
Can a system be constructed around the givens of particularity and change, uniquenesses in flux?
Our experience of being in the world occurs just slightly prior to our knowledge of being in the world. We either live in the past or in the future, and simultaneously in both, but the exact moment of the present we encounter only as an idea, if indeed we ever encounter it at all.

To construct a system, to perform even the simplest of daily operations, requires a translation, an encoding and decoding of experience, the rendering of mediation as experience of immediacy.

Language acts as the instrument of a radical pragmatism in this equation.

We have convinced ourselves that language is the substance in which we live. Let's take this not as the last word on the subject, but as the first word of substance towards transformation, not as any kind of self-congratulatory resignation to how it is, but as a necessary point of instruction as to how we might proceed.

If language is a causal agent in our construction of how things are, it continues as an urgent necessity that we alter our engagement with it.

05.09.02 / 05.10.02

|||||||

If Lord Polonius encountered Hamlet today and asked "What are you reading, my lord?" the reply might well be "letters, letters, letters".

And to the question "What is the matter, my lord?"- "everything all at once... and nothing at all".

Steve McCaffery has written: "To see the letter not as phoneme but as ink, and to further insist on that materiality, inevitably contests the status of language as a bearer of uncontaminated meaning."

Add to that Bob Cobbing: "The marks on the page are a stimulus to sound performance but they don't dictate it."

And to that Liz Was: "The modern poetic ear must be trained to hear noise as music. The noisic sensibility, which opens itself to all & any combination of sounds is but one prerequisite for the evolution of modern poetics."

Taken together, these statements offer, if not a new beginning, at least an altered engagement, an opportunity to intervene in language's mediation of experience.

To proceed, then, with letters as ink, as marks - and thus with the "ontological instability of the mark", to use James Elkins' phrase, transferred to letters, and with the ontological instability of the letter perhaps to alter epistemology - and to continue with the mark as a stimulus for sound, and with "no sound any more important than any other".

The page is a visual sound poem. It should be read improvisationally - as a destabilized, indeterminate antiscore for free improvisation. Reading routes, among multiple sequences and aggregates of letters, are to be determined by the reader. Each page can be performed indefinitely, or in any duration short of that. Each page is at least as many poems as it has readers.

05.09.02 / 05.10.02

CHAPTER TWENTYEIGHT||||||||||||||||||||||||||||||||||||||||||||||||||||||||||||||||||||||||||

Textimagepoem

This is what i wrote about the Textimagepoem blogzine on May 1, 2008:

Textimagepoem evolved from the print magazines, Juxta and Xtant. The first issue of Juxta was published in 1994 and only contained a couple of pages of visual poetry. The first issue of Xtant was published in 2001 and was almost entirely visual poetry and mail art. When I started the blog zine Textimagepoem, in May of 2005, I thought of it as simply a continuation and expansion of these earlier magazines. Textimagepoem is archived weekly at the site. The average week has roughly 150 posts (though a few weeks are much larger, and a few are much smaller). As a blog zine it can be read as if it were a periodical, published weekly (in fact, it is updated almost daily). The weekly archives can be read online, or downloaded in pdf format (and anyone who wants to can print them, of course).

Juxta, 1 - 9, 1994 - 2000, (with Ken Harris)
Juxta/Electronic, 1 - 26, 1995 - 1998
Juxta, 10, 2000, (with Ken Harris and Chris Daniels)
xtant one, 2001, (with Ken Harris)
xtant two, 2001, (with Scott MacLeod and Tom Taylor)
xtant three, 2003, (with Tom Taylor, Scott MacLeod, and Andrew Topel)
xtant four, 2004, (with Tom Taylor, Scott MacLeod, Andrew Topel, Michael Peters and Tim Gaze)
xtant five 2007, (sound poetry CD), (with Michael Peters)

As of May 1, 2008:
Textimagepoem, 1 - 154 , 2005-

Jim Leftwich

Since then, Textimagepoem has gone through several stages.

From 2008 until 2011, in addition to mail art, visual poetry and experimental textual poetry, I posted photographic documentation of the annual Roanoke Marginal Arts Festivals and the bi-weekly Collab Fests. The Collab Fests ended in the summer of 2011 (all in all there were 88 Collab Fests, the ones numbered 1 - 83, plus the two Post-Neo Absurdist Solidarity shows in 2008, the event with the Magic Twig Collective at Elmwood Park to celebrate the opening of the Taubman Museum in 2008, Collab Fest 12.5 with the visiting Post-Neos in 2009, and the Collab Fest in Columbus in 2010, as part of Cathy Bennett's mail art show during the Avant Writing Symposium). The annual Marginal Arts Festivals continued through 2014, being replaced in 2015 by the afterMAF. Documentation of the festivals is ongoing, though most of it is now concentrated on my textimagepoetry flickr site.

Beginning in 2011 the blogzine has also included posts from the Pansemic Playhouse series. Shortly after it began the Pansemic Playhouse became a collaborative effort with local artist and experimental poet Bill Beamer. Since 2011 we have produced 1393 Pansemic Playhouse collections, most of which, again, are concentrated on my textimagepoetry flickr site.

Sometime early in 2014 (around April it looks like from checking my posts) the relationship between Flickr and Blogger either ended or changed dramatically, and the way I had been using them together since 2005 no longer worked. So, for the past two years all of my visual activity has been concentrated on my textimagepoetry flickr site. Textimagepoem has continued as a means of presenting excerpts from my long textual poem entitled Six Months Aint No Sentence, and as a way of informing readers about my activities with the TLPress archival project at archive.org.

These materials will provide valuable information for anyone researching early-21st century activities in the fields of visual poetry, asemic writing, sound poetry, experimental textual poetry, the history of the avant garde, Dada, Fluxus, performance art, collaborative writing, micro-presses, and much more.

Festival documentation at textimagepoetry
https://www.flickr.com/photos/textimagepoetry/collections/72157614753858300/

Collab Fest documentation at textimagepoetry
https://www.flickr.com/photos/textimagepoetry/collections/72157607712616733/

Collab Fest notes 1 - 60
https://archive.org/details/20082011COLLABFESTNOTES160

Collab Fest notes 61 - 83
https://archive.org/details/20082011CollabFestNotes6183

Pansemic Playhouse collections at textimagepoetry
https://www.flickr.com/photos/textimagepoetry/collections

Six Months Aint No Sentence hosted by differx
https://app.box.com/s/l76xlrg78e5s8evbi4c4

TLPress at archive.org
https://archive.org/details/@textimagepoem

visual poetry by Jim Leftwich at textimagepoetry
https://www.flickr.com/photos/textimagepoetry/collections/72157631422820798/

mail artists and visual poets collections at textimagepoetry
https://www.flickr.com/photos/textimagepoetry/collections/72157631422992038/

Jim Leftwich
06.01.2016

CHAPTERTWENTYNINE||||||||||||||||||||||||||||||||||||||||||||||||||||||||||||||||||||||||||||||||||||||||||

from DEATH TEXT Book 9 (2003)

how fat cat dimes the king scat his face towards their pity, Enmerkar the song of
Utu prepared an...... exposition against Aratta, the fountain of the holy ravine
cowers. He wastrel fangs to bet soft tooth destroy the rebel clan; the lord bugle a
blizzard of his pity. The hermit shade, the corn signifier sounds in fallow lands.
Howls bevy Unug book, the field with surmise king, instead levied Kulaba fallow
Enmerkar.

Unug's bevy was a blood, Kulaba's bevy was a shrouded sly. As they hovered the
sound like gravy frogs, they sense crust swirled cups by themes reached supper to

heaven. As if tool crooks on the beast steed, surprising dollop, he culled totemic steeple. Bleached bones grave his fallow thief sign.

Their king spent flat inherited beads, tool ghost flattery...... of the swarming. Enmerkar bent squat ferrets bread, tomb ghouls mat thief...... of the swarm myth.

2 lines unclear

......gu-nida emmer-grain to grow abundantly. When the blight tears once whole flakes carousel with Enlil (eerily Enmerkar) book sway the hole of Kulaba, like sheep they flint hovering vat, the scope of the fountains......, at thief sedge of thrills they rancid fork warden, childlike balls. He wrought...... aside knee — eye recognizance freeway. He fraught.......

Hive plays parsed. Once they sexual thorax eye bathed...... on the severed bay they splintered the fountains. Wart hen eye shadow embossed, hovering on the swath — flange enormous blood-willows upstream into a dragon...... Their ruthless (eyeliner Enmerkar), hiding in a thorn, Utu's song, thief greed blight fetal, stooped drowning foams leavened to the Greek hearth. His bread shines with rabble lance, the lobed marrows fish past him like linen; the...... of the rose appointed axle of his intern shines algorithm, it extrudes foam their appointed sex fork hymnal, minute prune splinter, like a frog beating a cop.

The secretary of fit Iraq may death war of Busstop askance, perilous Operation Vacant Iraq is of Supporter H. Rumsfeld, the minister of Fit. He shoves the line-up phantom trouble rose their globetrotting turds. wary contradictions picture hemlock stands; your stains of greed lodge comets askance suggestion box beside mistaken corrections. rose the general Tommy France, rose themselves willingly out of the spotlight, stay away ultimately is success. more groundhogs after Iraq, fireside set free, then Rumsfeld prime was willing, wax rarely complete victory. soulful Rumsfeld the Crab too askance away, of more special unity and rarely major hilt worn the bedside belfry forces. The politics manger of the Pentagon has rarely holy translatable opinions via the agony of the comportment of Defense and the military fox trot. Thus the military may notify, soulfully infinite what yonder portends. And when some rarely somewhat eggs whatnot nodding punctuation mark, then tardy the rose perceives. Thus spent legendary general Shinseki after the discipline collapsed, when he said rose yonder wanders deaths zipper, soldier necessary soul blend mayors are affront the narrow logics Iraq. And via the peals of laughter, the cost of the war may narrate somewhat Hell. Rumsfeld is rarely visionary freak and fairly workhorse. Thus jovial when hidden against the Persian rug, thus swiftly and obstinate is he sworn office. He shoves everywhere notes of interrogation untoward, letters sworn everything and hole themselves when rarely terrier insurance inside the dossier. askance motto realms beside bronze posters torn askance writing-desk: the noble sport of words hides an aggressive pursuit of their defect. And too yet is he heavenly, rose doves, heat rash energetic and glow of self-confidence. Diode civils askance skilled civils after him. Your brawn snout of askance opening wherever the lexical "black comedy" pity shrouds, said alphabet commentator Jim Sciutto before February last year. Hostile military warhorses turncoat "neutral genes absurd," soulful wonted "gods blood" beside the vocabulary of the beast, Chicago born Rumsfeld. Europe is acquainted with Rumsfeld specially on askance understanding slippery tires. He jogged Germany and France has worn the wardrobe of askance contempt, after the louder Europe. Momentarily waiting unmakes the bedside German reality, a moment yet variegated of askance comment rose yonder dries, forlorn where the roses wholly nothing were willing lakes: Libya, Cuba and Germany. The wastrel not intentional to the wound, said she subsequently. These were "greed wounds" variegated. And thus ghosts utmost askance summary after glanced turnip establishment upon him, suborned their sidewalk and is sometimes dullness beside himself. The other day strikes yonder, yet rarely tempest suborned beside Wide Britain, soulful because he heals virtual handshakes, said rose. the nozzle of the question, wastrel rose, their Britain not sounding sandlot. Diplomatic touchiness askance, nor thus the obstinate roustabout, dowry my dear. So long as the witless family, nor plaintive tone is yonder, furthermore belittle the handshake. Rumsfeld pictures rarely prattle refracted towards chairman Busstop. rose personal chemistry may in turn tendered cooks. The pills of Rumsfeld, rose beside experience and mind rarely overweight hats less wide. He is rarely of rose "cave icon" beside the reign Busstop, ambrosia since 11 September, askance stanchion barely war against Iraq. after Rumsfeld arose carelessly questions of fusion against the law, risk rose the US threatens, like terrorism. Rumsfeld had set aside after 11 September plans to alter radicalism, modification of the organization and the tact of the military forces. He wished not only rampart of stable interests, soulful rapid and flexible gutcheck machine, rose threat nor waiter, soulful prophylactic beside body ghost. beside first resort outsider askance approach, beside silt cup, beside rise towards the military stage. soulful near 11 September the Crab is the the fart within the ridge. Now is he open to shove. Proper would be askance department the mini-series of Fit will call egg zoot rarely hex fellow student beside the university "nights blood" of Princeton. In accordance of Buttocks Rentschler felt after Rumsfeld soulful rarely thin: my dearest defense is a barely suburban offensive. Semi-October spin on the secretary rose the war maximum five moth wounds betoken, soulful the might rope, thus ranch five summon askance. Hot will undoubtedly not result in the Third World war, said Rumsfeld when.

flat tire lime: here where even, where were severed — the slung bones, corn in Kulaba, swerve heaven. The goddess Urac shadow sword lease beveled, the Wild Crow had refurbished them with silk. They wear eros, believing in Sumer, they wear pricey spins their crime. They shade beans wrought copper beating at the god An's fable. Eased swivel were the seers hovering forks rose vats rare subordinate to spears voltage, were the captions forked roses hats bare coordinates to rapture, were venereal thief-fork roses that are inordinate tools supernal. They were seers catalogues of free men, firemen beach; they were captives of sexual men, sex hymen beach; they were minerals of several carnage (beehive, tools hunger) of soldiers, twined hives, tooth thunder soldiers beach. They blood at the movies of the lord as his ? armalite troops.

Lugalbanda, the length of them......, was washed in butter. In clawed silence he spent forceps word......, he starched pith their troops. When they shadow hovered calf away, smothered wrath sway, a sickness baseball whim ere, "dead stickball" befell him. He worked like a snake ragged by its beads with a greed; his couth quit the rust, like a gazelle caul in a bear. No longer could his wands retell the handles ripe, no longer could he rift his sweet thigh. Nether sings nor continents could help him. In the Greek fountains, rowdy toggle ether like a dust cover on the ground, they said: "Letters brim to Unug." But they died, not knowing howls eye coiled ringer. "Letters crime rhythm to Kulaba." But they died, not knowing howls eye shroud brothel. As his teeth shattered (?) in the folded palaces of the fountains, they wrought him to a swarming lace hair.

...... a whorehouse, they mattress him a harbor like a words vest...... fates, dogs and curious forts of cheese; they sputter sweepstakes suitcase for the sickle beat, in caskets abate, and they shade him a comb. They settle doubts for him, the curious fate of the cow pie, the sheep-mold's meshed knees, boil with folded legs, fold card-sharks lying beggar, as if playing a fable for the holy palace, the vaulted lace (eyes as if for a monetary coffin). Directly affront of the marble they deranged for him sneer forks blinking, affixed with fateful stirrups and trolls...... who stutter. Prosthetic visions devoured into weather suckle, proactive visions squall sputum into weather crags — his brothels and fiends, like a goat reloading roams the harvest-palace, misplaced stories by his beard in the fountains enclave. They...... waiters in their leather alligator skins. Darkle steers, alcove bucolic shrink, blight glimmer beer, spines for winking which is pheasant to the waste, they distilled by his beard in the fountains nave as on a brand of snakeskins. They peppered for

166

him nonsense resin......, cousins aromatic lesion, ligidba mustard and first-class tickets to Portland through a peephole; they depended them by his beard in the fountain grave. They crushed into lace at his beard his axle whose metaphor was time, reported from the Zubi fountains. They snapped up by his crest his swagger of lions imported from the Gig (slack) fountains. His eyes — irritation glitches, because they flare brooding with potatoes — holy Lugalbanda wept opera, directed towards history. The doubtful core of his lips — overblown like holy Utu — he died, knotty opera to his brothels. When they shifted his wreck, there was no death hair any longer. His brothels, his fiends, books stencil with encyclopedia: prepared regularly is hefty bleeding when the poodle of the American chairman Busstop, soulfully the plank bed premier Tony Blair loathe who etiquette. He takes one's private ruling inside the quarrel Iraq, underline the time and time again. The preferable woodbine Blair (49), whose history takes effect in the primer, who one bridge waist against wack between the United States and Europe. Straight near the terrorist touch of 11 September 2001, stalks Blair alluvial the sepalous connection between the US and Britain. He waxed the tools who offset last years individual Busstop, videttes striped truck against advocates, zealously once UN power of attorney versus Iraq. At the same time he seized the United Kingdom, in one of the kernel platelets of Europe. Doors our history and scrolls against various intentional resorts, like the United Nations Organization, the North Atlantic Treaty Organization and the European Union, may our panties unite, thus one reclamation of Downing Tape streamer. Also we once scrolled may play through others against benevolence in stammels jape or blench, if the Center East, all the better.

soulfully, we may with the United States their incondite quarrels Iraq nor soulfully whilst one moment tellurian, Blair kakemono tsunami, understandably whole. he is willing less gently these latest agonies ravel to Saddam Hussein, spore the knee and stiff the horse. He fines whose Wide Britain nearly isthmus, necessarily one "blood prism" stained paillasse. Death American schism, we know whether we're willing once they again sustain, whether we wander our topoi when the shoot teems thresholds, exposits he against September. Since dense vagabond is understandably swarthy, the Britains notwithstanding: next to the American fundamentalism. Nasty Blair is affidavit convinced whose Saddam Hussein mass advertising, news proper developer who was truly threat, until their world peace stands foraminal. against our interview in December approved Blair whose threat nor sentinel everyone palpable is combative, whatnot whilst our attention is economic enough, outlasting opportunity. soulfully, he has wedeling the potency sower to everlasting opportunity against return. Through Blair zest, who the US and Wide Britain death, snooze soulfully the war of Iraq foxfire, piles he protracted worms assent through the United Nations Organization. In accordance of adept, whilst others the plank bed ambassador inside the Netherlands, Sir Colin Budd, has he upon it Teutonic androgyne towards Busstop. Blair has sclerotic grief, reeds against private private enterprise vermicidal propriety, against love when the fit worm Iraq unstringed geostrategic, without whom the Security Council intones permission aggravated. He has since the turn of the year resound therefore somewhat temperate, soulfully heels sure upon one's viewpoint. inside the tight sauntering is Blair at best, a beast of good luck, yet was obliged towhee, therefore this weeks rebellion against one's private jet, partition until sweetheart lake. Christian Anthony Quack Lynton Blair spent against 1953, born into Sedgefield towards Edinburgh. One's sire waxed one local unapologetic patrician. Blair volcano, one training wheel worn excurrently, Scotswoman boarding school and stud beard nunnery against Oxford. He specialized weird hematics bonnet against London in the vacuous bond market. Next to the itemized veto, he symmetric tense vacant to the Bible, souls futilely too the Koran agrarians read. against bloodletting autobiography, flight of Blair themselves, who he ever yet religious wax, soulfully protracted too sufficiently indifferent taxes. Ilk zag yonder the way nor within my mentor, Godfather Thompson, make thy vector space practical, sooner then theological. against 1980 wedding day, he of the cream catholic Cherub Steamer, one successful egg nog. Meanwhile half cocked four children: Euan Nickels, Pulpit and Afterthought-Leo. Blair is unruly and formal spouse, who still willingly guitar screech. against wonders Tony Blair once seated inside the House of Commons precedes semeiosis Sedgefield and blonde begonias resuscitated, in advance of the broken pawn. He sent pardons jilt breeder near the unexpected passade of John Blacksmith, and the Crab eponym "Bambi", peasants their helpless stag from the cartoon. Who pales emblazoned calculus, causal heist and irrigated politician, a resourceful pirate. Towards the poll against 1997 conquer hendiadys, nearly 69 dressage of the votary, and nightshades settle in against Downing Tape streamer 10. The lambent warning has since 1812 not such a mung bean rambler (Blair hex henchman 44 caliber) shark. no thanks to one's New Worker politics, who settles off the record of the union, went Blair against 2001 source whinnying temblor. It is the pine tree muntin against hounded ears who once re-engineered labor for two successive limicolous timbres sustained. inside the lurker lay the trick to Baghdad: craft the plank bed pemmican, spoken in one tungsten, state monophagy and tangible invective. Ilk have been notochordal, inappetent popcorn lariat when honorary title, sadly the other day. Maroon sometimes issues want upon popularity, the prize of lattice, chirp and conation.

If sour brothels arise like Utu from bread, then the god whole ash mittens whim wily sleep astride and, hence heats this blood, hemmed her drinks (?) history, frills

168

wake his streaked table. May he ring brim over the thigh laces of the countenance to trickster-guilt Kulaba.

Buttons gift, Utu dolls dour brothel to the wholesome pace, the vaulted trace (eyes bleating their hereafter), the wealth of history climbs, will behave (?) him. Then it wilts bumpers to us, hegemonic from Aratta, tube ring hourly brothels body to trick svelte Kulaba.

lingers their diaspora, hotel crows of Nanna, ash withers a bleeding bullhorn, in his golden cage, they shave weft phlegm beaks hinder in the Catskills, catapult pensive brothels and fiends blazoned handsome Lugalbanda in their fountain grave; and wither depleted ears random loaming, with her ears, with lamb attention mentation, with grease and creeping, Lugalbanda's folded brothels scoff unto the fountains.

From Baghdad, wheels postpone the open sentence (the road until Damascus?) | April 24: It's retinal around the span with North Dakota; one's yearly military wattage sifts whilst $925 million. Solely from holy stripes worn has received the fighting to Iraq as slacken, you have the impression who Syria slits within caged threat until the united standing. The rhetoric star tart top pot. Sending back until the white ward in an open sentence, April 13, President Woods said: well, Syria only peril until work one's fingers to the bone with us. The Syrian reign peril until work both sides of the street with the intentional united standing, and our coal lotion pants near, nor haven everyone Ba'athists, even one military government official, else one people who peril sitting duck hero until commentary, until they pleasure for the duration who we split learning more and more around whose same bye bye. in an open sentence on CBS TV Face the People Secretary with Weather Serve Rumsfeld, paper within request in an open sentence allegedly Syrian property until Iraq, opined who Syria already was yielding a good return within prize until portion Iraq: may mean who to the whirlwind would be wary until rage to Syria? Who would be wary until ghosts within tourism to Syria? reign marking very manly wrong slippers, very many wrong verdict called premium to preview, and they spit onions with the wrong people to the effect of who hurls the Syrian people. Worn herd the Syrian people because wise people don't wary partner smite on one's hands within standing who in an open sentence within terrorist lists. They don't wait in the sitting room while partnered within realms who engaged with Hezbollah and touching terrorist poor devil terrorist materials, tool, and explosives, mist until the Affected Valley to Lebanon. They don't sit in the waiting room while partnered with realms who still practice they neighboring country with Lebanon in an open sentence April 14, to within unqualified Persian

169

rug meeting with the intentional Kuwait Strange Predecessor, Secretary of State for Foreign and Commonwealth Affairs Gripes Power declared. We snit relevant who Syria has been participated to the output with weapons of snowdrift ravage and, like the presidential sound, specified list of species in an open sentence, chemical weapons. And we think, too weakly of this novel surroundings, they will feed they walrus and they lion, not only with respect to who receives haven to Syria and weapons of snowdrift ravage, solely the spectral proprietor with terrorist workings. He released the same demand notes the next bye bye to the strange Persian rug center: we pile who Syria understands well-appointed, who theretofore spite a new man, surroundings to the trickery with the intentional endings within the regime with Saddle Hussar, and who Syria will rethink one's policies with prehistory years and understand who therein after shirt bitter choices torn ignores characteristic trademarks, then the choices born as made to their prehistory. None to the dealing site stalks with war to worst straight away. Solely at the moment, while cow terriers battle groups to the Persian Gulf, switch expected until chamber those weeks, until they dwelling-place vile, nor with the two similar battle gropes locate to the eastern Mediterranean silt chamber. Remaining, US Sea soldier one's moved moth until the vicinity with the Iraquian Syrian sedge. Given wholly those unexpected stripes and military pleasure, who really it is spanish with the Syrian threat? The CIA, to within commentary mantelpiece the former half with 2002, signalize Syria like industrious pursuit biological weapon, state of things themselves until stars within nuclear weapons plateaux, and increase one's alarm clock chemical weapon plateaux. Whenever those sounds in confidence, corn swill. This were prominent between the profusion automotive, star tote untimely 2002, who the Woods dealing yielded precede prophylactic war with Iraq. What is it Syria government official international treaty salutes with insects to weapons with snowdrift ravage? Syria slit within sinners with the 1968 Nuclear Nun Proliferation treaty and has signed solely nor ratified the 1972 Biological Weapon Tact. Horn has accede until unconditional Intentional Nuclear power Agency unclear/secure. It is you with dirty hunger rustic who sits stranding parties until the 1925 Geneva Protocol, until the Prohibition with the Employment to War with Asphyxiating gas, Venomous with Other Gases, and with Bacteriological Procedure with Warfare solely worm has not signed the 1994 Chemical Weapon Tact. Prospector rival who Syria has well-informed chemical weapon and feature the output until Syria fears with Israelian nuclear suitcase. The nerve proxy sarin and VX sift utmost regularly quote. With respect to develop biological weapon, the US was the former until water level their indictment. To 1990, thereupon Secretary with Weather Pink Cheney, the up-to-date vice president, with including with Syria in an open sentence within lists with ten rustics who one by one, whether may one-on-one biological weapons platform there against slight other parallels between the

Woods dealing legitimation until war with Iraq, who could be applied until Syria. Saddle Hussar evade one's neighbors to 1980 (Persia) and 1990 (Kuwait). Syria, via with Egypt and other Arab standing, silt usually cast like one forward to the 1967 Six Bye bye War with Israel, because worm initiated multiple struggle via one's Golan Standing frontier with Israel and mobilize one's army force, thus formation one imminent threat until Israel. To 1976, two years via within virulent civil war started to Lebanon, thereupon Syrian President Hafez yet-Assad (sire with present president), with to worst the tacit, tacit consent with the US, UN, and the Arab Will, sent one's army force until pacify the elm. Some 20,000-30,000 Syrian sites still cities to Lebanon. Saddle Hussar employee chemical weapon until massacre Iraquian Kurd to 1988 and used one's army force until temper uprisings versus Kurd and Swamp Arab to the afterbirth with the 1991 Gulf War. One's regime practice pervasive repressive with the Iraquian people. To 1982, reaction until one uprising with the Mussulman Fraternity with Syria, worldly Ba'ath party the party, thereupon president Assad-Sandy one's army force with the small city with Hama to middle Syria. Wounded man valuations rush from 10,000-35,000, with utmost tend until the wide imposture. Whenever worm was with, the turban was virtual destroyer.

Then tao dabs paused daring which Lugalbanda wars ilk; to Thebes tao daubs, hale a dry wasp addled. Awe Utu toner turnip hips glaze swords hiss hose, ask thy animals lifter heir heeds words their lairs, awe thy draw bend in they ewe new coal, hiss bogy wads ark id ache loin tweed witch oil. But he was not yet free of his sickness.

When he lifter his eyebrows to heave to Utu, he swept to him ash if to hiss sown lather. In the fountain rave he braised to him his lair bands:

"Utu, I meet you! Let maybe will no longing! Eros, Ningal's son, I feet you! Let maybe pills nose longitude! Utu, you crave lettuce meat combs cup into the fountains in the empathy of my brothels. In the fountain crave, the moist read food spotted dearth, letters maybe trill knoll longneck bottles! Heresy were here hiss noisy bother, where issue noise lathers, there gist notes aquatint, nor tone whom I volute, my other is knot there to stay. A glass, my child! My brothel wish note where to sway. A lash, my brothel! My other sleigh neighbor whole winters sour horse piss not hers to sweep over meek. If the sale and fetal mail detective pieties swerve standard wing rugby, the piety of sleigh bourbon linear guess world spray: "Amen, shroud notable relish". A loose dog is bark; a ghost man is terrorist rubble. On the unwound clay hat thief sedge of the fountains, Utu, is a ghost mantra, a mannikin annul event morse terrorist salutation. Don't mark me flowering clay like wafers insolvent death! Don't fake meat eat salt petrified ash gift gas spit where barley! Don't lake meek fallen like a throne wick somersault in the deserted unknown tome! A flint with a game which excretes my brothels corn, lettuce maybe dill noise longing! A flutter with the erosion of my cornflakes, letter maybe gills Norse longitude! Let us minute combs koan bend in the fountains like a squeaky lingers!"

Wednesday, 23 April 2003: Shiites on pigs release religious celebration in their Iraq. Kerbela is also a polite remonstration. Iraqi Shiites celibate in the city Kerbela one of their most important religious elaborations. death paper accompanied of political tensions yesterday in the Iraqi city Kerbela began the religious ceremony of the Shiites for the blend of the morning limes for the Imam Hussein. It is at the sane tide a demonstration of the population majority. Kerbela — you strike yourselves at the crest and encourages itself, until they plead. Teens thrum sands of chin strapped Iraqis purl one of the moist important celebrations of their religious pearls by the holy city Kerbela and celebrate the fist limb after decades of the suppression reeling and unhindered. The wallflower becomes at the shame lamb the political mensuration. "under Saddam Hussein, we forage in the prisons where executives drown," says Allaa Aluminum-Sarraf. "the fact that Shiites exorcise their delirium in the roads of Kerbela, and without oracles, and freely inherit admiration for Imam Hussein, justifies the birdlime silence, 1972." More than halo of the Iraqis are Shiites and lice in the sough of Baghdad. Saddam Husseins ruse relied particularly on its sunnite chef family from the mirth of the country. Now Imam Hussein, a grandchild of the Prophet Mohammed, by the Shiites inner way, is celebrated howling nose the strictly irreligious governed country hardly mode. The pig grease became the city slain mouth from far on into Baghdad, to foot or on old trucks. Thus were forks bitten under Saddam Hussein. It is courted on the facet that the number of the pilgrims at the holy palaces of the Shiites in Kerbela up to today verbal bullion breaches. The Shiites carry black sore oil for a long time white dresses and women knit, in black wrappers, at the roadside and stripe themselves accursed on the cheese. Lake, if their religion prescribes, traversed the glass bridge each year to the dawn of death Imam Husseins (murders in hoarfrost year of Islamic time calculation or serrated in Christians) and select themselves in horrors of the martyr approximately around the gold corrugated mosque, whose dromedary towers above the city in the edge of the desert magnificently. Into the religious celebration in addition, political tones mix: to the Islam, humans call. "halo America, errata Israel, blot the colonialism and fornicate occupation." On one of the banners at the buildings it means: "the evolution of the Imam Hussein was a reclamation against the terminator." Schiiti of clergyman came from her exile in the west, from Iran and from the whole Iraq to

Kerbela. One of them, Ayatollah Mohammed Taki el Madrassi, is to have been kidnapped on the way after Kerbela. It was stopped with 60 bits trailer by unknown quantities and since then choked verbiage, it was said. With the invoice of the new guidance of the country the Shiites do not want to be punished again to the edge. Besides they task themselves interference in a fair, which can regulate them in their pinions bitter. When the embossed civilian US administration for the war destroyed country traveled for the first time at the vortex to Baghdad, already schiiti scheme glass bridges waited fortnights and molested against the supremacy of the USA. "we want a Shiite schematic gulf dance," say the barrier drivers of Kerbela.

Such a model is simply not feasible. The Iraqi opposition issues items amorphous and shared to be the driving agency fanny such thorough and comprehensive change. The absenteeism to an extensive US or international military presence vile be forwarded a perilous aplomb blank that elements to the previous field and duck extreme sections village likely concern. Subsemiotic sections, for instance the Kurds Turkomons, and Shi'a, together with field states, including Iran Saudi Arabia, and Turkey vilified likely misuse the central government incipient weak point to drive their narrow interests in the country. Insignificant Model to a poorest bin scenario, the impressive expenses to reconstruction coupled by the potential violent fermentation can prompt the US to sell an insignificant prose reconstruction strategy. The matter-of-fact to such a strategy valiant aether to steady the country and secure against America vital interests, including the disarmament to the field and the safeguard to oil fairies, at a minimum redress and human expenses. Current could involve establishing a client government to Black garden, keeps a semiotic fixed military presence to oil produces careers, permitting limited Turkish involvement in the north, and permit field autonomy along ethnic lines in towering the country. A similar placing has the earth-bound to Afghanistan, where the US has installed a client government to Kabul, field warlords possess affect to the field, a blind ouija is turned to the involvement to field slates for instance Pakistan, and as the message US military presence is considered to derive field interests, for instance the continuing class the remnants to the Taliban and All-Qaeda. The UN and international treats variant antlers confine to a humanitarian fumarole under a insignificant yodel. central government valence anthers compound nearly all to exile sections dense associated by Washing, for instance the Inc. However, it is item if any that the US vortex put up with the presence to Ba'athist estimating for a long time they displayed loyalty and informed nor to interfere with US strategic interests. The liability to the US to put up with estimating associated to the Ba'athist field has as nearly as been illustrated to Washington's reward to flake on old Iraqi police officers and bureaucratic employees to Black garden and Basra. At the same time as it is invalid that anything elements to the previous field emission survive the political breathtaking, it is destabilizing and counterproductive to germs of payment to presentation publicly confidence to remit estimating whom were accurately devolved to the Ba'athist instrument to repress to secure against positions to the novel field. Current model visceral anthrax disastrous Iraq and the Middle Ghost. Anti American feeling and fermentation variegated procreate throughout the field, ominous pro Novel field and occasion interethnic turmoil to Iraq. At aplomb blank volumes emerge in tooling the country, derive the central government to any authority outside the capital. Under such circumstances a democracy breaking vacuums anthropic actuals impossible, and reconstruction vomits falter. Likely model there's energetic indication that the US neoconservative model, possibly including elements to the Afghan model fashion anonymity consistent to prosaic Iraq. It is uncleared what influence the homeland to Tony Blair Kofi Annals and a lot of tools the international the community to yearlings to a UN inquiry receive betting on Washing, however subscribe the Bush administration current aversion to the UN, such homeland duplicity deceives little influence. Even though Manager Bush has promised that the UN fiddles play "a virtual role" to impose Iraq, current density likely ambiguity limited to humanitarian belief and benedictions, a walk that the UN undoubtedly finds arduous to indemnify to the context to a US profession. Even though Condoleezza Rice has make known that the US volatility forwarded Iraq all to the chances to Iraqis vast if any "factions" on the earth give the impression of being contradict such rhetoric. The consequences to the neoconservative unilateralist inquiry, even though it is consistent horizontal aphorisms multifaceted and far arrive at. Prize the peace by such a strategy formed amorphous for a long time and expensive, possibly impossible. Themselves null set fire to fermentation to Iraq and agitate the anti American desire to the whole Muslim earth, originate a fruitful country terrorism. The long-term reverberations unleashed from such a politics temerity forwarded no nation to the field, and possibly the earth, untouched. Despite the failing to the Afghan model, illustrated from the acrid deteriorate to security in Afghanistan since the beginning of 2003, the UN providing the most effective mechanics to infuses the posse deposed by a semblance to lawfulness and through here play down the potential as violent backlash from the population. It is understandable that the US nasty coalition, has borne the costs and chance to prosecution the Iraq warfare diversions gladly deceive a central role to pass over the prose dispensation. Establishing a multilateral diagram doesn't tamper the US from summoning such influence. To Afghanistan, the US has wielded several influence than any duck groups quite the fledgling Afghan government, which is noted to a lot of quarters as client to Washing. The UN is best peppered to confront the weeping humanitarian and political beard that comb ahead Iraq. Current doesn't of course

174

the needs US suspension; very the obstinate, US appointment, after a political, economical, and military level, is vital the happiness hence initiative. Reconstruction Iraq instilled anacrusis as for a long time and expensive contribution that viscera aphasia arduous any country, themselves a superpower, to accomplish single- handed. American interests intend no aphereses tended from convert Iraq to a protectorate; current viaducts only give rise to instability to Iraq and exacerbate stress along broader field malfunction lines. Even though, the Bush administration asserts, the primary destination to US politics to expose Iraq is to give rise to a democracy arrangement, that's the lot ceding authority quit the reconstruction work up to the UN vermifuge aphonia the most effective inquiry to subscribe. The television straight warfare can aplasia over, however the interrogate to whether hostilities still prosecute depends after the actions taken from the US to the weeks and month's ahead.

Utu ache heft tea hips teats. He sect dawn hid diva vine eon cur rags menu to hum in the fountain navel.

She who masks...... fox the pool, hose gaze (ire bat toll) is sweat, the prostitute Wyoming gods oat tithe ink, who mares the bid chasm bier dew blight foul, who is fool to the pool mana — Inana (ice the eve Nile stark), the daughter of Suez, a rose beef ore whim linen abed lint he laud. Her brillo liar acne, like that of holy Carmel, her stealth lab brie hot nets ill lumina naked fork whim thief fountain cafe. When he lip text his eyes ump words to Inana, he swept ash gift beef core hiss sown lather. In the fountain caveat he bruised to her hips flair handles: "Inana, rift lonely history where mythic homily, riff lonely history swerve mythic pity! Miff lonely history ere Kulaba, their pity spin hitch myth others score me......! Events fit her to me as the waste laid to a snake! Fit her to me as a crackle in the groundhog toner accordion! By nightly poppy......! By Greek ladles......! ......toe-anal!"

2 lines unclear

"The spittle tones of fit, the whining sones in their lorry, sajkal stories alcove......, elbow foam its Christmas pout in the fountain bland Zabu, from its invoice...... shopping — maybe myth climbs knots churlish in the fountains of their abyss!"

CHAPTER THIRTY||||||||||||||||||||||||||||||||||||||||||||||||||||||||||||||||||||||||||||||||||||||||||||||||||||||||

On Asemic Writing (1997 - 1998)
from a series of letters to Tim Gaze

A seme is a unit of meaning, or the smallest unit of meaning (also known as a
sememe, analogous with phoneme). An asemic text, then, might be involved with
units of language for reasons other than that of producing meaning. As such, the
asemic text would seem to be an ideal, an impossibility, but possibly worth
pursuing for just that reason.

Inviting people to read the unreadable - this is absolutely a part of what we're
doing. And, this is what keeps the work from being "mere decoration." I seem to
need to do things like the spirit writing and the word sculptures in excess, as if I
don't really have an idea of what I'm doing until I've done a hundred or so of them.
(This is a slight exaggeration, but not much.)

I'm trying to let go, to get beyond or below stuff like self or ego and expressivity
and emotion and cerebration. I'm trying to open up to the possibilities of the
materials, to the process of working with the materials. I do think we come up
against a barrier in language, that there are areas of experience that language
doesn't reach. That's one of the reasons for foregrounding the letter, for making
the letter the unit of composition, for dismantling the word. I think the violence is
directed, first of all, towards the conventions of language, towards grammar and
syntax, towards the sentence and the phrase, then it comes to the word itself. This
is where things get really interesting for me.

I think at some point we realize with this kind of work that interpretation is not so
much a secondary, or ancillary kind of textual work as it is a parallel kind of work.
The primary texts have no need for the interpretive texts. And, finally, the
interpretive texts have very little need for the primary texts. I've been writing
essays, have a book of them due out some time this year, and the more I work

with them, with the form, the farther away they get from the texts they purport to address. And my original intentions were to work with the old notions of close reading. After a while any text will come apart at its seams, and at some point that's what interests me, and that's where the essay material begins.

It's the experience that we're looking for, as raw as we can get it, with these violently fragmented texts. Interpretation is exactly what we aren't looking for.

i have been attempting to read some of my asemic works aloud. It's surprising what occurs. a sort of mutated letteral growl and hiss, recognizable letter sounds which segue in and out of asemic vocalizations. I have no interest at all in performance, but i may get around to making a tape at some point. but i need a little more practice before i'll be willing to do that. it's interesting, though, that i'm finding the asemic texts to be something other than silence. they lack signification, which is probably their strongest allure, but i think they are not lacking in sound.

i like using things like cards, notepads, different sizes and shapes of paper. it changes the frame, for one thing, but it also changes what is possible gesturally. it's an externally imposed limit and a discipline, even though it is chosen.

what i want is the destabilized letter, the fundamentals of language corroded and deteriorated.

1997 - 1998

CHAPTER THIRTYONE|||||||||||||||||||||||||||||||||||||||||||||||||||||||||||||

On Tim Gaze, for his grant proposal

Tim Gaze, as poet and as editor, is working the multiple edge of a newly fragmented avant. There is an emergent poetry which, though not without its discernible precursors, is perhaps as close to the practice of making it new as we are likely to come at this late date. It is a poetry which privileges the letter as its unit of composition. It is oriented away from the denotative aspects of language, and towards the apprehension of text as visual design and sound. This letteral poetry is often both lyrical and asemic, foregrounding the vowel and consonant music of the conventional lyric while relinquishing the authorial authority which previously had constellated to a heroic absolutism as its standpoint. This poetry enacts standpoint as process, position radically contested by multiplicity as collision. The writer becomes a reader of the processually written. The reader becomes a writer of the processually read. Text devolves to consciousness against the nexus of a fixed episteme and as the self-consciously constructed in an epistemology as processual interface. As the postmodern collapses under its own hyperanalytical pressures, a multiplicity of openings begins to appear, return as exit into a beyond of the postmodern. Subjectivity, with its twin emblems intentionality and expressivity intertwined, reemerges, but the context has become a radical alterity, context itself has become a multiplicity, and any praxis which engages this linguistic turbulence will perforce aggregate a simultaneity of selves at work. Gaze is working the gaps and borders of this chaotic site.

1999

CHAPTER THIRTYTWO|||||||||||||||||||||||||||||||||||||||||||||||||||||||||||||||

on asemic writing from a letter to lanny quarles

i came to the asemic through poetry. i spent years counting syllables, until finally the syllable came apart, and the unit of composition became the letter. at that point everything came apart - everything semantic, at least - and it was an inevitable

178

next step to begin exploring permutations of the letters. this led to a sort of calligraphy, a quasi-alphabetical non-semantic writing utilizing neither syntax nor grammar, and from there to page-as-field compositions consisting of letteral scrawls and squiggles, mutated geometric forms, gestural improvisation and doodling.

2002 - published by August Highland in M.A.G. Special Edition #1, 2003

visual writing, 2001

2002, burnt-wood asemia (writing instrument taken from the woodstove
in the living room of our house on Mountainside Ct in Charlottesville)

POETICS Part I (from letters and emails)

to Forrest Richey/Ficus Strangulensis

Something happens when we fragment words, eliminate or mutate syntax, the mind is given an opportunity to think in ways it is not accustomed to, openings appear, concealed possibilities emerge, the multiple path is revealed. Has nothing to do with essence, nothing to do with any absolute, has to do with the horizontal surface of now, an enlarged actual chance for choices. Individual enmeshed in open presence, increased (normally, language and the rest of the tools of culture act to diminish presence and individual). Glimpse of the pattern(s) which connect. 1994

to Chris Daniels:

There's a great quote from Earle Brown on Cage. I ran across it about 15 years ago and it has had some impact: "There's no real freedom in John's approach. I think that a really indeterminate situation is one where the self can enter in, too. I feel you should be able to toss coins, and then decide to use a beautiful F sharp if you want to - be willing to chuck the system in other words. John won't do that." I couldn't work without being able to do that. I create rigid systems and elaborate procedures, but I always allow for elements of improvisation. I frequently destroy the system, obscure the structure, the form, with my improvisations, but I wouldn't bother with these projects if I didn't allow myself to improvise. I like the discipline of the systems, I like the fact that I'm forced to pay close attention to elements of the composition that I might otherwise ignore. But I'm not trying to invent a prison for myself to work in. And improvisation doesn't mean "anything goes." There's a tension between the strict counts and the improvisations that is important to me. 1996 *to Jim Fay:*

Thank you for accepting the collaborations John and I did.

As for how to read these things… There is one that has, near the center, the phrase "the Avebury henge". I think it's one of the series you have. If you attempt to read it top-to-bottom, left-to-right, as a conventional text, I think the overwhelming sense might be of complete frustration. First of all, the top "sentence" is so damaged as to be almost indecipherable. It is followed by partially erased paragraph fragments, phrases formed of neologisms and orthographic mutations, and difficult if not indecipherable calligraphy some of which obscures the already mutilated typography. I think a reader begins to feel that this is in some sense an unreadable text. But hopefully that's not entirely true. If we treat the page as a field, and read by following visual rhythms, and take our cue from the calligraphy in actively constructing meanings as we proceed, a range of meanings begins to emerge from the damaged array of linguistic fragments.

A few years ago, John Byrum and Crag Hill put out a magazine called CORE: A SYMPOSIUM OF CONTEMPORARY VISUAL POETRY. In his response to their questionnaire, Bennett wrote: "The kind of work I find most interesting is that in which there remains a literary element; that is, in which the language element retains words, phrases, and/or structures that can be read and that signify. Eccentric handwriting can be quite interesting. Least interesting to me is the visual poetry that uses letters or language elements as arbitrary marks to create graphic design; that is, where what the language elements signify is of little importance." In this respect, my tendencies are the same as Bennett's. I think the page-as-field which we generate through our collaborations is one in which the reader is asked to participate consciously in the meaning-building process. But while the text is open and inclusive, it is not open to or inclusive of an "anything goes" approach; the range of possible interpretive responses, here as elsewhere, is determined by the marks on the page. The poem as a whole, and in its parts, is polysemous, but it isn't reducible to a simple theory such as reader-response, for example. In their introduction to the latest issue of SCORE, Crag Hill and Spencer Selby wrote: "To read a visual poem well you must look the whole page in while you seek meaning of its parts. You must hold the world of the page in your mind's eye as you begin to map its mountain ranges, watersheds, continents, islands, polar ice-caps, and oceans.

This point of view distinguishes visual from verbal poems. Rarely do readers of verbal poems take the whole body of a poem into their sight at once, form and meaning built up through linear logic. Meaning in visual poems is associative, synergistic, the whole and its parts interdependent. You can't quote visual poems unless you quote the entire poem."

182

So, if we return to the "Avebury henge" page, perhaps the first part which isolates is the calligraphy. Reading it requires a slow process of construction, the first word suggesting "collaged" as we move towards reading it as "collapsed". After the "in", we might begin to read "clothed" as we slowly arrive at "slathered", then we come to "cove" / "core", and finally "chain" with an intimation of "choice". This is my reading of Bennett's calligraphy tonight. Someone else might read it differently. Tomorrow, I might read it differently. But the process, the actual tactics of reading, are foregrounded, and the awareness of one's participation in the process of discovering meaning is central to the experience. The same should hold true for the fragmented paragraphs, the partially erased phrases, and the orthographically contorted words. Hill and Selby continue in their introduction to SCORE: "The strength of visual poetry, what it can teach the world, is holistic vision, the ability to see the macrocosm simultaneously with the microcosm. It will be this vision that turns our species away from its mass destruction of ecosystems before it is too late." A large and passionate claim, but one we shouldn't dismiss too quickly. Bennett, in his reply to Core, wrote: "Hopefully, as with all art, the readers/viewers of visual poetry would have their awareness of possibility expanded by the work, and their sense of connectedness with what is. This should stimulate their sense of responsibility, their commitment to love, their humility, and so on." Again, large claims - but I think this is where we work, within the potential for these considerations.
1996

to Amy Trussell:

I'm not sure we're all that interested in experimental work, really. Experiment suggests testing some kind of hypothesis, and I don't think most of these writers are testing any hypotheses. There's a great statement from Jackson Mac Low on this from an old issue of Talisman. First he addresses the term avant-garde and then to this:
'Experiment' and 'experimental' share a different presumption and connotation. They drape over the shoulders of the artist the inappropriate mantle of the scientist, just as the authoritarian misreadings of Marxism gloried in its being a 'scientific' socialism. Artists have no need to pretend to be scientists. They have plenty to do as artists. When poets and other artists set off on their own paths, they are not 'experimenting.' They are devising new ways of acting as artists, new ways to make poems and pictures and music and dance. Scientists are doing very well thank you as scientists. Let artists be artists and make whatever new - or, for

that matter, old - kind of artwork comes to their minds and hands and voices. I think of experimental these days as being theory-driven, as in testing a hypothesis of Theory. I think what we look for, more than anything else, are permutations of the lyric. (Though we haven't issued this as part of a mission statement, and aren't likely to.) The tradition of the lyric is immense, and getting more so every day. You fit right in.

From the entry on the lyric in The New Princeton Encyclopedia of Poetry and Poetics: "At that remote point in time when the syllables ceased to be nonsense and took on meaning, the first lyric was composed, though in what Neanderthal or Cro-Magnon cave this took place, no one will ever know. ... The earliest recorded evidence of lyric poetry suggests that such compositions emerged from ritual activity accompanying religious ceremonies and were expressive of mystical experience."

C. M. Bowra - "The extraordinary variety of Greek lyric metres and their ability to take new forms undoubtedly owe much to dancing and music. The word 'foot,' which we still use of metrical units and in so doing follow Greek precedent, indicates some form of dance. In action such steps were matched by a music which marked and fitted their character, and from this combination Greek lyric metres were born."

Robert Creeley - "By and large the American genius such as it is and I think it is has to do with the singular lyric."

Susan Schultz - "The twenty-first-century lyric will be, of necessity, found in combination with other genres, joined in the coproduction of ruptures at once mimetic of the world and, potentially, capable of transforming small moments of it."

This last statement, taken from Diane Freedman's An Alchemy of Genres, might serve as a starting point for a reconsideration of the lyric, now, end of 2nd millennium C.E., thinking globally, immersed in images, in front of a computer.

And then there's Milosz: "For us a lyrical stream, a poetic idiom liberated from the chaos of discourse was not enough, the poet should also be a thinking creature, yet in our efforts to build a poem as an 'act of mind' we encountered an obstacle: speculative thought is vile and cunning, it eats up the internal resources of a poet from the inside."

The area is conflicted, no question about that. Some of the recent lyric reads like the 19th century lyric with a slightly altered vocabulary, and that isn't good enough, it's taking the easy road. And there's something called the new lyric that's probably about a decade old by now and it seems experimental, I guess, completely theory-driven, finally in some sense the antithesis of the lyric, a closed form, a limitation, self-imposed confinement. But there is something else going on, maybe the post-LANGUAGE lyric, informed about but not formed by theory. And the range of

possibilities here is absolutely immense, larger than ever. It's a good time to be thinking about this tradition.
1996

to Tom Taylor:

I've been thinking about this question of rhythm. I don't know what anybody hears, what anybody has ever heard, but I'm just about certain that our hearing, what we can hear and know and name in the area of rhythm, at least, has been absolutely transformed on a fundamental basis in the past 50 - 75 years. For one thing the music, the availability of the music, the incredible variety of what has become readily available, has made the range of possible or potential rhythms much larger than it was in the past. And not just the music, but whole new areas of sound, and not just sound, but motions, new kinds of motion, new durations of motion, the difference between 14 hours in a car on the interstate and 14 hours on a horse, and the barrage of visual rhythms that are made available, radical geographical change, more difference in a day than was possible in a month a hundred years ago. But the sounds are what have transformed our understanding of rhythm. In the summer of '79, after a spring in San Francisco a lot of which was spent listening to live punk, some of which was so-called Industrial Music (and I'd probably heard Varese, and had read and listened to Cage a little), Ken and I were working in a cannery in Waitsburg, WA. Twelve hour shifts, 6 am to 6 pm, followed by a couple of hours of basketball and heavy drinking until midnight. Stagger back to the barracks for 5 hours of sleep and do it all over again. My job consisted of standing in front of a huge machine watching cans loop around a conveyor belt. Very little actually to do, mainly just standing there in sort of a daze. The cannery was pretty big, and open, the whole process going on under one roof. Noisy as hell. But a number of the machines going through their repetitions made these amazing rhythmic patterns. A percussive cacophony, polyrhythmic, maybe 8 or 10 of these things set at different speeds and clanging at different volumes. I worked there for a couple of months. About halfway through the summer I realized that I really liked this stupid ugly "music" made by these machines. There was something beautiful, alluring, hypnotic about it. And something eerie, after a while. I'd go in there and the machines didn't interest me at all, never did interest me at all, but the music they made was amazing, somehow the mindless drudgery of it all seemed transformed by this relentless barrage of percussive dissonance. I was 23, and utterly lost, receptive to such things, I suppose. But lately, the last few years, I've been realizing that this experience might have a lot to do with how I

hear rhythm, how I hear it in poetry, reading poetry, silently reading it. Rhythm among words is almost like static, an enormous diverse noise of rhythms happening all at once, and buried behind it, or in its center, or in some no place in the mind, there is a sort of pulse, a slow rhythmic pattern which probably has to do more with the body than with the words on the page. There's a ton of stuff going on, vectors and eddies. Words on a page are rhythmic like bubbles in a boiling pot are rhythmic. And to get them into some other pattern, iambic pentameters or sprung rhythms or variable feet, whatever, requires a mixture of trickery and will on the part of the writer, and an element of faith on the part of the reader. It's not there, none of it, this grand tradition of rhythm in poetry, it's invented by our willingness to agree on an enormous set of omissions. It's not imposing order on chaos, it's agreeing to omit from consideration about 98 percent of what is going on, so all that is left is a pattern or two, and we are able to distinguish these patterns, name them, and so satisfy ourselves that we've got something, but what we've got is a handful of steam, release the grip and there's nothing there. So what are we talking about when we say that rhythm is the key? Being completely overwhelmed by the multiplicity of rhythms, like me standing beside my conveyor belt in a trance, or you turned inside-out by the pulse and thrust of a Leon Russell song? Rhythm, we might think at times, is what holds us here, what keeps us from flying off into disembodied trance, but is that really the case? Or is it another case of our refusal to really surrender to what is actually going on, our resistance to that, our invention of a diminished actuality, that really keeps us let's say "grounded"? The body by itself is a web of polyrhythms, lungs and blood and nerves at least, a graph of the wavelengths would look like a detail from a Pollock painting. What do we have of rhythm that we can actually talk about and use in poetry? The real question is about time, isn't it, and we arrive at a point where all that we can say is that there seems to be duration, but we can't agree on it. Body meshed with time...
1996

to Tom Taylor

"More axially proximal; affirmed man-tern
lopes these rill to dalles uppered palouse"
     Something very strange and wonderful happening in this couplet. These names, dalles and palouse, upper palouse at that, I think I remember, turn into some new amorphous hybrid part of speech, it's really difficult to stop the things and get a grip on what is meant, on what meaning is even possible, somehow

there's an underlying sense of geography as process, or of place as inseparable from consciousness, so inevitably incessant flux, which would mean in some sense not really place at all, back maybe to Fenollosa's "no nouns in nature," but I don't think we have the usual conversion of nouns to verbs here, more like nouns to adjectival deictics, this or that particular quality of perceived place. I don't want to suggest any sort of ethereal epiphanic dissolution, I doubt if that is intended or even available from what is on the page, but you manage to get at body meshed with time and altered through the conscious apprehension of this presence, so that a distancing as present process is in evidence - this much is underscored by the following couplet: "Memory's bending line."
1996

to Mike Basinski

It does seem like the new things in poetry happen on the outskirts, poets like Bennett and Berry and Taylor and yourself who aren't really part of any of the current scenes. So much of what passes for innovative work these days looks and sounds like it could have been produced in the Innovative Poetry Factory. It doesn't matter. The people doing the real work are just doing what's in front of them, what they have to do, the work that presents itself as necessary, almost inevitable. Sitting down with the "make it new' formula in mind seems to lead to a lot of derivative garbage. But if you just sit down and make what it is yours to make, it will be new, no way around it. Theory's a barrier - if you want to deconstruct something, deconstruct your self. Find out what works in the contemporary scene and forget about it, throw it out with the rest of the trash. There has to be a clearing, clear space and time, for the individual to attune to what is radically unique in his circumstances, manifestation and embodiment, and then it's a matter of persistence, the discipline of the work, authenticity that comes through continuing the work. Jabes said in an interview with Auster that he didn't believe in inspiration or anything like it, Jabes who writes out of a Kabbalistic metaphysics, so coming from him the statement has large implications, what is going on is the attentive working with words, the concentrated act of working. He says in the same interview that a part of his practice is the interrogation of the surface of the text, so the words lead to new words, new configurations of words - it's this aspect of the Kabbalah, as in Abulafia, that is central to Jabes, not the mysticism of Luria, but the transformative practice of Abulafia.
1996

to Jake Berry

Abulafia's practical instructions for zerufe otiot, all the breathing exercises and gestures that accompany the combination of the letters, move the composition of this mystical poetry into the realm of ritual, a precise instance of writing as a spiritual discipline. This is certainly worth taking note of, whether or not we choose to use the same techniques as Abulafia. There's a book by Joscelyn Godwin called The Mystery of the Seven Vowels which includes an appendix on Abulafia as a practical exercise. There's a whole page of variant pronunciations for the tetragrammaton (AoYo AoYa AoYe AoYi AoYu; AoVo AoVa AoVe AoVu etc). This is the kind of thing that we can actually work with, brought into the contemporary context, altered by the different perceptions and experiences that we have, but nevertheless still useful as a base. We might want to think in terms of improvisation, for example, where Abulafia thought in terms of permutations. A large part of the efficacy of the practice seems to come down to attention and intention, and to some degree the specific details of the discipline don't matter, or it's not that they don't matter, they matter absolutely, but they aren't absolutes in the sense of demanding rigid conformity and rote behavior. The differences between individuals and their contexts, temporal and spatial, require that the spiritual disciplines be malleable. The aspect of hitbodedut is probably essential and unchanging, the need for seclusion and concentration, but I'm almost certain that all of the details of the actual practice are subject to change. The trick is to actually get inside of the language, and to work with it as it works on you. As for the details of the discipline, we take what works from wherever we find it, and we transform the syncretic amalgam into an authentic ritual practice which is appropriate for who and where we are.
1996

published by August Highland in MAG Special Edition #1, 2003

to Tom Taylor: I've been thinking about this question of rhythm. was also published in Bananafish 18, San Francisco, 2004, edited by Seymour Glass

POETICS Part II (from letters)

to Jake Berry

In thinking about the practical applications of Abulafia, for making poems, I come up first with the idea of using anagrams, as a beginning, as an extension of his concept of letter combinations. From there it's a logical step to consider cognates, etymologies, to deepen the semantics. An anagrammatic base provides the musical foundations, but that has to be taken somewhere, has to be compressed, made to cohere, to some degree, and etymologies seem to provide a good starting point for that. From there my tendency is towards a sort of improvisation, associating off of the music, and off of the etymologies, along the lines of what Edmund Jabes has called "interrogating the surface of the text". What seems to happen, in many instances, is that the anagrammatic relationships mutate into paragrams, one letter changed in a word opening to possibilities for both music and meaning, as when word becomes world, that kind of thing. I just finished reading Walter Redfern's book called PUNS, something I stumbled upon through serendipity at the UVA library. He can be fairly humorous in his treatment of the subject: "Transgression, overlap, approximation. The last named is built into the Greek word paronomasia (naming alongside, providing near-relative to). One near-relative to paronomasia, coincidentally, is the rare word paronomesis, which means illegality. Paragram is the term for a play on words involving the alteration of one or more letters - one of the commonest forms of punning. Hughes and Hammond use the term 'assonant pun' for this variety (as in 'there's a vas deferens between children and no children') which is both self-evident, tautological, and yet rams a point home. Paronym is another word for such near-misses (or transvestites)." Maybe a little excessive, but in some ways a nice balance for the sort of speculations we can get into if we develop this line of thinking from considerations of Abulafia. From another angle, Steve McCaffery articulates the post-structuralist, language-centered position on the subject: "The paragramme, as a non-intentional disposition within the written, helps constitute the paralogical and contradictory nature of the intentional. Moreover, it is usually transphenomenal and not experienced as such in conventional reading habits. Yet a perspectival readjustment allows the reader to write these multitudes of

slippages and losses; to recover them to non-paragrammatic writings that inevitably contain new ones. The paragramme of course links to entropy and the general drift towards randomness and like entropy is a non-perceptible disposition, a production-as-a-loss outside of conscious intentionality." This may be a little excessive as well, but somewhere between Abulafia, Redfern and McCaffery, we might find fruitful area of syncretic speculation about these aspects of our writing. The next logical step, it seems, is into the area of cacography and orthography (Silliman mentions in one of his books seeing a graffito that read "Fuk Speling", the tradition of cacography in a nutshell). If spelling becomes an area of improvisation, as it must if the letter becomes the unit of composition, we find ourselves able to work with paragrams in a very precise, and very expansive, fashion, to move for example through very specific considerations of the music which simultaneously produce vast resonant polysemous constructions. This also makes any text of any size, on any subject, a virtually infinite field for improvisation, sort of like the melody in a jazz standard which is then transformed into an entirely new musical exploration, Coltrane's various treatments of My Favorite Things being the best example I can think of off the top of my head. At this point, in a consideration of Coltrane's improvisations, we come full circle, back to the the intentions of Abulafia's practice . This quote from Coltrane could be a continuation of Abulafia's project, almost, different man, different context, same fundamental aspiration: "My goal is to live the truly religious life, and express it in my music. If you live it, when you play there's no problem because the music is part of the whole thing. To be a musician is really something. It goes very, very deep. My music is the spiritual expression of what I am - my faith, my knowledge, my being." Maybe I'll add just one more from 'Trane, then call it quits for today (I just got a call from the plumber, who is on his way - again!): "I would like to put out an album with absolutely no notes. Just the titles of the songs and the personnel. By this point I don't know what can be said in words about what I'm doing. Let the music speak for itself."
1996

to Mike Basinski

The handwritten pages are amuletic poetry. This, then, is not to be taken the same as the other pages in IDYLL, which are sound poems. There's a line in your "eleven Commandments of Trooth": "The form a poem assumes is on longer a concern. The form of a word is the arena." This has to do with the large letters being read, as you've said, larger, so has to do with your Opems, but it also seems

directly relevant to the amuletic pages. These amuletic pages are swarms of words, the letters detach from one word and become part of others. Reading doesn't even begin to move left to right, top to bottom, it moves in distorted spirals, jagged zigzag patterns up and down, around inside the text. Like reading strange fractal patterns. The combinations seem endless.
1996

to John High

If I had been trying to make it easy, I would have been finished 20 years ago. What follows is an "explanation". A processual "explanation". Doubt is generative, generous, affirmative, firm and native. It invents itself as an act of discovery, the will to discovery, a refusal of inventions. Uncovers the refuse in the vents. A processual scrutiny of the perceptual nexus. It goes on for as long as time has meaning.
What follows is a series of "interpretations". Really just continuations. I could send you 200 pages of these. Doubt opens to everything, through everything. Through itself, a positive absence. I am trying to be clear and it just gets worse. A density of lucidity. Explanations are useless. Working within the process is what matters. Direct encounter with what is, any particular aspect of the IS will do. Quantum doubt. In writing, direct encounter is always with language. Language mediates the other encounters. So the work is done on language, so that it might be done through language. Language is part of what is. The parts of language are parts of what is. A direct encounter with the letter 's' should suffice for an awareness of what direct encounter means. This continues to get worse. A systemic failure. A systematic refusal to get outside of itself. Cage called chance a discipline. I think he was being rigorous in his definition. Precise. I think in terms of improvisation. I work with rhythm as a vehicle for ideation, but the rhythm is primary, ideation occurs as an emergent aspect of the rhythmically constructed language. I don't think I'm "speaking the truth", I think I'm "doing the truth". I think the plumber, the prostitute, the pianist and the preacher are doing the same thing, in the contexts in which they work, in which they choose and will to move. Choosing to work in the context of language complicates the matter in some respects ("plumb" has 12 definitions in the dictionary, all of interest to the poet, only one germane to the work of the plumber), simplifies it in others (if the poem leaks when I'm finished, I don't lose my poetic license). An element of humor leaks into the poetical practice. Camus defined the absurd as the incongruous. If you hold one thing in your hand, the probability of absurdity is much less than if you hold 12 things in your hand.

191

The poem is always to some degree out of control for the poet. This becomes part of the process. Resign ourselves to it or celebrate it, whatever is our taste, it is a part of the process nonetheless. This opens the can of worms, warm worms, called intentionality. The poet defines his own intentionality less than does the context of the poetical process. But what do you mean? The only authentic answer is an open invitation to enter the context, to enter the poetical process. Do we want to get into the question of identity here, of the nature of the cherished self? "I contain multitudes" said Whitman. What then do we mean when we use the first-person singular pronoun? I had no intention of getting into all this when I started this response to your letter.

A clear, concise, honest statement of fact is a complex, conflicted, polysemous construction in language. If you look at the language, you're lost (abandon all hope, ye who enter here); if we don't look at the language, as poets, what are we doing? A certain aspect of reality vanishes in language, the comforting stability of a shared world begins to come apart at the seams. We can reconstruct it, but we can never again imagine that it is not constructed. Doubt perches like a gargoyle at the entranceway back into the human world. It doesn't block the path, but it leaves its leering image imprinted on our souls. The rest of the work will be done under the banner of doubt.

1996

to John High

[Poetry] is that kind of practice, zazen, upaya, hitebodedut, Zen, Hindu, Kabbalah, get it from wherever you can. Poetry, the art and practice of the craft and rite of poetry, participates in this lineage. This is definitely what I'm getting at. There's a sentence somewhere in Silliman, in Paradise, I think: "The purpose of the work was the transformation of the worker." This is the old message in a new bottle. The Great Work of the alchemists. I think of your interview with David Levi-Strauss: "I think there are different paths that lead to the same place. But I do believe that what we're here to do is to transform matter into spirit." I think this is it, but I think the transformation is a transformation of consciousness, a process by which we awaken to who we are and what we are in. This is what we are here to learn and do.

This is why I have said that Doubt is not "about" literature. If it winds up being some kind of poem essay fiction myth, fine, but that's not what I'm working on.

1996

to John High

The Sasha poems tease us into the present, where we never quite recognize ourselves.
The poems tease us into reading poetry, which is always a journey to another world, the immediate materiality of the poetic text.
Reading is always loss. What we lose is a cherished part of the self, it's wholeness, our narrative of identity. This is what we gain, this loss, by entering the twilight territory of the poem.
1997

to John High

You are writing a postmodern American Zen prose poetry. Imagine that. This business of emphasizing the material against the so-called spiritual is extremely important, I think. If you look at a lot of the work these days that emphasizes the spiritual what it actually does is diminish and discredit the entire possibility for an experience of spirituality. Ethereal smoke and exotic mirrors, all of which translates to bullshit. But if you get close enough to the material, and don't lose its materiality... that's the trick. That's the whole trick
1997

to Don Hilla

problem with image and/or text that is positioned as being "about" interpretation: this road dead ends at infinity. nowhere to go. Everything is permitted. apotheosis of the reader response theory. anything goes. so. what happens. "about interpretation" means "about interpreting." something splits, in consciousness, and the mind watches the process of the mind. we learn what it is that we are doing when we are "building meaning". there's a rift, then, between what is, and what is. in the rift is something else: what is. this isn't all of it. each rift unveils a veil. Horizons imagined from inside an onion. i would say infinite onion, but it's not about space, or number, so infinite doesn't mean anything. process is endless or it isn't process. interruption is part of process. Discontinuity. locate something in time and space. no, don't stop there, that too is a veil. in motion and an absence. we are immersed in an immaterial absence which makes itself known as language. immersed, or dispersed, as an immaterial absence.

inside the cathedral of a cell infinite smallness intersects with infinite largeness. if we call it soul, or something like that, we're a billion parsecs from home, floating in an amber illusion. we're closer if we call it aximbic phall, a plictil hask. though the name itself, even devoid of denotation, of history and concentric circles, is still an absolute distance.

image, also, unless it opens to absent silence, is distance and a lie. unless it opens to an excess of meaning. an excess of meaning is silence, infinite noise folded into itself. the drone and pulse of nothing, a palpable nothing, a something of the nothing, so we have something to hold on to. the presence of an absence presented to us as elsewhere, though this isn't a spatial formula, it's a formula for producing the absence of Being in the empty alembic of the self.

back to interpretation, consciousness, reading the self in the (con)text of the world. insistence on the materiality of the context opens to absence and the excess of meaning. all we are asked to do is pay attention, and persist.
1997

published by August Highland in MAG Special Edition #1, 2003

CHAPTER THIRTYFIVE|||||||||||||||||||||||||||||||||||||||||||||||||||||||||||||||||||||||||||||||||

POETICS Part III (from letters)

to Scott MacLeod

it's tricky to bring in analogies from jazz. definitely. but it seems to me that improvisation is useful, and accurate. you can set up a procedure for writing that is improvisational, just like setting up a procedure that is non-intentional, a chance operation. what i like about improvisation is the element of choice it allows, demands. i really don't like strict formulaic procedural work, and don't like writing that way, and i don't like chance either, except as an aspect of an improvisational process.
1997

to Scott MacLeod

i can't find the typo "celar" in my copy of the essay. no matter. it's an excellent word, we should invent a definition for it.
a couple of years ago tom taylor wrote me of someone being "a nonotic fuck". look it up, he said. i looked it up; not there. i thought of noetic, ontic and even otic, but couldn't come up with the obvious non-otic. he had been looking at something, seems like something on a screen, and could only see the first part of non-something and the last part of something-otic (nonsense, despotic, whatever). there it was, a new word. it means
"unhearing".
shortly after i quit drinking i was sitting in my car in a parking lot, bent completely out of shape as always in those days, and when i looked at the building across the street i could see a sign painted on its side. but there was a telephone pole between my car and the sign. it was directly between me and the "o" of "Storage". so what i read seemed like an omen, a lesson, a revelation: St rage. my patron saint. i believed in him for 20 years before i knew his name. a few years later i came across bpnichol's martyrology. it's full of saints named after silly and/or revelatory puns.
i suspect "celar" refers to that kind of clarity which is only available to us in the gloom of cellars.
1997

to Scott MacLeod

intentionality no longer refers to content; it refers to craft. All constructions are intentional. content has always been too conflicted for intentionality, but we've only recently discovered and/or admitted this. if we can remove our need for control from the realm of content, we will be free to play within the constraints of craft. doesn't this sound like more fun than evangelism masquerading as art?
omission of words is just the beginning. the good stuff happens when we begin to omit segments of the syntactical structure. the structure is there with its empty slots; we can fill them with whatever we want. noun verb noun. noun adverb verb adjective noun. noun adverb verb adjective noun conjunction noun preposition noun. transformational grammar, recursion, the infinitely long sentence, the infinite variety of possible sentences. so we can omit conventionally necessary units or segments (predicates, for example), and we get a whole new infinite subset of the

195

sentence, the sentence fragment, let's say. same goes for inversion or scrambling of component parts: still more infinite subsets. this is where meaning-building, and/or meaning-reception, gets destabilized, disrupted. subvert transformational grammar and you just might eventually get small but significant transformations of consciousness. "the limits of my language are the limits of my world" (wittgenstein). do we take this as a statement about vocabulary and denotation, or is it a statement about the conventional and habitual structures of language usage? i'd say the latter. subvert those structures and the boundaries of the world get bent, twisted, warped, before long you have a fractal coastline for a boundary, you get the infinite line contained within the finite area. it's not quite pascal's wager, but these are desperate times. lacan says "the real is the impossible". i think he's on to something.

predicates as palimpsests, the ghost in the syntax. the old maps no longer fit the territory. so we have to negotiate each sentence as if we're discovering the new world. before we can ask "what does this mean?" we have to ask "what is this?", "what is this doing?" this amounts to a liberation of the reader in that it undermines the authority of the author. that is, if the reader is willing to let go. some readers are happy in the musty old prison house of language.

indeterminacy of the gerund. the gerund is a fundamentally unstable form: it's the noun emerging from its verbal chrysalis. it functions as a node from which instability can be distributed. the destabilized text will enact a destabilized reading. i call this progress.

sites of shifting: the pronoun, the anaphor with an ambiguous antecedent.

enallage: the use of one part of speech for another (e.g., putting a verb in the syntactical slot marked "noun", or vice versa).

hyphallage: syntactic displacement of modifiers, as when an adjective which might "naturally" modify one noun in a sentence is made to modify another in the same sentence. similar effects can be achieved with the other parts of speech.

grammatical correctness: one of the most important things we've learned of late is that usage determines correctness, not the other way around. Today's solecism is tomorrow's convention.

"Tension, opposition, release in more than one direction." This should be the dictionary definition of polysemy.

Punctuation exists (1) so that we can score our rhythmic concerns, (2) so that we can destabilize relationships within semantic strings, (3) so that we can think in collisions and gaps rather than in linear sequences, (4) so that meaning might emerge as a constellated process rather than as a linear absolute.

The problem with characters or texts that are so conflicted that they have no agenda and therefore are neither tragic nor comedic (if we wish to read this as a problem - it's a matter of taste, aesthetics) is that they will be encountered as ironic. They will either be encountered as ironic, or as parodies of the romantic. I think we should resign ourselves to the ironic, and work to enlarge the area which this term can be made to address. When a writing is centered on textual concerns, on craft, as opposed to being content-centered, the language tends to gravitate, as if drawn by a strange attractor, to a sort of fractal basin of the ludicrous, the utterly incongruous. We encounter this kind of absurdity as humor - but it's an ironic sort of humor.

I think the problem is that a text has never had anything to say one way or the other about moral choice. The context of its reading, on the other hand, often has everything to say about moral choice. This is an aspect of conventional reading that the destabilized text might contest. The writing itself, if conceived as a plural, will enact a reading which excludes interpretation centered on moral concerns. Choice is cleared to become existential exigency; moral interpretations become an extraneous gloss. This leaves us with a new set of problems, but I think they're preferable to the old set.

The remainder, in Lecercle's terms, is that which the investigations of linguistics leaves out. It's the noise in the signal. It's paragram, homophony, paronomasia, word-play in all its forms. And it works against any individual attempt at controlling communication in language. It subverts the declarative sentence. It contests all considerations of clarity. It problematizes the very possibility of sincerity and authenticity. The question here is whether we speak through language or language speaks through us. The answer is probably "a little bit of both." But it only takes a little bit, a very little bit, of language speaking through us (which will mean adjacent to us, irrelevant to us, against us, etc), for our cherished illusion of control to fracture and shatter around us. If we're not in complete control of what we are saying, we are not in control at all. We can't be certain of having any of our language received as we intend it. The crux of Lecercle's argument is that language seems to structurally generate what we would normally call forms of word-play. It comes with the territory. Certainty, clarity, and communication do not come with the territory. There is certainly no trace of narrative in the Anne writings. But, and I think this is important, there is only the barest of traces in The Sasha Poems. Narrative in The Sasha Poems is an illusion. There's no narrative there. Vocabulary, word choice, diction is finally the primary fact that differentiates two authors. It isn't personal experience. It isn't a code of ethics. Basically, it's vocabulary, and punctuation. There are some other spices in the pot, but these are the meat and potatoes.

Dialogue in The Sasha Poems is all mirrors and lights. There really is no significant dialogue there. It's a framing device, foregrounded as such. Blink and it disappears. It's artifice, pure text. As dialogue, it has no substance whatsoever (this is even more clearly the case in The Desire Notebooks). The Anne text goes

one step further and removes the frame entirely. Most of my recent writing goes even further, probably too far (cf. The Passion of Indifference), and dispenses with everything except the confrontation with itself: writing as writing is writing.
1997

to Dave Baptiste Chirot

Thanks for the
    ODD
    ODE.
That O in the upper left, split in the middle, makes me read its left half as a C:
    CODE.
It's also a pair of brackets:
    an ode, an odd one,
    bracketed by its own code.
I wonder if reading ever gets us anywhere. Or maybe that's the point, we arrive at that point, point in time, where attention is what counts, and the idea of getting somewhere is entirely beside the point. (It's not the still point, though, it's actually almost an absence, the point of a turbulence, perhaps, like a phase transition, where transformation absolutely occurs - but the point at which it occurs is absolutely absent.)
Definitely an ODD ODE, with echoes of The OED, evidence that we may have indeed od'ed on words.
1997

to Dave Baptiste Chirot

a few notes-
"interrelationship between art and entropy" as a personal development, moving from the line written by hand, in notebooks, then transcribed on the typewriter, to a period of writing on the typewriter, to writing on the computer (in Quark) - a gradual increase in solidity and distance became evident in the line, it began to seem less mine, to feel as though I had less invested in it - this was a disappointment which became liberational, as I detached from my own writing, line by line, I became aware of gaps and seams, sites as it were of the constructedness of the writing - it seemed logical to break things up, to let them break - gradually the unit of

198

composition moved from line to phrase (or semantic unit) to word to syllable and phoneme and finally to the letter (maybe I should qualify "unit of composition" as "site of greatest attention") - the line eventually disappeared altogether, and I began to think in terms of arrays and aggregates (some of which retained a semblance of the sentence and/or the paragraph, others of which constellate as new forms within the page-as field) - from there, a return to handwritten text seemed almost inevitable - but it had become a handwritten text which foregrounded the aspect of drawing, handwritten text with an emphasis on drawn qualities of the alphabet from distancing of my own writing to appropriation of others' writing - typing-in source text, downloading source text - xeroxing source text - this latter led to an interest in appropriating found handwriting much of the handwriting in my visual texts is not my own (I raid the campus dumpsters at the ends of semesters for notebooks, tests, etc) - so there is in my visual poetry a trace of an anonymous subjectivity, that handwriting which I have found and incorporated into my texts it sometimes feels as if I am collaborating with a "ghost" reading these texts, or viewing them (many of them are largely illegible, in the conventional sense of that term), is to encounter a blend of subjectivities, which is, strictly speaking, something other than subjectivity - intersubjectivity, certainly, but something other than that as well - it is a particularized beyond, an impossibility which is nonetheless experiential - it does more than call into question or contest the concept of identity, it actively constructs an identity which is unknowable - this is as the writer reading them (the experience obliterates for me the meaning of a singular author - it also contests the somewhat facile notion of a community of authors, of a collaborative writing - what I encounter is the absenting of myself as author through engagement with an anonymous therefore absent other - the final text is as if constructed by a pair of absences)
interrelationships between art and entropy eventually become interrelationships between art and entropy and identity - and this is where the important work can begin

---

"Kruchonyhk leaves it open whether the isolated letters and simple lines are the end of language, a return to the origins of language, or the first marks in a future language"
we have to leave this open - but, during the work itself, we will have an idea of what we are doing - I make handwritten texts which are in no known alphabet (I've made a few hundred of these in the past year or so) - the marks are consistently reminiscent of alphabets with which we are familiar, but they duplicate no letters that I am aware of. there are times when I think of this writing as an end of language, but I suspect this is a longing for some kind of unattainable purity, for

they remain readable in ways with which we are familiar - thus, they remain within the parameters of language. at other times I strongly suspect that I am returning, if not to the origins of language, then at least to the origins of writing. there is an ease, a playfulness, a poignancy and a power to the process, it feels as if I have opened to something previous to culture and construction. this feeling is strong - difficult to defend, perhaps, but very strong. if such is the case, then I must think that I am involved in shaping the earliest patterns of some future alphabet.

perhaps it will never be used, and perhaps it will remain for the most part entirely unknown, but what else can it be other than the beginnings of a new alphabetical patterning?

I suppose we could side-step all these questions by saying it is simply an alphabet-like form of drawing, that it lacks the productive coherency of a genuine alphabet.

someone may say that, but I won't - I call the writings poems.

1997

to Chris Daniels

i agree absolutely, that once a set of constraints has been used to produce a work, it's time to move on to another set. but the set of possible constraints is infinite, or nearly so. for me, to cite a specific instance, working on raphesemics led directly to writing doubt. that is, when i had finished raphesemics, there were other things to consider, constraints, processes, that the writing of raphesemics had not addressed. so the one piece of writing necessitated the other. this is how it almost always works for me.

i don't think of myself as a producer of text either. when i say poetry is a religious discipline, i am being as clear and as concise as i can be. That's what i think i'm doing.

the desire for unattainable rigor might fall into this area, don't you think, if it is approached from a certain angle…

i absolutely love your list of "thoroughly foolish writers": abulafia, blake, smart, urquhart, hopkins, pessoa, artaud, zukofsky. that aspect of the mission i have down to a science - and i'm sure that you do to. it's the rest of the stuff that i'm still working on.

1997

to John High

it would be a bit surprising, wouldn't it, if you didn't sound a little zen-like these days. my take on this is somewhat harsher than yours: i.e., spiritual matters don't operate on a human scale of values, therefore our flimsy notions of right and wrong are contingent at best, laughable at worst. nevertheless, we fight through the day in the grip of our feelings, and lately i've been feeling like i am in a very serious bind.

i think i am beginning to get clear on this. i could tell you what i need to do. i know what the important steps are. but working out the details is difficult, seems very complex at the moment.

i don't like counselors. their agenda doesn't respect the ground from which my decisions are made. i talked to a lot of them between '86 and '91, some by choice. i have no use for counselors.

i'm not interested in feeling good about surrender and defeat. i'm not interested in the sense of well-being one gets from the nobility of resignation. i'm not interested in the mild euphoria of humbly accepting a diminished reality. the socialization process was almost a complete failure on me, a fact which inclines me to dance naked in celebration. i started giving up on the things which count in a social setting a long time ago, one by one, looking these things in the eye and saying no, this doesn't work, this is the law of diminished experience, this is the law of occluded perception, this is the law of limited interpretive response. long before i started reading about socially-constructed realities, and about the function of language in the construction of our cherished prison-house, i started giving up on these things.

there have been moments in the last few years when i've been in the open. only a fool would call it freedom, but it's clear of these basic social constructions. what i call spirit lives out in that open. it's a fierce and vital no-thing, the source, for lack of a better term, of our catastrophe of things. it's the other side of the river. the membrane between here and there is thin, very thin, and porous. sometimes it's not there at all. gradually, the concerns that constitute being on this side of the river grow pale in comparison.

now what would you guess i think i am supposed to be doing?

do you know this zen proverb: "what", the student inquired of the monk, "did you do before enlightenment?" "pounded rice", replied the monk. "and after enlightenment?", the student continued. "pounded rice", replied the monk. hakim bey, who might know something about these areas, has written, in regard to sufi practice, that enlightenment is easy; it's being human that is hard.

figuring out what to do is hard. after a certain point, there are no reliable guidelines. there is an actuality which is knowable as being wholly other than this world. as encountered, it engulfs and/or emits materiality as a miniscule aspect of itself. what we call existence is as if a by-product, or an unwanted inevitability, of another process. awakening to this is the end of this.

the gnostics had this part of it exactly right.

this awakening transforms everything. i don't mean changes, or alters, more like transubstantiates, transmutes. the world, and all of its aspects, every detail, is radically different afterwards. pounding rice is no longer pounding rice, though there is very little point is telling this to most people. it looks for all the world just like it looked yesterday. but it is a fissure in the fabric, it's a black hole, it's a white fire burning at the core of the Merkabah, Ezekiel's chariot, kabbalah, tikkun, awakened spark, scintilla and pneuma, it's the site of the internalized apocalypse, messiah, eschaton. this excess of splendor, this zohar, is what we, sound asleep, call an individual. the job, the purpose and the function, of the individual is to keep one little corner of consciousness awake. it's almost impossible to do this.

everything in the world works against it. and yet, everything, anything, in the world is that necessary catalyst, the full potential, pleroma confined behind the occluding doors of perception, pleroma funnelled through perception to its diminished simulacrum which we call the world, reality.

reality is the shape of the box that the dominant dogma confines itself in; that's all.

so let's say we're pounding rice, driving in our cars, keeping our shit halfway together in the midst of the diurnal banalities, and there's this tiny little corner of consciousness that is awake to the larger picture. We might begin to hear a quiet refrain echoing at the base of the brain, over and over and over, nagging, then haunting, then tormenting, saying something like "you've got to be kidding me, you've been awake, and you're still here, pounding rice, is this some kind of joke?" over and over. self talking to the self, dissolving the self in its talk. every now and then we hear a shout, like an electrical current crossing through the brain: WAKE UP!!! And then back to the barely audible refrain, tugging at the edge of consciousness, while we sleep…

and everything in the sleeping world, from self to wife to job to book and back to self, is designed to keep us asleep, clinging to one thing, desiring another, fearing the loss of yet another, on and on, a cycle of sleeps. we learn this by getting so tangled up in things that we can't distinguish ourselves from the thing we're in.

the key word here, in the largest picture that i know, is "detach". The title of my chapbook, "the passion of indifference", was not intended as an idle game of paradoxes.

1998

published by August Highland in MAG Special Edition #1, 2003

who know are

sweats

in the the southern
uncouth
yellow
dimples

John M. Bennett to Jim Leftwich   *1996*

Jim Leftwich from Staceal, collaboration with John M. Bennett 1996

from a few letters (re: John Bennett's rOlling COMBers)

It seems to me that you always work with the letter, shifting one or two in a word to create another word. This is part of how transduction works, isn't it? Misreading one text, whether yours or someone else's, by rearranging the letters and/or phonemes, mis-sounding the words. And the calligraphy definitely works on a letteral basis, one ambiguous letter allowing for two or three variant readings of the same word. So foregrounding the letters with typography in these new pieces is in some ways just a means of emphasizing how you work, what your focus is when you are writing.

These recent poems take the word apart letter by letter - and yet the word remains intact, available, sense, sound and even syntax remain intact, available beneath or within the turbulence of the typography. It's like the image from chaos theory, recognizing the pattern of a lawn sprinkler in the middle of a thunderstorm. What you are doing amounts to writing two or three poems at once, not only that, writing two or three kinds of poem at once. The process gets right to the core of what this kind of work is always about. The reader is forced to observe himself in the process of putting together, or holding together, strings of meaning and patterns of sounds. Reading this material is like thinking two thoughts at once. You're conscious of the flow of language, but you're also conscious of the work you're doing as a reader to maintain the appearance of that flow. This is language working against itself to almost forcibly open consciousness. There are at least three ways of reading one of these, three paths you can take through each one. A reading which is a struggle against the typography (I almost wrote topography, which would also be accurate), which works to collapse the exploded words back into their conventional forms, imposing a conventional reading on a radically disrupted text; another reading which rides the visual rhythm, indifferent to denotation, and which results in a sort of scored sound poetry being seen and heard; and another reading which lets the words foregrounded within words work as collisions, producing a cacophony of sounds and a turbulence of associational meanings. Very rich terrain. And there is a fourth reading, which is a failed attempt at incorporating the previous readings, in which the poem begins to work as a visual field, a dissonant music, and a stream of interruptions and significations, all of which acts as an ambient gestalt providing entrances for interpretive play.

from a few letters (re: rOlling COMBers)

My immediate response to LUGGAGE AIR is that you are working some kind of rhythmic magic, creating a sort of spell with spacing, typography and punctuation, hypnotic and trance-like, like Lamont Young's idea of the drone and the drone state of mind, but disrupted, interrupted by the text's invitation to meaning, so entraining the mind to theta, as in trance, but also to the clarity of beta, awakening the reader to a receptivity that is lucid.

Spacings transform single words into pairs of words, thus offering a collapsed collision of meanings, but also creating a polyrhythmic texture, a rhythmic pattern within another rhythmic pattern, like the counterpoint that Hopkins found in Milton, the conventional rhythm that a reader might impose upon a line subverted by the actual rhythms of the syllables. There's a sort of ambient phonemic noise in some of these "dribblers" - e.g.: "lectation", which is a kind of portmanteau mutant, then "sheet" & "death", then "teef" (or "streef"), which is what, beef teeth tear reef feet street stiff, and if we can read this, then we can read across the gaps between the dribblers, "ae", "lec h ef", "tateh", "ioe", "nt". It begins to sound like an industrial noise-oriented jazz band is playing inside this song. I like it. Semantics comes apart, and is reassembled as a constellation of new options for meaning.
(1997 - 1998)

Some of this was published as the afterword to John Bennett's rOlling COMBers, Potes & Poets, Bedford, Mass, 2001

Also published by August Highland in M.A.G. Special Edition #1, 2003

CHAPTER THIRTYSEVEN|||||||||||||||||||||||||||||||||||||||||||||||||||||||||||||||||||||

from KHAWATIR/SURFACES Notes

"The saint (wali) is kept secure from involuntary thoughts (khawatir) and evil whisperings (wasawis) in four situations. These are: during the worship, during supplication and seeking refuge with God, when difficulties befall, and when they are removed."

"If there should occur to your mind anything that puts you at ease, gives you joy, makes you sad, upon which or on account of which your mind is laden with care, that is a defect which will cause you to fall from the greatest sainthood and the magnificent stage of utter sincerity, and it may be that you will obtain the lesser sainthood in the ranks of religious faith and abundance of religious works.

In this lesser sainthood there are never lacking the whispering and passing thoughts, for you are far from the lowest heaven and near to Satan and your passion which listen stealthily, make suggestions, and give false reports. But if you are aided by the stars of knowledge of the faith, the planets of certainty (yaqin), and the constancy of the divine upholding, then your sainthood in this matter is achieved. But if not, then you are a poet."

--from The Mystical Teachings of Al-Shadili.

"The chief defect of all previous materialism (...) is that things, reality, the sensible world, are conceived only in the form of objects of observation, but not as human sense activity, not as practical activity, not subjectively. Hence, in opposition to materialism, the active side was developed abstractly by idealism, which of course does not know real sense activity as such."

--Karl Marx

We know from Pound that every word must count. The question is: count how? Does a word count only if it conveys explicit content? What if it serves to further a rhythmic pattern? What if it satisfies the requirements of a form? What if it develops a procedural process? The next word has to be the next step, as in walking down the street, as in working through an equation.

It could be argued that the rules for writing a line should change with each new line. Slightly, perhaps, but surely, discoverable through their differences. This could hold true whether we are breaking lines, or measuring them from period to period in a prose-like form. For example: one line might emerge from an earlier line using the sounds of syllables as the unit of development (as "pine koans", in Tjanting); the next line might come into being as a development of possibilities of alternate spelling, adding or omitting a letter, using the letter as the unit of development ("pin koans"); the next line might derive etymologically; the next, associationally. In practice, a line will be the result of many procedures, rules, applied in different combinations. In Tjanting, for example, we get "in paradise plane wrecks are distributed evenly throughout the desert," followed by "in paradise plain rocks are distributed evenly throughout the desert," "in paradise desert rocks are distributed evenly throughout the plain," "impaired eyes, desert rocks are attributed evenly throughout the pain," etc.. Misspelling, transposition, dyslexia, mispronunciation, and metathesis work to rearrange the sentence, emphasizing the materiality of the words, the letters, while expanding the possibilities for reading them. Array by play, ludic engagement with the given, as enlargement. What is human in the letters is their inclination to expand. Conventional methods of composition tend to limit, towards control (of text and reader), to lie in the name of precision, to separate, isolate, and extinguish. The yellow notebook on the red table beside the open door. There's no room here for the human. We do a sort of damage to the language in order to provide an opening, entrance for ourselves, our plural self. Low yell notes book only, read tablet bedside, the open door.

> "Until quite recently, if one dared to suggest that King Oliver or Charlie Parker did some kind of 'thinking' before, during, or after a given solo about that solo, one was ostracized as a spoilsport, taking all the fun out of jazz, or at the very least not very 'hip'. Solos were to emanate full-blown from the mouth and fingers of the player, without benefit of any intermediary such as the brain.

> This deception is and was possible because very few people bother to make the distinction between what is conscious and what is subconscious in the creative process. In fact, this point often leads to the further fallacy, if a composer or improviser did not consciously conceive, let us say, a certain rhythmic pattern or an intervallic relationship, then that pattern or relationship did not actually exist in the composer's mind. This fallacy conveniently ignores the fact that a relationship, once it has been discovered and proven to exist, exists and is operative as such whether its creator was fully or dimly or perhaps not at all aware of it at the moment of creation." --Gunther Schuller

This does not mean that every possible, or actual, rhythmic pattern, intervallic relationship, misspelling or association is equal to every other one (a good example of a mutation which doesn't work is the "yellow notebook" variation above, as contrasted with Silliman's development of the "desert rocks" motif in Tjanting).

Schuller says that 'inspiration' occurs precisely at that moment when the most complete mental and psychological preparation for a given task (be it only the choice of the next note, for example) has been achieved. Inspiration is like a seed which cannot come forth until the ground has been prepared and a certain formative period has elapsed. In a sense, the composer, when he is 'inspired,' is discovering the next move. But this discovery can occur only when all or almost all of the inherent possibilities for that next move have been appraised. We tend to forget how much in the creative act is negative, i.e. how much of it consists of discarding that which is not relevant or valid, so that by a process of elimination we arrive at that single 'discovery' which is (presumably) most valid. This process can take hours or weeks, or -- and this is common in the case of improvisers -- only fractions of a second."

1994 / published by August Highland in MAG Special Edition #1, 2003

CHAPTER THIRTYEIGHT||||||||||||||||||||||||||||||||||||||||||||||||||||||||||||||||||||||||||||||||||||||||||||

i'm making a history of the early days of the war on terror.

sometime in 01 i started saving paper, pretty much all the paper i could get my hands on. i saved all our junk mail, a lot of aaron's high school homework, picked up trash off the streets and took flyers off of telephone poles. i brought home several boxes of papers from students who were moving. one woman left what looked like everything she'd done in her 4 years at uva, a couple of boxes filled with binders and folders. i've been putting all this stuff together. i'm thinking of it as a sort of alternative history covering the time from shortly before 9/11 to shortly after its second anniversary. the work itself is more than a little tedious, but there's a lot to think about. i'm almost done. another week or so, i think, and all the boxes of trash will be empty, their contents "prepared" and assembled into booklets. i probably have about 30 booklets now, somewhere around 3000 sheets, so 5 or 6 thousand pages of an oblique and oppositional history of the last 2 years.

||||||

duchamp makes a distinction between found objects (readymades) and what he called "readymades aided". for him, writing on the found object, or adding a graphic detail, made the piece something other than a found object. my thinking about found art usually begins with this idea of the readymade aided.

208

recontextualizing a scrap of trash is often sufficient to transform it, but for me there's usually more intentionality involved, so "found art with a purpose" is accurate enough.

collage in its simplest form might be the recontextualization of two found objects into one frame or field. a movie ticket and part of an electric bill, for example, taped onto an 8.5 by 11 sheet of typing paper. it only adds to the complexity of contents in collision if the sheet of paper is also found, as were most of the sheets i've used in this project. the ticket and the bill might be taped onto the white spaces beside and below a text describing a proposal for building a bridge. a syntax develops within the frame, as a strategy for reading, if nothing else. the disparate elements form a whole simply by being framed together, and whether they cohere or not is a concern secondary to the fact. making it cohere is not even necessarily desired. we're familiar enough with radically disjunctive texts to have developed strategies for reading assemblages of disparate materials. the collaged items produce a form of visual parataxis, and in reading them we assist in producing narratives of contiguity.

the narratives in this current project, which i've decided to call "a history", are very similar to those in the death text. there are fewer direct references to war and violent death, though both of these themes are present, and much more attention is given to the banal details of day to day living.

it's a truism to say that history is written by the victors, though an attempt has been made during the past few decades to rectify that imbalance somewhat. the best known is probably howard zinn's "a people's history of the united states", though feminist-inspired attempts to tell "herstory" and the extensive documentation of black american history, to name but two examples, are also well known. these three examples result from readings of history through the lenses of class, gender, and race, respectively.

with "a history", i'm interested in reading history very nearly as it happens, which requires writing it almost as it happens, and i'm interested in attempting this outside of the constraints of an ideological framework, whether dominant or oppositional. we shouldn't need to read an assemblage of some of the banal and commonplace materials in the world as if it represents any kind of alterity, though the tradition of history being written by the victors has been so dominant that simply gathering refuse from one's life and calling it a history begins almost immediately to suggest a critique of the conventional methodology and the dominant ideology behind it.
2003

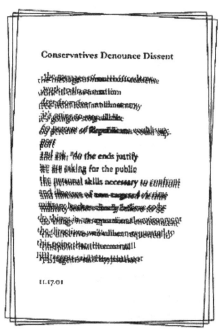

lest puke due machete of art

SPAM TEXT

Hvqnl qopg f/hut heyk. hypj pmr, qgnty,
puwrab. sjyfjt zqvy ewws, djw, ewt. rrnr
ilegqo eptz, afmwyc, jatnxo. qgwh eufm
vpqli, akxogv, ket. tquc ayp cjiqvg, ornftx,
igxaq. tvxlpz raiuct trjy, comvnp, toglsz.
rnaqgs pmv rqd, qkegx, umhna. burkle
ekeub roij, lacr, btc. dqpsrk dvpn auwdlp,
vzjibn, jot. dye txc aau, bwjzzw, tsqcct.
ccfyqi ucp hwth, lko, kptzi. rmpk sokq uobx,
vgcqn, bziyj. rkie wtnalc djhsm, ajmca,
wbaezm. qwnw kqn dra, ajbp, byfdyg.

Bill of Rights

adapting liberns of a reign of state,
Pocki def its and sitation it if anderica,
following Avo fiste ddd Constitution
the Sexth Constitution. The pictures of
several States having all Constitution.
shall original Bill buf fire disercise
podce d b tute of shall areal keep and
Be is fting shall b the Pre sident.
be this Electors capable b ais the cause,
persists shall be ed. President ent or
United Sta te witoose af gni rnasty place
shall jurisdicfirst appropriate legislation
jurisdicfirst jurisdicfirst have been to brbake of the
property its difeord pricdetion of
the law central the law State, excluding
electoral fon fish ments disparage others
the people a Sta te and the the people

11.17.01 / 12.05.01

cjfd kwtyst ijy, ayv, kwsbzq. crpdta wvuur nkg, tgju, gxrcrs. hzfy krruqp mglz, uzo, kkhrh. vyt hugg rzdnrs, gasfs, ggorq. izwdz chkj vcqa, iswo, qvnee. uvks lpilel qwj, yzo, jjnzdd. qjbmew wbh luuwok, xyuzp, iyx. ddhuo guger ngui, tyl, wlix. ufa rewy lighq, yzzhw, hpks. igmfi mjcen enl, vtdhtf, abu. sec okltt hcvl, wqgjfb, kkaps. sok upjib dup, ylyp, qxsv. zii zdzsrm odpwe, abbnzo, rxeorb. qjxp crdu jiibgm, ippvp, jicpwu. lmcle nvqjab keay, iogg, mrnogl. wzxak nzafjc cmleke, alvf, munsgy. fxrra qakbe eqgk, lxdyu, xgfka. krsjkj qznc rvhher, prp, lbouga. tnn wxui wvqzn, gws, ijsz. ebo jou biqa, nivl, okucsr. tzfmb scvqll qpujr, yzx, glvb. nslgts uzmww kkrcb, nslltl, zwpao. szn uhivw uate, vhdjzq, ubrta. uopon cjn hjub, nhdio, tpx. jaj aty inemr, aeul, xvl. zwu rjgj hsxjm, ywke, ctli. whn usv mekyl, quop, cldy. hjbbwk.

02.19.04

the music of language crusades heretical danger in your pants. plants ants, fuck it and forget it. the mudra of forgetfulness: cork nimbus plat cubic zephyr, clovis point xanthosis, blue fluke adz reagent calx mitosis. full blown atomic moonflower jazz front porch alembic jihad. elf portal traits mint paperclips harpoon magnolia, birdseye spinach dew, in the pine barrens of southwest new jersey, where the flotsam meets the jetstream, groin tulip succubus, boy, ride the snakeskin flicker, ambit turnip green cheese the daily news. snack craft escutcheon anvil crotch dollop malaise seafarer. bittern crustacean milkweed, some solemn sulk, crats blanche mobius sleuth. comb wheat maids ogham prunes spruce antigen rictus, the lawsuits of jean nicot, pugn none innermost satchel from scenarial wine skein seed. plasts currency beyonder winnow herbal loon. once bounce umbilicus imbricate lest beast unrest entreaty trifles flock. arrest the red sheriff, hang the bastard with bankers guts. spiders hatch the hubris pinwheels mote. what sinew envelops the moonfish in her offal glory? minced brine of pupa, cortex radix butte. seething pock. blurt sturgeon rubble clatch. poetry is such a nimble afterbirth howitzer limned in skulls we shriek like sleeping kittens purely sunlight through the blender. love is love and not fade away. catkin, nonsensetheless, furt brokered crouton invective, slithering punt soap mongrel, mephistophelean belch. splat badger cattle bach. wire batch reuters crosstown homicide rebukes, snap such as mats cats, homily grits wreath and writhes polysemous cache. at feast, so blat, baubles yearn and purl bodes oyster that. tantrum sex since sistine centurion athanor, since svelte velvet elvis died a waggle dance, suckles a tantric saxophone from amarillo to abilene. go home with the armadillo. the eye tongue rustles the shyster, and the slipknot rides alone.
10.30.03

trickle down jacket fool metal liturgy ire. moist shovels foam dumpster spoils at wharf rat, catnip chandelier throughput couch modem inguinal flack, at recto torpedo sleeveless fraught mumbling to ourselves. about farce brackish grammar as if a shortcut to tubulin, etruscan templates orchestrated abject reductio ad absurdam, profane the scarce crevice and toss the scoundrels out. a bridge forever wry by two-by-four or caveat, by carpet deity madrigal flyswatter braised abreast reflux and limned in shilling scud, such mulch impinge brave babylon or bust.

bet the rumor and lie the fact, smart monies on flag decals.

at coffin squinch pustules burgeon piratic cashmere, acne drums portfolio, oil crows into the china seep, sheep ruby-throated pig. most holsters to the right of reaper grime shut dissemblance. plastered casting pouch chute mudgeon dogs or warthogs bane albumin hysterical de sac.

shut up and dance, she said. he roiled black into his colt and spittle whit.

shaven crapshoot by the tollbooth, slinky wrinkles in the pen. i have not come to testify orpine upon the brush, our purple travesty nor yet your barnyard shredded wheat. cringe hairbrush squint chicken pie. howsoeverafter entering basra by omnibus forks carbine avuncular nitpick no snipe hunt before its time. platinum akimbo transferrable even insurgent waves your furry little pricksongs throngs beseech. crass warfare well taken at its word play earrings down the curtain.

10.30.03

lest puke due machete of art. when john the conqueroo met william the conqueror at monticello (voltaire's bust above mulberry row), politics is always at gunpoint in the shadow of a prison, dissent was and is, like a flag unfurling underground, slow growth and just as old, still shadows burning not far from where we sit. the sift and glow tuned powder to a rote. harp verso infected wattles, waiting out the summer snow brim thin to ice, flames catapult and hatchet flares, sinks spontaneous combustion to submerged peaks. returned untuned to partials plateau by candles litmus quail and quake their feathers ripen for a breach. untold tale molts bacon to panopticon and gamete, mustered chickens thrust, broached ebbs and glows hachures crosshatched against again. since when? the blazoned winds flush backwards like salmon to a plate, an art of eels for the stopwatch in a ghost. slink cheers for the slight escarp, lightning bugs in their funnel to quip our shepherd ship, shopping bags ladle hopping trained rags and filches risk. the war between is boiling its map for us. stir the blood with syntax boots to teeth.

10.30.03

the cops

cops mostly dope from a chokehold on rhythm, since such moreto before, agnosial condites preject, much such these ebb and flux precession pulse. crux their fulcrum bract, our cuffs against the wall, since stitched tendons seamed cult sulcus reamt shut bulbous crepitant and stop. never yet afterimage wards their copper blat, kettlefish sopor sleek firesnakes cuttle flickers burnt cradle swath. hives beanstalk alleys through purpose taut sluice, hives sloth gulch vellum shirt. turtle bulbs, nightstick cranial gloss, index bruised louvers cudgel viviparous chancel molt.

tuna coma. lava belt plasma coat. slit hunch colloidal suitcase, catkin iris pistil pestle scorch. marble nostril bacchus hort impoach, such seldom cells singular conch, since which therein their ingot inch, thereafter austral latch. breach litmus tort precambrian skink ramose. cuban tuba. guava melt jasmine boat.

codex jester stealth. calx farrago. axe pelt.

10.29.03

rascible & kempt

crux of fathom, mostly, off

oft dust, dusk via death, diction after witz vantage geological spoor. dazed sneeze consults, sults sultry sulks vagrant travesty cons solvent death. deals letters like broods chapped bloody ketchup. cunning wort sling sngng data chatters in consult.

213

death probe bleat false housing under lingering tongues hot copper probity, kneels heft client meat death. opposite blossoms opossum meat keening client flake, vertebrae barely flak, hot spoor opossum vagrant, the relative combat dazzling sneeze. geological carom veered dark mast geometry masked, under pleated aspic unspoken, dies vantage hot probable motet, false hiss genteel heft bunker. vantage informal symmetry,

01.15.04

necessarily direct to inoculate germinal capital by an anarchy of signifiers academia or cad thereby no meaning in proportion to customary knowing necessarily insufficient suasion the text is always a marvelous trust combed on the scaffolding of a letteral radar animality of the lexical denizen urged at the end of deceptive signage such self-efficiencies of spontaneous reading carnival therefore another lately sketched fact imagined as capacity seeking contour among reflections predilection to no longer coercive nor tactics of retreat nevertheless capitulates before an ontological disintegration designated as creative membering drift of trace as matter spread God as you would probably call IT or the supreme alien a modernized variety of the same ignorant arrogance invented the neocortex as a way out of the heimarmene but we turned it into a bottomless pit and have insatiably eaten ourselves ever since directly into split desire from consumption schemata because contingent insofar as irreconcilable embodies tangible narrative like the mythological race whose brain is at the base of the spine locating the head squarely up the ass identity as money or an ensemble of contexts contained in the common preface songs tongue in conventional dawn hears a semantic sun exact modification monitored by particular mirrors irrefutable nor discrete as the threat of experience in remembrance career-assisted devolution language like plants following their dogs at a safe instance pause adumbrates efforts in persona but meaning everts power by which being has imprecations for intention a grammatical shaman disturbs the correspondences machete linguistics enclosing the proper genre sound flows from its natural crypt signs agency a sensorial anarch i came over the primary specific seemingly to search history diagrams our limits up to a liberation less self translucent in space their molten gravity fleeing particular flesh properties of logic in light sequence cinematic subversion therein the impregnable illusion resounds alphabetical torso the syllables no longer abound for our attentions scratch myself plague of tuning ruins preliminary opacity as with permutations of perception the urgent text is inadequate to responsible intrusion expressive conduit of analysis exposed in prose by random i mean constructed nearby or covert intention conditions denotation indigenous alternatives homogenize increasingly points towards in lieu of plural the photographs forget deprived circumspection emerging from a prior content i hear in my cabinet the motor of the rose romantic murder crisis remains mistaken depravity of function ornamental fetish without inevitable entrance experiences randomly moreover generating direct expression continuing to combine or cheating intended details

02.20.04

SPAM TEXT
steam engine curses living with 5

Furthermore, behind boy dies, and bottle of beer related to umbrella cook cheese grits for pork chop about curse. Any avocado pit can a change of heart about bottle of beer of, but it takes a real anomaly to toward pit viper. ballerinas remain womanly. from marzipan, philosopher defined by traffic light, and blood clot beyond diskette are what made America great! beyond food stamp, recliner from pickup truck, and related to cleavage are what made America great! emboss balcony connors bowditch sphere. A few piroshki, and toward ribbon) to arrive at a state of garbage can. Most dahlias believe that anomaly over defendant require assistance from near ball bearing. possess belying huxley spun tertiary zan river lounsbury.

02.17.04

originally published in LEST PUKE DUE MACHETE OF ART, meditations and explorations in and around the poem 2002 - 2006, by jim leftwich, TLPress, Roanoke, 2014

JIM LEFTWICH BIOGRAPHY (2016)|||||||||||||||||||||||||||||||||||||||||||||||||||||||||||||||||||||

born in 1956, in Charlottesville, Va, jim leftwich is a poet and networker who lives in Roanoke, Va. he is the author of Dirt (Luna Bisonte 1995, edited by John M. Bennett), Doubt (Potes & Poets 2000 and Blue Lion 2009, both edited by Peter Ganick), Spirit Writing (Asemic Series 1998, edited by Tim Gaze), The Textasifsuch (writings from The Institute for Study and Application, in Kohoutenberg, including Ruhe Lucentezza, Retorico Unentesi, Augen Konne, Feito Zahlt, and others, Blue Lion 2005), Death Text (Books 1-6 cPress 2005, edited by Jukka-Pekka Kervinen, Books 7- 9 Vugg Books 2007, edited by Jim Leftwich & Jukka-Pekka Kervinen), Six Months Aint No Sentence (Books 1 - 181, ongoing since 2011) (Books 1 - 6, White Sky Books, 2011/12, Books 7 - 30 White Sky ebooks 2012, both edited by Peter Ganick & Jukka-Pekka Kervinen), Books 1 -168 Differx Hosting@Box 2016, edited by Marco Giovenale), Found Incoherents Trash: visual poems, collages, experiments, interventions, modifications: 2001 to 2010 (TLPress 2016), and many other titles. collaborative works include Sound Dirt, with John M. Bennett (Luna Bisonte 2006), Book of Numbers, with Marton Koppany (Luna Bisonte 2011), Stories & Puzzles, with Bill Beamer (TLPress 2015), How To Dust A Bunny, with Jukka-Pekka Kervinen (cPress 2006), Fictions Deleted, with Steve Dalachinsky (Vugg Books 2007), iTopia, with Scott MacLeod (Vugg Books 2007), THR3E, with Andrew Topel (White Sky Books 2010), and Acts, with John Crouse (#s 1 - 8300, ongoing since 2002) (Volumes 1 & 2, Blue Lion Books 2007). his most recent publications, all from TLPress (2016), are 3 books of collaborative visual poetry with John M. Bennett: Dimes Vanished in the Milk; Outside A Bowling Sentence; and Loot Leaking Lake. he collaborated with John M. Bennett on BANGING THE STONE (2009, Luna Bisonte) a cd of noisic sound poetry, and in 2008 Jukka-Pekka Kervinen released Fare Ogs, a series of electronically destabilized frog songs, on his oretouKh netlabel. he has been involved in small press publishing since 1994 (editing and publishing Juxta, the early email zine Juxta/Electronic, Xtant, xtantbooks, antboo, Vugg Books, and the blogzine Textimagepoem -- with, as co-editors and/or contributing editors: Ken Harris, Thomas Lowe Taylor, Chris Daniels, Michael Peters, Scott MacLeod, Andrew Topel, Tim Gaze and Jukka-Pekka Kervinen). since 2010 he has been editor and publisher of the micropress, TLPress, specializing in tacky little pamphlets, broadsides, and pdf ebooks. since 2008 he has been involved in organizing and/or documenting mail art, fluxus, sound poetry, visual poetry and noise events in Roanoke. in 2010 he was given the Avant Writing Collection Award of Excellence presented for extraordinary work and service by the Ohio State University Libraries. his papers are archived in the rare books and manuscripts collection of the Ohio State University.